STANLEY KUBRICK'S 2001: A SPACE ODYSSEY

EDITED BY ROBERT KOLKER

STANLEY KUBRICK'S 2001: A SPACE ODYSSEY

NEW ESSAYS

2006

OXFORD
UNIVERSITY PRESS

Oxford University Press, Inc., publishes works that further
Oxford University's objective of excellence
in research, scholarship, and education.

Oxford New York
Auckland Cape Town Dar es Salaam Hong Kong Karachi
Kuala Lumpur Madrid Melbourne Mexico City Nairobi
New Delhi Shanghai Taipei Toronto

With offices in
Argentina Austria Brazil Chile Czech Republic France Greece
Guatemala Hungary Italy Japan Poland Portugal Singapore
South Korea Switzerland Thailand Turkey Ukraine Vietnam

Published by Oxford University Press, Inc.
198 Madison Avenue, New York, New York 10016

www.oup.com

Library of Congress Cataloging-in-Publication Data
Stanley Kubrick's 2001: a space odyssey : new essays /
[edited by] Robert Kolker.
p. cm.
ISBN-13 978-0-19-517452-6; 978-0-19-517453-3 (pbk.)
ISBN 0-19-517452-6; 0-19-517453-4 (pbk.)
1. 2001, a space odyssey (Motion picture) I. Kolker, Robert Phillip.
PN1997.T86S73 2006
791.43'72—dc22 2005016290

9 8 7 6 5 4 3 2 1

Printed in the United States of America
on acid-free paper

Thanks to everyone at OUP: copyeditor Merryl Sloane,
production editor Stacey Hamilton, Abby Russell,
and Elissa Morris, a wonderful and gracious editor.

STANLEY KUBRICK'S 2001: A SPACE ODYSSEY

Contents

Introduction

ROBERT KOLKER

I first saw *2001* in 1968, on a gigantic Cinerama screen in a London theater. I was overwhelmed by the images and only somewhat impressed by what the images were trying to tell me. I left frankly questioning what all the fuss was about. On subsequent viewings, in slightly more intimate surroundings, on smaller screens back home in New York, the film began to grow and grow on each successive screening. Each viewing opened up more questions and more answers—and even more admiration. *2001* became one of the touchstones for my love of film and a major factor in my desire to make the study of film part of my intellectual life. I realized, as I would with all subsequent Kubrick films, that it is a kind of double, triple, quadruple play, revealing more meanings on each viewing—and more mysteries.

On its initial release, *2001* was advertised as "The Ultimate Trip," a smart appeal to the counterculture of the 1960s. It was played for its spectacle and the psychedelic quality of the images that make up the "Stargate" sequence near its conclusion. But it was, of course, another film entirely, a deeply serious, richly textured, enigmatic, meditative spectacle of a film, so complex and so unyielding in its answers that its cowriter, science fiction author Arthur C. Clarke, wrote "novelizations" to try and explain it. Kubrick himself, with the exception of a few tightly controlled interviews, remained silent. Control was the way Kubrick survived as a completely independent filmmaker. He continued to edit *2001* in the projection booth before its New York premiere. He was concerned that it was too long. At one point during its first New York run, a sheet of paper was handed out (I cannot recall if it was signed by Kubrick) to the people on line that explained that Bowman's reentry into the vacuum of the ship's airlock was scientifically accurate. Kubrick was very keen on *2001*'s scientific accuracy. But by and large, the important matters of the film—the validity of extraterrestrial life, the willingness of humans to devoid themselves of feeling, the relationship of men to machines—he left to the film itself and to an audience that he trusted would stay with it, understand it, even if it provided no final answers to the questions it posed.

I was not the only one who responded to the film with growing enthusiasm and with the experience of seeing something new every time I watched it. *2001* was enormously popular at the time of its release and is now generally regarded as one of the most important films ever made. Significantly, it continues to reveal meaning. Objects and ideas, movements, gestures, and words, invisible once, suddenly become obvious, even though "obvious" in a film like this does not make them any more comprehensible. Even though its prophetic year has passed, it still speaks to us about our past and future, our relationship to the unknowns of the universe, and cautions us about the ways in which we deal with the technologies we invent.

2001: A Space Odyssey is a film that shows and hides, gives and takes away, promises to reveal great secrets of the universe and then reneges. This is a film of spectacular images developed slowly, contemplatively, even elegiacally. It has little dialogue; it shows more than it tells, and what it shows is not always what we think we see. Kubrick is not being perverse; he was very consciously making a difficult film, which itself is something of a contradiction in terms, since we do not usually equate difficulty with watching a movie. We expect to be given a clear plot and obvious emotion, not confronted with complex ideas and insoluble problems.

In order to understand some of this, it will be helpful to put the film in context, two contexts in fact. One is the cinematic and cultural history that surrounds it; the other is the body of Kubrick's work—and with the filmmaker's death in 1999 after the completion of *Eyes Wide Shut*, that body of work is complete. Stanley Kubrick is a director to whom the term *auteur* can be applied with little hesitation. He created and managed every aspect of his films, from inception through advertising and distribution. He often depended on writers to initiate the words of a project, but he created a final shooting script that was to his liking. The shooting itself (during which he would sometimes operate the camera or direct from a distance a second unit, who might be in another country making background shots), the visual design of the film, the actors' performances, every detail was under his control. The result is an amazing uniformity of production. Despite the differences in each of his films, they carry forward visual designs and narrative and thematic movements that make all of them cohere as Kubrick films. We need to understand *2001* in this light.

Let's examine briefly a general history of the films that, in important ways, made the creation and reception of Kubrick's film possible. *2001* appeared in a decade of intense cinematic experimentation, mostly from abroad. There was, earlier, Italian neorealism. Their country in ruins after World War II, Italian filmmakers turned to filming in the streets with nonprofessional actors, capturing a desolate world and a desperate people in ways that film had never done before. Neorealism influenced, in turn, the French New Wave, a group of film lovers and critics who discovered in American film a vitality and a sense of authorship that they took to heart when it came time to make their own films. These films, like those of the neorealists, were shot on location, and at the same time they grabbed hold of American film genres and turned them inside out. At one time or another during the late 1950s and 1960s, many New Wave directors, especially Jean-Luc Godard and François Truffaut, made gangster films—or at least their version of gangster films, like Godard's *Breathless* (1959). Kubrick, who started his career in the United States before moving to England in the early 1960s, had already made two gangster films, *Killer's Kiss* (1955) and *The Killing* (1956). This was a popular genre in the United States, which is one of the reasons the French New Wave took it on. Kubrick's versions of the gangster film, especially *The Killing*, looked forward to the kinds of existential gangster movies that the New Wave would create. Later, in America, under the direct influence of the New Wave, other experimental filmmakers emerged in Hollywood. Arthur Penn's *Bonnie and Clyde* (1967)—a gangster film—set a new style for films of violence; in 1972, Martin Scorsese made *Mean Streets*, another gangster film, one that turned filmmaking upside down for almost two decades. It became a model for almost every young filmmaker to follow in his or her first movie. With *M.A.S.H.* (1970), a war film, Robert Altman began an unprecedented string of films that went counter to Hollywood tradition in narrative structure. Many others followed.

2001 was part of this explosion of film, part of a culture in which filmmaker and audience alike took part in experimentation, in a reexamination and rediscovery of cinematic language. But Kubrick was ahead of the game before this. *The Killing*, with its exterior shooting and maddeningly complex time scheme, was a big influence on future directors of gangster movies; we can still see traces of it in the films of Quentin Tarantino. With *The Killing*—and the two films that preceded it, *Fear and Desire* (1953) and *Killer's Kiss* (1955)—he began what was to become a lifelong experiment in narrative and visual construction. He created what was to become, in effect, one long film about the ways that people attempt to impose themselves on their worlds, erecting enormous barriers, schemes, structures, and technologies to which they yield their power, lose their agency in the world, and via which are eventually destroyed.

Kubrick from the start experimented with the limits of film, intent upon using it to examine complex ideas with an unyielding intensity, always focusing on the ways in which people diminish their capacities in the world and, in *2001*, the universe. From his first film, *Fear and Desire*, through *Eyes Wide Shut* (1999), men in Kubrick's films act against their own best interests, or are driven by political forces they can't control (driven so far in *Dr. Strangelove* [1964] that they destroy the planet), or put themselves in situations where they are guaranteed to be undone by their own demons (think of Jack in *The Shining* [1980]). Kubrick saw all of this with a clarity of vision that was at the same time richly textured and deeply ironic. *A Clockwork Orange* (1971), for example, was condemned when it appeared for exalting violent behavior, and indeed the film does at first seem to condone Alex because he alone seems to have free will and vitality in an exhausted world. But look again. We are had by this film. Alex is indeed the only energetic presence and voice in his world. We are given no alternatives, and neither is he. He can be a thug and rapist, choreographing his energies on the stage of a world in ruin, or his violent ways can be taken away by the state, given back when it is in the state's interest to use it. Brainwashed, restored, violent, barely controlled, "I was cured alright," cries Alex at the end of the film, chillingly echoing Dr. Strangelove's cry, "Mein Führer, I can walk," when he rises from his wheelchair and the world explodes. Kubrick's films tend to end with overt or inverted violence, with a character and his universe either exploding or collapsing in.

Kubrick's characters almost always think they are in charge, masters of the bright, fluorescent worlds they inhabit. But they are never in control and not really characters at all, in the traditional movie sense. Kubrick's characters are *ideas* given human form, acting out their own processes of destruction. They are, in effect, part of the spaces that define them. In a Kubrick film, the mise-en-scène, the totality of the cinematic space created on the screen, is part of a usually destructive pattern the characters follow. Character and pattern, place and the figure inhabiting it are reflections of one another. Jack may "always" have been the caretaker of the Overlook Hotel, but the hotel and its "ghosts" also open the spaces of Jack's own growing madness. The painterly compositions of *Barry Lyndon* (1975) trap the characters in an illusion of civility and order that finally crushes them. Kubrick's images confine his characters and point to their breakdown. Within the spaces of these images, his characters always act out the same pattern—against their own best interests. They are rarely what they say, but always how they are seen. In *2001*, there is a startling image—one of many. Heywood Floyd calls his daughter from the space station. The Earth rotates behind him. Floyd pays absolutely no attention to it. He is the man of the future, with no emotions, oblivious to a universe he takes for granted and which, therefore, not taking him for granted, will swallow him up (figure 17).

Once we understand the coherent patterns in Kubrick's work, the complex articulations of human activity, which ironically undoes itself as it struggles without insight to become more than it is, the job of understanding *2001: A Space Odyssey* becomes a bit easier. You will certainly not find unanimity among the various interpretations offered in this book, but even the divergent views of the contributors become clearer when set in the context of the work of an artist whose ironic perceptions of the limits of human agency changed only in the ways they are represented from film to film.

We can also understand *2001* a little better when we put it in the context of its genre, the science fiction film, a mainstay of 1950s Hollywood production, and, like the war film, a favorite of Kubrick's. Science fiction films of the 1950s were made mainly on the cheap and were most often used as covert, allegorical political statements that gave voice to the big fear foisted on the culture: that aliens—of the communist variety—would infiltrate and subvert "our way of life." In science fiction films, like the none too subtly named *Red Planet Mars* (Harry Horner, 1952), *I Married a Monster from Outer Space* (Gene Fowler, Jr., 1958), or the notorious *Invasion of the Body Snatchers* (Don Siegal, 1956), "communists" were transformed into personality-robbing monsters from outer space. There were, to be sure, a few bigger budget, somewhat more speculative films, such as *Destination Moon* (Irving Pichel and George Pal, 1950) and *Forbidden Planet* (Fred Wilcox, 1956), that explored more interesting ideas. *Destination Moon* and George Pal and Byron Haskin's *Conquest of Space* (1955) nourished Kubrick's imagination of space as much as the mind-robbing monsters of alien invasion films (figures 1 and 2).

With *Dr. Strangelove; or, How I Stopped Worrying and Learned to Love the Bomb*, Kubrick made another kind of Cold War science fiction film. Here, the monsters are government and military officials, all of them half or fully mad, hell-bent on destroying the "enemy," which, of course, is themselves. *Strangelove* is a hilarious and hair-raising satire about the United States and the USSR gone mad with fear and vengeance, which results, inevitably, in their both blowing up the world. As Kubrick was making his science fiction film about space travel, the genre had already gone into a recessive mode. Few science fiction films were made after the 1950s (although one of the French New Wave directors, Jean-Luc Godard, made a parody of the genre, *Alphaville*, in 1965), and after *2001*, which appeared in 1968, it took almost another ten years for Kubrick's film to get absorbed and revive the genre, which happened with George Lucas's *Star Wars* in 1977. The genre hasn't flagged since, and almost every science fiction film now made bears a debt to *2001*. Kubrick made a number of decisions that changed the genre for good. He strove for scientific accuracy, calling in NASA and computer scientists to advise him. The texture of his film—the sets, the models, the very movements of the people—were more detailed and more imaginatively constructed than the flying saucers and mutant aliens in aluminum foil or rubber costumes that figured in most 1950s science fiction. In place of the anticommunist hogwash of the previous decade, and even though the film does contain some mockery of Cold War attitudes, he introduced a large measure of complexity, inquisitiveness, and ambiguity, which places his film closer to the best fiction literature than it is to science fiction cinema.[1]

That's why *2001* can be called a speculative, even a meditative film, a film that demands attention and a willingness to wonder. It asks us to do a number of things at once: to join its meditative pace, to be amazed at its spectacular images, and to go along with that rarest of all things, a film that poses a multitude of problems with no easy answers. In short, to use a word that has occurred often in analyses of *2001*, it is a complex film. As Annette Michelson says in her groundbreaking essay, written when the film first appeared, it elevates "doubt to an [a]esthetic principle" and demands "a kind of critical, apperceptive athleticism" in the act of interpretation.[2] Doubt and aesthetics—the last involving a concentrated gaze at an imaginative object of some intellectual and emotional complexity—are a bit out of style at this moment, when easy answers are demanded no matter how difficult and complex the questions may be and when art itself, along with all of the demands it puts on our time, attention, and critical faculties, is somewhat out of fashion itself, especially in film.

The great paradox of Kubrick's films is that they are intellectually rigorous and demanding; they are indisputably works of a creative, artistic imagination and they are also spectacular to watch, entertaining, as well as profoundly ironic, and always playing jokes on us. Despite the fact that many critics use the word "cold" when talking of his films, they are in fact on fire with ideas, prophecies of the way we live and what will become of us if we continue on our path, and a deep comprehension of the difficulties into which we get ourselves. They are funny, angry, jokey, not compassionate, rarely if ever offering redemption to their characters, but always showing us more than we have ever seen before and showing us with the passion of a filmmaker who sees, feels, and expresses his art deeply.

That is the main reason for this collection of essays: to reignite the passion of *2001: A Space Odyssey*, to rethink and reexamine its complexities, and, hopefully, to make the film accessible—though never completely comprehensible—to a new generation of viewers. It is time to reopen the film, resee it, attempt again to understand what it's doing. *2001* has had much written about it, but given its richness, its history, and the changes in its audience since its first release, more is ready to be said. Like the narratives of Kubrick's films, the critical responses they call forth move in a kind of eternal return, coming back again and again to reconsider, reinterpret, and even recreate their meanings.

In order to get fresh perspectives, I have looked to film scholars with broad areas of interest and, in two instances, to scholars who work in areas other than film—a historian and a computer scientist. I wanted to present new points of view and bring new methodologies of thinking and writing about films in general and about this film in particular.

Although they wrote their essays independently of one another, it is not surprising that almost all of the authors touch upon the film's major enigmas: the monoliths, which may or may not be artifacts of alien intelligence; the final sequences in which astronaut Dave Bowman is transported to an imaginary realm "beyond the infinite" and then mutated into a fetus circling the Earth; and *2001*'s most interesting character, HAL, the computer with more than human qualities. Each writer has come up with different perspectives to similar questions. Are the monoliths—those mysterious structures that seem to spur the movement of human progress whenever they appear—indeed extraterrestrial visitations, or are they symbolic representations of obstacles that must be overcome for the progression from ape to human to some kind of rebirth of a superhuman? This is a central question in a film that depends on an almost tactile sense of the visually real. Things are so strikingly present in such detail that, like the apes that first encounter the monoliths and Dr. Floyd, who reaches out to it when he sees it on the moon, we too want to touch it and know its meaning (figures 19 and 20). We see the monoliths, as do the characters in the film, but are they "real"? Of course not. They are images in a cinematic fantasy. But even within that fantasy, or fairy tale, as George Toles considers it, they may well be the visible projections of the human imagination's need to think beyond where it is currently stuck.

But, then, why does the overcoming of obstacles always involve violence? The ape sees the monolith and learns to use tools as weapons to kill. The discovery of the monolith found on the moon leads to HAL murdering the hibernating crewmen, Dave Bowman lobotomizing HAL, and Bowman's harrowing trip to another imaginative realm, where he is transformed. What exactly is the meaning of the film's last image? Bowman, passing from youth to old age in front of his own eyes in the timeless space of an alien though eerily familiar, dreamlike motel room, seems to pass through the monolith and become an encapsulated fetus circling the Earth (figures 23 and 35). Is this a rebirth into a new human race, or simply the entrapment of humanity gazing in fear and wonder in a way that none of the other characters in the film ever did?

With the monoliths and the mysteries of the Jupiter room, HAL is *2001*'s great enigma: a machine with intelligence and consciousness. A machine with feelings—in fact more feelings than any of the human characters inhabiting the film. A machine that kills. A machine whose lobotomy causes more emotions in the viewer (and itself) than anything that happens to the film's human characters. HAL is the overriding intelligence of this film's imaginary realm, the patriarch, the holder of knowledge and feeling, and, like the apes long before him, he is a killer.

Stephen Mamber, in his chapter on the spatial realms of *2001*, points out that the first time we see astronaut Dave Bowman is as a reflection in HAL's eye (figure 13). It is almost as if the worlds of the film take place in HAL's brain. Marcia Landy picks up on this idea and, working from the discipline of brain science and the work of the French philosopher Gilles Deleuze, speaks of the film as an odyssey through the brain, a "cerebral journey," a kind of cinematic history of intelligence and consciousness. This is expanded by Michael Mateas's essay on HAL and artificial intelligence. Mateas is a computer scientist, a humanist, and a proponent of what he terms "expressive" (as opposed to "artificial") intelligence. He reads HAL through the history of AI and the ways that Kubrick responded to and prophesied the various episodes and issues in the computer discipline of artificial intelligence.

We begin with Barton Palmer's investigation of the early reception of *2001: A Space Odyssey*. He points out that, on its release, the reviewers had more difficulty with the film's slow pace and open questions than did its audience. Contemporary viewers, especially younger ones, moved freely within its enigmatic images. But, while some film reviewers scoffed and dismissed it, other, more thoughtful critics began to examine it, and what they began to discover, Palmer points out, laid the field for the various critical interpretations that followed.

All interpretations proceed from the fact that Kubrick was the embodiment of the film auteur, in control of all facets of his work from inception through distribution. Auteurism is a seminal theory of film that speaks of the director as the driving, creative force of a film. James Gilbert, a historian who has written on various aspects of science and film, expands on this idea. His chapter provides a history of this particular director's restructuring and rethinking of the science fiction genre, in which Kubrick was interested for many years. *Dr. Strangelove*, as we noted, is a kind of satirical, political fantasy/science fiction, which points a direction toward *2001*. Even its final images of the B-52 flying toward its destination in Russia are similar to the strange trip through alien landscapes at the end of *2001*. Gilbert's chapter examines the film as the work of a guiding cinematic intelligence (not at all extraterrestrial), fully in control not only of his film but of the history and science that make it up.

Throughout this introduction, I've been stressing the *seriousness* of *2001*, which has a depth of speculation and thought not usually found in film. Jay Telotte addresses this "gravity" in both senses of the word. *2001: A Space Odyssey* shows us what it might be like to defy gravity and the known spatial coordinates that gravity makes possible. Kubrick takes great visual pleasure in the spectacle of antigravity activities—from walking, to eating, to going to the bathroom. Telotte expands upon this to examine the concept of trajectory in the film and its spatial movements of regeneration and birth. He plays upon the other meaning of "gravity": seriousness, weightiness, as opposed to weightlessness. Gravitas. Profundity.

There is a good connection between Jay Telotte's essay and Stephen Mamber's on Kubrick's use of space. Mamber categorizes the various spaces of the film, from the "realistic" to the imaginative, indicating how Kubrick creates boundaries and then makes them porous. Mamber also connects the spaces delineated in *2001* with those in other Kubrick's films, further indicating that, unique as it is, *2001* is still part of the fabric, the spatial density, of Kubrick's entire imaginative output.

Barry Grant's "Of Men and Monoliths" takes a slightly different turn to address the issues and spaces of gender in the film, from the dominance of men and the absence of women to the phallic nature of the space ships and the monoliths themselves. He understands this as part of a broader view of a male-dominated Earth and universe. But Grant recognizes that, finally, Kubrick goes beyond the usual gender boundaries. The end of the film offers an opportunity for a different way of being and understanding than the usual dichotomies of gender allow.

It is important to note that, as Kubrick's work matured, he questioned gender stereotypes more and more. *The Shining*, cowritten by a woman, Diane Johnson, is literally about the collapse of patriarchy and the end of woman hating. *Full Metal Jacket* (1987) turns the tables on marine machismo when a female sniper brings down the platoon. Kubrick's last film, *Eyes Wide Shut*, is a profound examination of domesticity and the enormous effect on a male's ego when he discovers that a woman has her own sexual fantasies and desires. Moving from the universal in the early part of his career to the microcosm of marriage at the end, Kubrick continued throughout to see the cycles of awareness and defeat, of male ego leading to some variety of emasculation, if not downright self-destruction. Gender was always on Kubrick's mind, coming more and more to consciousness as he and his work matured. But even as early as *2001*, Kubrick understood that maleness was an earthbound concept. Freed of the spatial constraints binding it to the Earth and its culture of male dominance, "man" becomes unmanned in an odyssey that releases consciousness and the body that contains it into spaces of imagination.

Marcia Landy's and Michael Mateas's chapters continue to explore the movements of intelligence and consciousness as they are figured in Kubrick's film. They come to it from different perspectives while expanding the spatial metaphors developed in the previous essays. Landy, as noted, examines the film through the discipline of brain science, seeing it as an imaginary journey through the brain itself. Mateas examines the film, and HAL in particular, through the work of computer science, specifically artificial intelligence. The latter was, of course, an abiding interest of Kubrick's, so much so that he planned a film called *AI*, which he was unable to make, but which Steven Spielberg took over after his death. Intelligence, natural or artificial, is part of the reigning paradox of all of Kubrick's films: human intelligence inevitably creates something that will ultimately turn on its owner and undo him. We see it in the fantastic robbery plot in *The Killing*, in the Doomsday Machine in *Dr. Strangelove*, in the Ludovico technique in *A Clockwork Orange*, in the mechanism of the aristocracy in *Barry Lyndon*, and so on throughout the films.

The pivot point in *2001* is HAL, a perfect machine that thinks and feels. Mateas puts this fantasy computer in the context of the real research being done on artificial intelligence—research that Kubrick himself used in creating HAL—and then extrapolates his own computational-based fantasy into the future of AI. He speculates on what would happen if HAL were lifted as a character from the narrative fiction of the film into another fiction: the interactive game. Considering the fact that HAL and the astronauts are engaged in a life-and-death game within the fiction of *2001*, this extrapolation is not extreme.

Susan White's chapter picks up a number of threads woven by the other contributors. She continues an exploration of gender in Kubrick's work, and she contextualizes *2001* within the body of that work. As all of the chapters demonstrate, Kubrick's films construct a coherent view of the world and the work of undoing performed by all of his characters. White examines *2001* as one among Kubrick's thirteen feature-length films. In so doing, it becomes somewhat different and a little clearer than when it is viewed in isolation. Some of its enigmas are less enigmatic, and its apparent, if mysterious, optimism at the chances of human rebirth begin to appear as somewhat less than optimistic. White follows a particular concern that is manifested throughout the films: the surge of violence and disorder that lurks beneath and often bursts out of their cold, distanced surfaces and impeccable, formal beauty. She calls this the "obscene shadow," the dark, hidden chaos that lies beneath the light. With this in mind, she pulls all of Kubrick's films together around *2001: A Space Odyssey* and, with this gathering, provides a space for a clear understanding.

Finally, George Toles comes to the film from a novel and satisfying perspective, viewing it as a fairy tale filled with riddles, trials, genies, and shape shifters. He sees it as a fantastic voyage and a film about seeing, memory, and meditation. Perhaps this take answers no more of the questions that the film continually poses, but it goes some way in helping us to ask better questions. In the end, none of the chapters adds up to a conclusion. And this is very important. The power of *2001* lies in the fact that it can have no conclusion. It is the perpetual generator of the imagination, taking us on its journey every time we join it, stimulating with its imagination the imagination of others, making meaning, making us continually want to find meaning, and eluding us every time.

Notes

1. For a fuller discussion of the context of Kubrick's films, see Robert Kolker, *A Cinema of Loneliness: Penn, Stone, Kubrick, Scorsese, Spielberg, Altman*, 3d ed. (New York: Oxford University Press, 2000), 97–174. Further exploration of the science fiction context is in Kolker, "*2001: A Space Odyssey*," in *Film Analysis: Norton Film Reader*, ed. Jeffrey Geiger and R. L. Rutsky (New York: Norton, 2005), 602–21.

2. Annette Michelson, "Bodies in Space: Films as 'Carnal Knowledge,'" in *The Making of* 2001: A Space Odyssey, ed. Stephanie Schwam (New York: Modern Library, 2000), 203, 204. Originally published in *Artforum* 7, no. 6 (February 1969).

1

2001

The Critical Reception and the Generation Gap

R. BARTON PALMER

Pauline Kael, the era's most influential critic and tastemaker, observed that the largely unforeseen success that Stanley Kubrick's *2001: A Space Odyssey* achieved at the box office was due to the younger viewers who crowded that nation's theaters to see it, turning the film's exhibition into one of the signal cultural events of the decade. And yet the enthusiasm of the fifteen- to twenty-five-year-olds for the film, so Kael opined, was not to be explained on purely cinematic grounds. Instead, *2001*'s appeal to the young was to be traced to the "new tribalism" that had emerged by the end of the 1960s.[1] Kael suggested that what most commentators at the time termed the "counterculture" had also responded enthusiastically earlier in the decade to European art films that were characterized by ostentatious visual and aural stylizations, which were indisputably prominent elements of Kubrick's new release as well.

Young people, however, had been drawn to *Juliet of the Spirits* or *8½* (Federico Fellini, 1965, 1963) not because the art film form intrigued them, but because they were interested in "using the movie to turn on," or so Kael maintained. *2001* supposedly followed in this tradition, quickly developing, upon its release in 1968, the similar reputation that "the movie will stone you—which is meant to be a recommendation."[2] Outraged by the success the film achieved despite her negative assessment and those of the critical establishment in general, Kael was prompted to take an especially jaundiced view of the more culturally adventurous among the baby boomer generation.[3]

The "new tribalism" explanation for the box office success of *2001* may have some (if undoubtedly limited) merit. At some theaters where the film became a cult attraction, recreational drug use in the auditorium was commonly reported. In any case, one obvious result of the film's surprising popularity with teenagers and young adults was an unintended promotion that quickly outstripped the more conventional advertising campaign plotted out by MGM. Prior to its release, the studio had been convinced it was not marketing a cult film, but yet another spectacular epic in the vein of *Lawrence of Arabia* and *How the West Was Won*, blockbusters with serious themes that had proven popular with older cinema goers earlier in the decade. Kael is correct in pointing out that the word on Kubrick's science fiction epic did not go out (at least initially) through newspaper or magazine spreads.[4]

What some considered to be the film's attractive qualities, including its visceral appeals, were not generally promoted by prominent reviewers, many of whom, like Kael, panned the production, at least initially (some recanted upon a second viewing once *2001*'s popularity became too widespread to deprecate). She scornfully observed, "'The tribes' tune in so fast that college students thousands of miles apart 'have heard' what a great trip *2001* is before it has even reached their city" (100). Kael left no doubt about how she felt about the reception accorded the film by this class of viewers: "Using movies to go on a trip has about as much connection with the art of the film as using one of those Doris Day–Rock Hudson jobs for ideas on how to redecorate your home—an earlier way of stoning yourself." Poor films like *2001*, she thought, can perhaps be used more easily than good ones "for such non-aesthetic purposes as shopping guides or aids to tripping" (101).

To be sure, the popularity of *2001* with the young in general and the counterculture in particular likely went far beyond the purview of what might be properly called the aesthetic. Yet the evidence suggests that many in those first, predominantly youthful audiences found more than an easy high. For the generation that came of age in the late 1960s, seeing the film (often numerous times) became a *rite de passage* thought to be the source of a special knowledge that distinguished them from their parents and "square" adults in general. Many reported undergoing religious conversions, rather than experiencing altered states, during the film's famous twenty-four-minute, dialogue-free final sequence: astronaut Bowman's rapid journey through the immensities of time and space, which ends with his transformation into a newborn "star child," whose glance back from space toward the Earth could be understood as foretelling some kind of renewal (see figure 35). If Bowman were freed from the familiar (including his own physical being), so might the human race, hitherto trapped by the linearity of historical unfolding and the destructive, iron laws of technological "progress," with its inextricable connection to violence.

The substantial appeal of the film to young adults proved quite enduring, but it was by no means intentional. A rerelease in 1974 was rather profitable, with those under twenty-five constituting once again a large percentage of the enthusiastic audiences. To be sure, the acceptance by young people of their parents' favored form of mass entertainment contributed more than a little to *2001*'s excellent box office. Many baby boomers, especially the college educated, had gotten hooked on the movies even though both the studio system and the filmmaking style that had created it for more than four decades were in the process of decay and reconfiguration. The crisis in the industry coincided with the changing demographics of the cinema-going public, prompting the production of films designed to appeal to the young. Yet this was a series to which *2001* was not designed to belong.

The youth-oriented films that set box office records at the end of the 1960s (notably Mike Nichols's *The Graduate*, also 1968, and Dennis Hopper's *Easy Rider*, 1969), were predictably Oedipal, staging compromised rebellions, in the tradition of J. D. Salinger, against middle-class values and institutions (marriage, settling down, productive employment, "responsibility") in the name of an ever-elusive personal freedom, a quest that could be shaped into either a comic or tragic conclusion. These youth films lent visual and narrative form to the many-sided conflict between the young and their parents that—along with a host of other social and political issues—became known as the "generation gap." In contrast, *2001* was written and directed by men in the never-to-be-trusted over-thirty group (the film's author, Arthur C. Clarke, and Stanley Kubrick belonged to an earlier generation, though this was typical of the period; the youth movement among Hollywood directors did not truly emerge until the 1970s).

Of course, *2001* is critical of the patriarchal establishment, broadly speaking. The film mercilessly debunks the then-current myth of the triumphant technocrat, whose claim to advance the frontiers of knowledge had found its most publicly celebrated reflex in the American victory over the Russians in the space race, ratified the year after the film's release by the first lunar landing. Kubrick's film offered a quite different view. In *2001*, arrogant scientists fail to understand and master the monolith that seems to announce the presence of a superior and powerful intelligence of some kind, giving an ironic twist to the vaunted concept of "mission control."

But there is more here than revolt and debunking. Kubrick was less invested either in mounting an assault on those supposedly in charge of society in the manner of his critically acclaimed *Dr. Strangelove* (1964) or in satirizing conventional pieties, as he does so effectively in *Lolita* (1962). Unlike any film ever released by Hollywood, *2001* offers a sweeping if provocatively reductive and ultimately ambiguous representation of human history that is deeply Spenglerian in its faulting of Enlightenment values, such as progress, humanism, and even civilization. It is hard to imagine, in fact, how Kubrick could have further undermined the ideological presuppositions of Hollywood storytelling, with its narrative driven by and centered on character, its embodiment of political or social questions in valued individual destinies capable of neat resolution, its conventional deployment of admirable protagonists and despicable antagonists, its devotion to arousing the sympathy and pathos necessary for the proverbial happy ending, and, perhaps most important, its confection of a closure that masked contradiction with a perfect knowledge of character and event. Such a sweeping rejection of those structures and themes so customary in the American commercial cinema certainly challenged the analytical and critical acumen of journalists and reviewers at the time.

2001 goes far beyond the single-minded Oedipality of adolescent revolt in order to raise, if not to definitively answer, the most vexing of metaphysical questions, including the debatable value of the emergence of hominids from purely instinctual behavior to tool making, murder, and eventually the transmissible culture that endows *Homo sapiens*, alone among creatures, with a history. That history, as the film makes manifest, stimulates man to entertain a curiosity about his origins and purpose, even as it provides him with the technological power to pursue the "truth" of his situation, which becomes the goal of the odyssey that Kubrick's narrative traces. In fact, a number of influential young viewers, as we shall see, were especially attracted to the teleology developed by Clarke and Kubrick, which was so different from both Christian eschatology and the gradual meliorism of traditional science, even as it similarly promised forms of redemption and renewal. Indeed, it seems that, contra Kael, the popularity of *2001* with the young had much to do with the film's themes (and the way these were advanced by an unfamiliar narrative strategy) and not only with the supposedly hallucinogenic effects of its visual and aural programs, however strikingly original and deeply affecting. Here was a film in which spectacle arguably dominated a seemingly deliberately banal, even meager, script. But it was also true that *2001* had something different to say, in the largest sense of that term, and had found a different way to say it. The establishment critics, for the most part, were simply not attuned to this message. But the film-going public evidently was. *2001* earned the third-best box office gross in 1968, finishing behind only the spectacularly successful *The Graduate* and *Funny Girl* and easily making the list of the then top-twenty grossing films of all time. With its initial and subsequent releases, domestic and worldwide, Kubrick's arty, intellectual film earned nearly $138 million, which was, at that time, an astounding figure.[5]

Kael's comments are contained in an essay provocatively entitled "Trash, Art, and the Movies," whose premise is that the movies are the "sullen art of displaced persons." The appeal of this "sullen art" resides in their being "slick, reasonably inventive, well-crafted," conforming to an aesthetic endorsed not only by those in the industry, but by most critics as well (87, 92). In Kael's view, films such as *2001* reject this aesthetic because they aspire to be art rather than entertainment but, paradoxically, "may be no more than trash in the latest, up-to-the-minute guises, using 'artistic techniques' to give trash the look of art." They are dangerous because they may make us forget that "most of the movies we enjoy are not works of art" (117, 89). To put this another way, Kael thinks that movies are what we enjoy "and what we enjoy has little to do with what we think of as art" (102). This is a debatable point at best, perhaps little more than a sophomoric rejection of official culture in the name of old-fashioned, just-plain-folks enjoyment. The dominant view in American culture, which she endorses, is that "[a]rt is still what teachers and ladies and foundations believe in, it's civilized and refined, cultivated and serious, cultural, beautiful, European, Oriental: it's what America isn't" (105). Kubrick went wrong, in other words, not only by making a movie that could be enjoyed by the brainless young, but also by making a film with artistic pretensions.

Kael's dismissal of the film, and the musings that serve as the underpinnings of that judgment, point toward the challenge that *2001* posed upon its initial release to long-dominant notions of movie value. Her analysis, while hostile, is also complex and perspicacious largely because it is unintentionally revelatory of the contradictory values at the center of the era's American film culture. *2001* deconstructs the usual opposition of high to low culture (art to trash), providing a subaesthetic form of enjoyment for some and advertising itself as having the same seriousness of theme and structure as the latest Fellini or Kurosawa release (although this intellectual content is nothing more, in her view, than "inspirational banality") (123). That a film made more or less within the mainstream commercial system could manage genuine visceral and intellectual appeal would become a commonplace judgment just a few years later, during that flourishing of popular American art cinema usually called the Hollywood Renaissance. The making of *2001*, and its controversial reception, are likely the first signs that such a revolution in cinema culture was in the offing.

In any event, the popularity of *2001* proved difficult to analyze and appreciate for most journalists and critics, who were accustomed in 1968, like Kael, to think of art film as serious, edifying rather than enjoyable, and European (or, at least, foreign). Celluloid entertainment was what Hollywood provided. It is indeed notable that the most articulate initial defense of Kubrick's achievement appeared in the *Harvard Crimson*, penned by youthful critics who were not so much under the spell of the "classic Hollywood text" as were Kael and company and who, perhaps for that reason, looked beyond the unfamiliarity of the director's structural innovations to find the film not only an excellent example of a standard Hollywood genre, the science fiction film, but also "huge and provocative" in its engagement with questions about "progress—physical, social, and technological."[6] Thus the generation gap not only explained the film's box office success, but to an important degree its critical reception as well.[7]

Establishment Views

Unlike Kael, Stanley Kauffmann found the enthusiasm of the hip young for the film less a cause for dismay than the director's supposed failure to adhere to the customary canons of cinematic correctness. His comments show that he was in implicit agreement with her judgment that Hollywood films should be "slick, reasonably inventive, well-crafted." But, again unlike Kael, he identifies and disparages precisely those aspects of the narrative structure that later critics were to consider central to Kubrick's substantial (and, arguably, never equaled) achievement. Kauffmann admitted that the five years of production and $10 million of funding (an amazing sum at the time) could be seen on the screen, a testimony to the director's strong visual sense and maniacal attention to detail, but he expressed puzzlement about how Kubrick was able to "concentrate on his ingenuity and ignore his talent."[8] The film goes wrong, he thinks, in "the first 30 seconds," presumably when, unlike the usual Hollywood product, it did not provide enough in the way of customary structural elements (particularly a main character to focus the story). Viewers like Kauffmann could not immediately orient themselves by identifying the film's genre and presumed narrative trajectory.

As did other critics at the time, Kauffmann found part of the problem to be what he called "sheer distention," the fact that, as originally released, the film ran 160 minutes, a full three hours including intermission (19 minutes were excised by Kubrick early in the initial release in an attempt to blunt this criticism). This objection, however, turns out to be something of a red herring. *2001* was hardly distinguished by excessive length. Since the early 1950s, Hollywood had been producing blockbusters whose claim to special status was, in part, established by their running longer than the 90- to 120-minute format that had been established as a standard by the early studio period. In 1960, Kubrick had himself contributed to the blockbuster series with *Spartacus*, a film he was called in to complete, which was 196 minutes long. Though the film ran nearly four hours with orchestral overture and intermission, *Spartacus* did not provoke complaints about "sheer distention," presumably because it did not otherwise ignore or violate established industry conventions.

Kauffmann, it becomes evident, was actually more displeased by the story that Kubrick and Clarke had fabricated than by the film's supposedly unjustified length. The film is divided into three sections whose connections, though many and subtle, deviate from the Aristotelian causality that had for decades lent the usual studio project such energetic forward motion. Kubrick's narration, particularly its leisurely pacing and omission of significant story information, was also a startling deviation from standard practice. Somewhat typically, Jeremy Bernstein, writing in the *New Yorker*, observed that "after reading the book, I realized that I really hadn't 'understood' the film, and I had especially not understood the ending."[9] Such a judgment presumes that "understanding" (that is, the kind of mastery of story and character that the

Hollywood film had traditionally provided) is what Kubrick wanted the film's viewers to carry away with them. Like Bernstein, Kauffmann did not see that the director was obviously aiming for an entirely different effect. He suggests that Clarke's short story ("The Sentinel") had "been amplified and padded to make it bear the weight of this three hour film," but, though he evidently read it, Kauffmann failed to note that the story the film tells, much transformed in the process of its "novelization," had also been reduced to its barest elements. There is but a minimal provision of information-laden dialogue and a near total absence of revealing title cards or clarifying voice-over.

In any case, Kauffmann suggests that the most obvious evidence of this "padding" is to be found in the conflict between the astronauts and the HAL computer, which, in his view, Kubrick "devised" in order to "fill in this lengthy trip with some sort of action." The real problem, however, has more to do with coherence than distention: "None of this man-versus-machine rivalry has anything to do with the main story, but it goes on so long that by the time we return to the main story, the ending feels appended" (41). And thus the presumed point of the whole picture is "sloughed off," though Kauffmann interestingly declines to identify what that point might be considered to be.[10] Even when the action is coherent, however, the film is "so dull, it even dulls our interest in the technical ingenuity for the sake of which Kubrick has allowed it to become dull" (41). Kauffmann presumably felt that Kubrick, "ignoring his talent," had proven either unable or unwilling to provide the film with a causally linked plot leading to an exciting, last-minute conclusion. In Kauffmann's view, the parts of the film do not connect readily to one another. Hollywood movies, Kauffmann judges, must build up to some point that is made with unmistakable clarity, which *2001* declines to do. Kubrick fails to produce a film that is "slick." *2001* winds up being "dull," the very opposite.

Writing in the *New York Times*, Renata Adler agrees, finding the film "just plain boring."[11] Like Kauffmann, Adler singles out for detailed attention only the conflict between Bowman and HAL. Significantly, this is the one section of the film that is handled in more or less traditional Hollywood fashion, with a suspenseful *agon* between characters, who are styled pretty much as good and evil, that is resolved after a lengthy struggle, which is more physical than psychological and climaxes in a violence that is as poignant as it is righteous. Expecting the rest of the film to fit this same pattern, Adler attributes its loose connections, lack of backstory, and final ambiguity to a failure of artistry: "It is as though Kubrick himself had become so rapt in the details of his fantasy that he lost track of, or interest in, the point of it all" (L 1).

Interestingly, Adler here glimpses an alternative interpretation of these formal features: that Kubrick is not, finally, interested in telling what is, in conventional terms, a "human" drama that might be summed up in some kind of message. Similarly, Kauffmann remarks on a central thematic contradiction of the film, that it shows space, on the one hand, as "thrillingly immense" but, on the other hand, as a place where men are "imprisoned, have *less* space than on earth." Controlled by the environment, the characters in the film are thus "dehumanized" (41), as they are in many Kubrick films.[12] Adler goes more to the heart of the matter, identifying what makes this film so different from the earlier ones made by the director: "One of the things that Kubrick has left out of his movie to a truly astonishing extent is people. It is about a half hour before anything but marvelous apes, tapirs, landscapes, and about an hour before the main human characters arrive" (26). Like Kauffmann, however, Adler fails to identify the thematic and narrative strategy of which this startling absence is the most significant example.

Understanding Kubrick's antihumanist perspective on human history proved difficult for many. After his first viewing of the film, Joseph Gelmis wrote that "because its characters are standardized, bland, depersonalized near-automatons who have surrendered their humanity to computers, the film is antidramatic and thus self-defeating."[13] When he saw it a second time, Gelmis became convinced that this was a film of "such extraordinary originality" that it upset "the members of the critical establishment because it exists outside their framework of apprehending and describing movies" (266). Yet he still declared, "Kubrick's depersonalized human beings are antidramatic and that is cinematically self-defeating. The pace is so leisurely and the characters so uninteresting that you may become impatient to get on with the plot." Thus, for him, "the film failed as drama [on] the first viewing because it did not keep me spellbound." Now he had come to see that "the tedium was the message" (267).

Among those first audiences, however, there were those who did not agree with this McLuhanesque conclusion that Kubrick's only aim was to deconstruct the desire of spectators for an engaging narrative that centered on sympathetic characters and was motored by a conventional plot.

A Youthful Perspective

Acknowledging his own initial failure to appreciate Kubrick's achievement, Gelmis observed that the establishment critics were "threatened" by the film "because the conventional standards don't apply." What was needed instead was "an innocent eye, an unconditioned reflex, and a flexible vocabulary" (266). *2001* found its most articulate champions in three Harvard students, who recognized it not only as a "superb science-fiction genre film" but also as "an attempt at metaphysical philosophy." Hunter, Kaplan, and Jaszi recognized that Kubrick's double desire to offer audiences an entertaining film that offered the conventional pleasures of genre and to make an intellectual statement might well be a "sure-fire audience baffler guaranteed to empty any theater of ten percent of its audience." That 10 percent, they might have gone on to say, would likely include the majority of the older generation of critics. If, as they affirm, Kubrick did his best work in the film with "plotless slow-paced material," whose purpose was to underline the "ritualistic behavior of apes, men, and machines with whom we are totally unfamiliar," then it was likely that many viewers would be unable to perceive an important, if never explicitly stated theme of the film, which is "the constantly shifting balance between man and his tools" (216–17).

This preoccupation with technology, broadly speaking, is, of course, the core theme of science fiction, whose signal quality as a genre is that it postulates another, imagined order of existence in which the rules of science, broadly speaking, can be plausibly made to apply. It is this concern with a plausibility established by an extended appeal, always logical and consonant with larger scientific truths, to the reader's sense of the physical and historical real that marks off science fiction like *2001* from superficially similar fantasies like *Star Wars* (1977). What distinguishes Kubrick's film as science fiction, so the *Harvard Crimson* reviewers accurately observe, is that he is able to achieve, "in terms of film technique and directorial approach . . . the audience's almost immediate acceptance of special effects as reality: after we have seen a stewardess walk up a wall and across the ceiling early in the film, we no longer question similar amazements and accept Kubrick's new world without question." Once the "credibility of the special effects" has been established, "we can suspend disbelief . . . and revel in the beauty and imagination of Kubrick/Clarke's space" (217).

The remainder of the review is devoted to a reading of the "challenging substance of the excellent screenplay," which is ably demonstrated to be much more than "inspirational banality" where "tedium" might be the only message. A brief summary will make this clear. In the "Dawn of Man" sequence, we witness the coupling of progress and destruction, as the first use of a tool by the primitive australopithecine hominid is to kill an opponent of a rival band and take possession of the water hole. Before this evolutionary leap, however, the black, rectangular monolith makes its first appearance, and this is the precise moment when the moon and sun are in orbital conjunction. Thus, "a theme of murder runs through simultaneously with that of progress." Thousands of years of human history are then elided by the cut from the bone to the spacecraft, an example of Bazinian associative montage that serves as "an effective, if simplistic, method of bypassing history" (218) (see figures 3 and 4).

The film's second section is set at the beginning of the new millennium, when space travel and exploration are much advanced. On the moon, scientists have discovered a monolith identical to the one that appeared to the apes (once again the moon and sun are in conjunctive orbit). The scientists are baffled by the monolith, but they do soon discover that it is emitting a powerful radio signal toward Jupiter. The conclusion is that some form of life on Jupiter might be responsible for the appearance of the monolith and it is to Jupiter that an expedition is sent some fourteen months later. Thus, the monolith "begins to represent something of a deity," inspiring "apes and man to make the crucial advance," first toward tool making and violence and then later toward traveling to Jupiter.

On that journey, the conflict between the HAL 9000 and the astronauts provides yet another meditation on the relationship between humans and their tools. In the opinion of the reviewers, the script development is, again, linear, as "the accepted relationship of man using machines is presented . . . then discarded in favor of an equal balance between the two." The irony is that HAL "proves [to be] a greater murderer than any of the men" as the film turns again "to the theme of inherent destruction in social and technological progress" (219). Ingeniously using his tools for purposes other than those for which they were intended, Bowman manages to "kill" the computer, in a "complex act [that] parallels that of the Australopithecus." This act is salvational, freeing Bowman from an excessive and dehumanizing dependence on tools; through it, he becomes "an archetypal new being: one worthy of the transcendental experience that follows" (220). This reading is perhaps a bit simplistic. Despite his defeat of the renegade computer, Bowman remains a tool of the monolith—although he does pass through it—and is imprisoned in his fetal sack as he circles the Earth.

After dismantling HAL, Bowman follows the monolith, which he spies floating in space, and enters some kind of time/space warp where he undergoes the startling and ultimately ambiguous remaking that turns him into a "star child" or some species of mutant. Kubrick, as the reviewers recognized however, is not interested in providing a clear message: "the intrinsic suggestiveness of the final image is such that any consistent theory about the nature of *2001* can be extended to apply to the last shot: there are no clear answers" (222). Perhaps the most remarkable fact about the *Harvard Crimson* review is not the sympathy and appreciation it shows for Kubrick's film, which is claimed to be a "superb" example, in its "dazzling technical perfection," of an unusual genre, that of "great philosophical-metaphysical films about human progress and man's relationship to the cosmos" (222). What is most remarkable is that it is the only major contemporary review to provide a close reading of the film's narrative and themes.

Last Words

Pauline Kael is certainly correct in suggesting that what was most interesting at the time about the success of *The Graduate* was not cinematic but "sociological." Sociology, as she sees it in this instance, confirms a time-honored truth: the more things change, the more they stay the same. It is remarkable, Kael observes, "how emotionally accessible modern youth is to the same old manipulation. The recurrence of certain themes in movies suggests that each generation wants romance restated in slightly new terms" (127). No doubt. Older viewers, in contrast, who are comfortable but also bored with the same formulas, are in the process of giving up the movies—because "they've seen it before." And this ennui affects critics of a certain age as well, and "this is why so many of the best movie critics quit." In what is probably not intended to be an autobiographical observation, she declares, "some become too tired, too frozen in fatigue, to respond to what *is* new" (127).

It may well be true, in part, that younger people do not truly know what is new because they do not have the experience to be properly comparative, a sine qua non of the critical task. We might argue that another element of that task should be a certain openness to innovation, as she herself observes: "One's moviegoing tastes and habits change." But then the cinema changes too. And yet Kael seems to ignore that simple truth. She presents as an unalterable fact the dictum that "[i]f we've grown up at the movies we know that good work is continuous not with the academic, respectable tradition but with the glimpses of something good in trash" (127). The younger generation, however, as the *Harvard Crimson* reviewers exemplify, was pleased to find that "the academic, respectable tradition," hitherto the more or less exclusive province of the international art cinema, had found itself a home in a Hollywood studio–financed and –distributed epic film. Of course, *2001* is in only a limited sense a Hollywood film in the tradition of that "trash" for which Pauline Kael affirms such affection.

An essential aspect of *2001*'s conception and production, in fact, is that Kubrick and the creative team he assembled worked outside the studio system, on the other side of the world, in a somewhat dismal place called Boreham Wood, north of London. What Kubrick regarded as the disastrous experience of directing *Spartacus* (after Kirk Douglas hired him after firing Anthony Mann) had soured him on Hollywood, and the changing nature of the industry, in which the studios that had once dominated production were reduced, as in this instance, to little more than banks, made workable both his desire for independence and his more or less permanent relocation outside of the United States. In a history that has been fully documented by others, especially Robert Kolker, the altered conditions of production and the evolving tastes of a younger audience led to a different kind of American film: visually sophisticated, intellectually engaging, intriguingly (dis)connected to genre, and unmindful, as appropriate, of the conventions that had for more than four decades determined the shape of the American commercial product.[14] *2001* is the first, or one of the first, films of this new tradition to make an impact on the marketplace. With the perfect hindsight that the passage of more than three decades provides, we can now clearly see that, contra Kael, the younger generation was not simply "mooning away in fixation on themselves and thinking this fixation had suddenly become an art" (127). As the *Harvard Crimson* reviewers eloquently demonstrate, *2001* was undoubtedly "art" in the tradition of the international art cinema. Although most within the older, established critical generation did not agree, here was a film that could sustain a careful and detailed reading even as it impressed with its technical sophistication and thematic richness. But a youthful enthusiasm for sophisticated science fiction and striking cinematic effects only identifies one kind of appreciative reading that Kubrick's enigmatic text might sustain, as the film's subsequent critical history, including the diverse perspectives collected in this volume, amply attests.

At the time of its initial release, there was a lone but significant indication of the substantial influence that *2001* was soon to exert on cinema studies, then in the process of finding a second home in the academy. Annette Michelson, one of the pioneers of serious film study in this country, devoted a long appreciative essay to *2001*, the only analysis from the period of the film's initial release that today holds more than an archaeological interest. Michelson acknowledges the groundbreaking nature of the director's accomplishment, which is to be seen in its unusual melding of form and content: "Kubrick's film has assumed the disquieting function of Epiphany . . . a disturbing structure, emitting, in its intensity of presence and perfection of surface, sets of signals."[15]

But these are not indecipherable. Kubrick, unlike Homer, is not to be imagined as nodding, nor, in Michelson's view, can he be accused of purveying meaninglessness as a theme, thus deconstructing the mainstream cinema's preoccupation with having a "point." Instead, the film propounds profound ideas about the human experience, the nature of art, and the history of the medium itself; its message is not defined entirely by the high seriousness of its engagement with genre. Like the enigmatic monolith that sets into motion the events of human history that the film traces, *2001* is "endlessly suggestive, projects a syncretic heritage of myths, fantasies, cosmologies and aspirations" (56). In stark contrast to both establishment critics and youthful fans, Michelson finds that "everything about it is interesting," but especially the fact that its form and substance merge inextricably in a "'formal' statement on the nature of movement in its space" (56). Thus Kubrick takes as his subject the notion of "'arrival and departure.' . . . [The film's] narrative [becomes] a voyage of discovery, a progress toward disembodiment, [and] explores . . . the structural potentialities of haptic disorientation as agent of cognition" (56).

Yet, the richness of Kubrick's film is not exhausted by its epistemological movement, by its use of the medium to disengage, disorient, and instruct. Michelson also recognizes that the director's accomplishment was to insert himself into the mainstream tradition of Hollywood filmmaking, whose primal purpose, as the young fans of *2001* instinctively recognized, was always to provide an alternative universe into which the spectator was invited, even impelled. On this level, Kubrick was no less successful than Howard Hawks, Lewis Milestone, and Michael Curtiz, as well as other skilled purveyors of studio-era screen epics: "The film of adventure and of action, of action as adventure is an event . . . and it offers, of course, the delights and terrors [that] occasions of that sort generally provide, [by] positing a space which, overflowing screen and field and vision, converts the theatre into a vessel, and its viewers into passengers" (63). And so the knowledge the film offers is ultimately of the body, or "carnal," the ultimate special effect to which "youth in us, discarding the spectator's decorum, responds" (63). Michelson too saw clearly that *2001* was, in many senses, the ultimate trip.

Notes

1. Pauline Kael, "Trash, Art, and the Movies," in *Going Steady* (Boston: Little, Brown, 1970), 100. Further references will be noted in the text.

2. Kael's view about the appeal of *2001*'s images was echoed by Jeremy Bernstein, writing in the *New Yorker* (September 21, 1968):

> What appears to have happened is that *2001* has uncovered a large public—especially of young people brought up on the visual stimuli of television—for whom visual beauty is sufficient reason for the existence of a film, and who do not need the prop of a conventional plot with a clearly articulated dénouement. (180)

Television theorists might dispute Bernstein's point since, conventionally at least, the audio track is considered to dominate the visual in that medium. Evolved from radio, television is "talky" compared to the movies, which first developed without sound and with only printed language. If the younger generation in the 1960s was accepting of a cinema of spectacular images, it seems more likely the result of the interest of Hollywood, after 1950, in producing visually striking and color films (often shot in widescreen format) in order to compete with television, which was restricted through most of that era to small, ill-defined, and black-and-white images.

3. John Russell Taylor also noted a generational gap in the audience for *2001*, but drew a different conclusion from that fact. The second time he watched the film, he sat next to an especially enthusiastic young viewer and observed:

> [H]is attention was not functioning in the same sort of way that his parents' was, and that mine was. He was, that is to say, not in the slightest worried by a nagging need to make connections, or to understand how one moment, one spectacular effect, fitted in with, led up to or led on from another. He was accepting it like, dare one say, an LSD trip, in which a succession of thrilling impressions are flashed on to a brain free of the trammels of rational thought.

Here was an audience interested in "a whole new way of assimilating narrative," not as "an articulated plot, but [as] a succession of vivid moments." From the *London Times*, in *The Making of Kubrick's* 2001, ed. Jerome Agel (New York: Signet, 1968), 171–72. Taylor raises an interesting point about how *2001* was probably enjoyed by many. Kubrick's artful deployment of images and sound may well have influenced (perhaps inaugurated) one of the most important and enduring elements of the current cinema, its fascination with something close to "pure" spectacle.

4. An important exception must be made for Albert Rosenfield's ten-page spread (mostly stills from the film) in *Life*, April 15, 1968, 24–34. Anticipating the judgment of later film scholars, Rosenfield observes that the film "dazzles the eyes and gnaws at the mind," going beyond the "realm of literal science-fiction into a puzzling, provoking exercise in philosophy" (27).

5. Figures are from "All Time Rental Champs," *Variety*, January 7, 1976.

6. Tim Hunter, with Stephen Kaplan and Peter Jaszi, "The *Harvard Crimson* Review of *2001*," in Agel, *The Making of Kubrick's* 2001, 215. Further references will be noted in the text.

7. There are, as one might expect, notable exceptions to this general rule. West Coast critics were generally more enthusiastic about Kubrick's accomplishment, notably Gene Youngblood (*Los Angeles Free Press*) and Charles Champlin (*Los Angeles Times*), both of whom strongly praised the film, while Penelope Gilliatt, writing in the *New Yorker* (April 13, 1968), though somewhat puzzled by what she had viewed, conceded that *2001* "is some sort of great film, and an unforgettable endeavor" (151).

8. Stanley Kauffmann, "Lost in the Stars," *New Republic*, May 4, 1968, 24. Further references will be noted in the text.

9. "Chain Reaction," in the *New Yorker*, September 21, 1968, 180. Thomas Allen Nelson provides a thorough and insightful commentary on the relationship between the film, on the one hand, and the two literary texts (the short story and the novel) produced by Clarke. He observes:

> Throughout the novel, Clarke combines these evocations of exploration and wandering amid the lonely expanses of space with an elaborate superstructure of explanatory material that ultimately has the effect of subordinating "mystery" to the speculations of science. The film, by contrast, is more open-ended than Clarke's novel, perhaps because Kubrick realized that mystery, whether futuristic or historical, becomes trivialized on the screen once it assumes a definable, objective shape. . . . Kubrick internally organizes *2001* in ways that likewise combine a minimum of explanatory clarity with a maximum of visual ambiguity.

Kubrick: Inside a Film Artist's Maze, rev. ed. (Bloomington: Indiana University Press, 2000), 106–8.

10. Other reviewers were also unhappy with or dismayed by the film's failure to make some obvious point. Robert Hatch, for example, declared that "the ambiguity of these closing scenes is the more disappointing because at least twice in its progress this most ambitious and often most thrilling of space films promises some energy of communication." *Nation*, June 3, 1968, 74. *Variety* (April, 3, 1968) agreed, observing that the "film ends on a confused note, never really tackling the 'other life' situation and evidently leaving interpretation up to the individual viewer. To many this will smack of indecision or hasty scripting" (6). The perspicacious Arthur Schlesinger, Jr., rhetorically asked: "But what is one to make of the astronaut's finding the image of himself in a French eighteenth-century drawing room, his aging, his death, his rebirth? . . . The concluding statement is too private, too profound, or perhaps too shallow for immediate comprehension." *Vogue*, June 1968, 76.

11. I quote here from the second of her two reviews of the film in the *New York Times*, April 21, 1968, L1. Further references will be noted in the text.

12. As Robert Kolker observes, "Kubrick's narratives are about the lack of cohesion, center, community, about people caught up in a process that has become so rigid that it can be neither escaped nor mitigated—a stability that destroys." *A Cinema of Loneliness*, 3d ed. (Oxford: Oxford University Press, 2000), 110.

13. "*Space Odyssey* Fails Most Gloriously," *Newsday*, April 4, 1968, in Agel, *The Making of Kubrick's* 2001, 264. Further references to this and the other two reviews by Gelmis, also collected in Agel, will be noted in the text.

14. Kolker's *A Cinema of Loneliness* is usefully supplemented by James Monaco's *American Film Now*, rev. ed. (New York: Penguin, 1984).

15. Annette Michelson, "Bodies in Space: Film as Carnal Knowledge," *Artforum* 7 (February 1969): 57. Further references are noted in the text.

2

Auteur with a Capital *A*

JAMES GILBERT

The prospect of human venture into space has always raised the disconcerting prospect of discovering either *nothing* or *something*. While the loneliness of nihilism has always been possible, it lacks dramatic potential. To find *something* is a very different story. Since its inception, science fiction has become the popular medium for portraying that something—the presence in the universe that challenges (or confirms) the anthropocentric presumptions of the great monotheistic civilizations of Western society. As Stanley Kubrick was fond of noting, the psychologist Carl Jung predicted that any encounter with transcendent intelligence would tear the reins from our hands, "and we would find ourselves without dreams. We would find our intellectual and spiritual aspirations so outmoded as to leave us completely paralyzed." Quite aptly, therefore, Kubrick said of his film masterpiece, *2001: A Space Odyssey*: "I will say that the God concept is at the heart of *2001*—but not any traditional, anthropomorphic image of God."[1] He recognized that space travel is nothing less than a voyage into time: into the future and into the past, toward end time and back to creation.

Beginning in the nineteenth century, two potent ideas introduced the questions that science fiction was invented to answer. The first centered on Darwin's theory of natural selection, raising questions about how, in fact, humans could have developed from a chance roll of the evolutionary dice. The second engaged Mary Shelley's classic picture of man as the simultaneous inventor of technology and creator of monsters. Theologians and, more broadly, a whole host of imaginative thinkers have struggled with the problem of the human place in a universe that might only incidentally, if at all, be concerned with the fate of mankind. Simultaneously, they have worried over the human tendency to embody ambition, greed, and aggression in technology. Both of these preoccupations occupy the very center of Kubrick and (science fiction author) Arthur Clarke's space travel film. But, unlike a good deal of contemporary science fiction either in literary or film form, which manages to resolve the plot with a glance at God, or reaffirm the limits on human aspiration defined by the religious and philosophic traditions of sin, pride, and hubris, *2001* steps into a different sort of beyond. This idiosyncratic vision of man's encounter with a higher intelligence is accompanied by the suggestion that humans err in presuming to be the anthropomorphic model for God. The result is a remarkable personal conversation about the implications of decentering man within the universe. In this regard, Arthur Clarke's offhand remark about the film rings with unintended truth. "While the film was being made," he explained, "I made the comment that MGM is making the first ten-million-dollar religious movie, only they don't know it yet."[2] The film's millennial title alone should have suggested a spiritual project to anyone aware of the mathematics of apocalyptic thinking.

Science is the vehicle for Kubrick's spiritual quest in outer space in much the same way that it energized a huge body of speculative fiction about "ETs." The possibilities that science raises and the certainties that it challenges constitute perennial problems and periodically demand a revision of God images and belief structures. As the director put it during an interview for *Rolling Stone* magazine, "On the deepest psychological level, the film's plot symbolized the search for God, and it finally postulates what is little less than a scientific definition of God."[3]

In the 1960s, as the Apollo missions swung closer to a moon landing, *2001* spoiled the impact of that landing for us all. More realistic than reality itself, and certainly more dramatic, the film depicted man's venture into space within a rich mix of mythological allusions. It presented a picture of space in ways that the real astronauts could not. With stunning clarity, it demonstrated weightlessness, imagined the moonscape, and pictured the passage of meteors. At the same time, it interpreted the whole experience within a broader framework of mythological and religious symbolism. It combined science and technology with philosophy, anthropology, and religion in ways that were unthinkable to the more conservatively scripted American moon explorers of 1969.[4]

It is noteworthy that almost simultaneously in this period, Protestant evangelical thinkers were constructing a case that used science as the vehicle to speculate upon divine beginnings and endings, to salvage their view of a universe that was purposefully man-centered. In 1962, John Whitcombe and

Henry Morris published their influential reformulation of creation science, *The Genesis Flood: The Biblical Record and Its Scientific Implications*. In this challenge to Darwinism and modern astronomy, the engineer and the theologian confronted the huge problem of explaining away evolutionary science. Quite understandably, they chose to attack the theory of uniformitarianism: "the belief that existing physical processes, acting essentially as at present, are sufficient to account for all past changes and for the present state of the astronomic, geologic, and biologic universe." A world that operated by the slow and inexorable shifts that Darwin had made central to evolutionary theory could never, they affirmed, create an intelligent being such as a man. Evolution could not, on its own, prompted by blind and chance forces, create anything so splendid. It was precisely at this point of radical doubt that Kubrick and Clarke began their famous story of a journey beyond the stars.[5]

Their reason for engaging evolution is, curiously, the same as the creation scientists: there is no drama in evolution, however persuasive a theory it might be. Without outside intervention, there is no tale to tell; in other words, there is only the Nothingness that has always remained a possibility in man's encounter with the Universe. Unlike the preposterous pulp-fiction worlds of Mars and Venus created by Edgar Rice Burroughs, for example, where an energetic evolutionary force has created an elaborate hierarchy of intelligent beasts and beings, Clarke and Kubrick looked to outside intervention to spur the slow, steady state of terrestrial change. If the only tie to evangelical creation science is this question mark about evolution, it nonetheless reveals the moral and aesthetic problems of a Darwinian explanation that *2001* chose to confront. For the encounter with ETs implies nothing less than a new explanation of the origins of humans and the prediction of their future. Evolution might have remained a driving force in this universe, but, like the explanations of the late Stephen J. Gould, it was a force that operated to the rhythm of "punctuated equilibrium"—or put simply, long periods of slow development interrupted by catastrophic change.[6] *2001* is a film that explains such cataclysms.

But punctuated equilibrium and catastrophic change are neither strictly religious nor scientific concepts for Clarke and Kubrick. Even if the narrative of the film is the long story of the creation and resurrection of mankind, it is nonetheless true that this is not strictly a religious or scientific account. That is what Kubrick meant when he described the theme as an oxymoron—a "scientific definition of God." It is why the film encompasses more time than perhaps any other film made, for no less a period could contain such expansive narrative ideas from evolution itself or prophetic religion.

Yet this religious-science emphasis does not begin to exhaust the meanings of the film. Indeed, *2001* is layered with allusions to several of the principal secular and pagan mythologies of Western civilization. As Kubrick noted, it would not reach millions of viewers unless it explored "the universal myths and archetypes of both our shared cultural experience and our collective unconscious."[7]

Sometimes these mythological allusions are explicit, as in the notion of the Odyssey, which is suggested not only by the film's title but also by the various names given to characters or locations. If the astronaut Bowman is a latter-day Odysseus and outer space the tempest-tossed Mediterranean, the classical references nevertheless remain intentionally incomplete and undeveloped. The astronauts do not undergo the variety of adventures that kept the Greek hero and his crew from returning home. So too with other stories that are invoked, such as Nietzsche's Superman, called forth by the leaping chords of Richard Strauss's *Also Sprach Zarathustra*, which is played at the beginning; when ape-men first use the tool/weapon they have been inspired to discover during the first section of the film; and in the birth of the star child at the end. As Alexander Walker paraphrases this theme, the film is Kubrick's story of the nature of intelligence: "He roots intelligence in the mythological past, before man has begun to use it, then ends intelligence in the metaphysical future, where man cannot yet grasp its latest transformation."[8]

In addition to such analogies, there is, of course, the theme of man and modern technology run amok. Kubrick makes this point repeatedly, for example, in the affectless human reactions of the "Moon Station" sequence, in the robotlike astronauts Poole and Bowman, and finally, most dangerously, in the computer HAL, who turns murderer when he believes (wrongly) that the mission to Jupiter is endangered. This too, is a retelling of older myths—of the sorcerer's apprentice, of Frankenstein, of course, and of the countless science fiction films and stories that repeated this warning. From the havoc caused by out-of-control science in H. G. Wells to the cerebral considerations of Isaac Asimov in his brilliant examination of technological control, *I Robot* (1950), this variety of science fiction fits the description of what Susan Sontag has called "the imagination of disaster" as the defining characteristic of the genre.[9]

Beyond the obvious references to mythical stories and older literary plots and science fiction clichés, critics have found symbolic meanings of a different sort in the film. For example, the monolith left by the aliens has been regarded as the God beyond God. Some critics have discovered Freudian symbolism in the rebirth of the fetus after a voyage through a womblike tunnel of light, or in the breaking glass as Bowman eats his last supper in the Louis XVI motel/zoo/observation room. Others have described the monolith as a representation of pure form, or discovered in Jupiter a symbol of the father.[10] The possibilities are legion, and I believe that this is intentionally so.

But why this layered—some might say confused—structure, with bits and pieces of myth cited and partially developed, with suggestive images that cannot quite be unified into a persuasive and coherent whole? Why a story that competes with one of the most fundamental accounts of our civilization, the Bible, in presenting the beginnings and the endings of human existence but that is yet not a truly religious depiction? Why a clearly designated discussion of evolution that, in the end, denies or seriously modifies Darwin? There are, I believe, a number of plausible explanations: the pride of the autodidact eager to display his omnivorous reading; the long period of development and incomplete modifications to the plot and its execution; the powerful presence of Arthur Clarke, who conceived of the film in somewhat different terms than Kubrick; and the likely possibility that confusion or diverse clues were intentional and that the various and even conflicting possibilities were part of Kubrick's purpose to promote multiple interpretations of his work. This is what he meant by calling the film a "mythological documentary." As Clarke put it, "We set out quite consciously and deliberately—calculatedly if you like—to create a myth, an adventure, but still be totally plausible, realistic, intelligent."[11] Without, of course, quite saying what it all meant.

In addition to myth and symbol, there were certain related intellectual enthusiasms that Kubrick also wished to interject in the film. First among these was the director's strong belief in the existence of extraterrestrial beings. Although Arthur Clarke claims to have saved him from a naïve belief in UFOs and flying saucers, Kubrick's enthusiasm was based upon substantial science or, better, probable scientific speculations. As he said in an interview, he was fascinated by the "scientific probability that the universe was full of intelligent civilizations and advanced entities." Allying himself with "most astronomers and other scientists interested in the whole question," he affirmed that he too was "strongly convinced that the universe is crawling with life, much of it, since the numbers are so staggering, equal to us in intelligence, or superior, simply because human intelligence has existed for so relatively short a period."[12]

It was also Kubrick's belief that evolution had worked in a particular fashion: that the human discovery of tools was embedded in the development of warfare. In other words, man's progress was as much determined by destruction as by advance; the race was truly descended from Cain and Abel. This attitude certainly expressed his ambiguity about technology, whatever his enthusiasms for cryonics and space travel. Like much of the science fiction from which he hoped to differentiate his work, he retained an edge of suspicion about technology and a tendency to emphasize the dark side of mechanical progress.[13]

In justifying his allusions to multiple myths, Kubrick sometimes cited Joseph Campbell's anthropological study of mythologies, *Hero with a Thousand Faces*; J. G. Frazier's *Golden Bough*; and his own adherence to the psychology of Jung. What links these works is their exploration of the symbolic dimension of culture. In other words, they are about the myth-making genius of human beings and societies as much as they are about specific stories. This capacity of the imagination to hold varieties of mythic ideas in a kind of synchronous tension justifies the partial references that intersperse the film. In this sense, even the allusions to Christianity are cast within the larger schema of multiple mythologies.[14]

What some critics have treated as confusion and intentional obfuscation—and they may partially be right about this—also reveals Kubrick's purpose of opening up speculation about possible interpretations. The director purposely chose to convey meaning through visual signs and symbols, aiming at both the conscious and unconscious aspects of the viewer, rather than explication through text. By making what is essentially a silent film, with language used sparingly to convey certain necessary narrative cues or to act as a counterpoint to visual messages, Kubrick made it more difficult to determine precisely what he intended. Because visual metaphor is generally less specific or concrete in content than speech, it was tempting because it was possible to layer multiple meanings into the structure of the film. As he put it in an interview with *Playboy* magazine in 1968:

> *2001* is a nonverbal experience; out of two hours and 19 minutes of film, there are only a little less than 40 minutes of dialogue. I tried to create a *visual* experience, one that bypasses verbalized pigeon-holing and directly penetrates the subconscious with an emotional and philosophic content. To convolute McLuhan, in *2001*, the message is the medium.[15]

If true, there exists an interesting paradox. Kubrick and Clarke never stopped talking about possible interpretations of the film, and Clarke's novel (published after the release of the film) carefully explained many of the more obscure meanings and suggested interpretations that would surely have been beyond the consciousness—or unconscious—of the average viewer. For example, that the room in part 4, after Bowman passes through the Stargate, was furnished in Louis XVI style, or that these living quarters were actually an observation chamber furnished out of Bowman's own memories are not obvious without considerable prompting. Kubrick, critics, and the legion of interpreters writing about the film have added meanings that ordinary viewers, by themselves, would ever see. How, for example, was the viewer to know that Kubrick had, in his own words, filmed "a human zoo approximating a hospital" that was constructed out of Bowman's "dreams and imagination"? For good reason Arthur Clarke seemed unable to let go of the story, rewriting it three more times before his death, in novels entitled *2010: Odyssey Two*, *2061: Odyssey Three*, and *3001: The Final Odyssey*. Indeed, for a film whose meanings were purportedly individual and subconscious, *2001* has been subjected to a remarkable degree of scrutiny and intellectualization, more than making up for the silences of the film itself. The aura of commentary has become as much a part of the experience of the film as the viewing of it.[16]

In the creation, filming, and final editing of *2001*, Kubrick transformed a relatively concrete, if brief, short story by Arthur Clarke into an increasingly elliptical and suggestive narrative in which speech, on the few occasions it is used, imparts important information or elsewhere reveals, in its banality, the absence of meaningful communication. As Frederick Ordway, NASA astronomer, rocket expert, and technical advisor on the film, noted, Kubrick cut elements of voice-over commentary that explained several of the key scenes of the film. It was thus left to Clarke, Kubrick, and various critics to reintroduce those missing elements in interviews and articles on the film—and especially in Clarke's novelized version.[17] For example, in describing how aliens changed the ape-men, he helpfully explains that the monolith probed their minds and implanted ideas: "It was a slow, tedious business, but the crystal monolith was patient."[18]

Because he demanded so much from visual symbols, Kubrick moved ever closer to the aesthetics of silent film, defined by the camera work and montage. Such consequences were surely anticipated. As Kubrick noted, "words are a terrible straitjacket." By suppressing speech, the director returned the science fiction movie to its origins in the masterpiece of Georges Méliès, whose 1902 *Trip to the Moon* first demonstrated the possibilities of using montage as a kind of new language in which the miraculous or extraordinary could be spliced into the narrative through special effects (figure 16). In *2001*, the silence only underscores and calls attention to the significance of the camera work itself. Kubrick's meticulous care in creating verisimilitude, technological plausibility, and the depiction of space-travel reality equally matches his care in depicting multiple symbols and metaphors. Both interact in the deep silences of space.[19]

But, of course, silent films were and are neither completely silent nor always without words. By titling parts of the film "The Dawn of Man," "Jupiter Mission," "Jupiter and Beyond the Infinite," Kubrick borrowed another tactic from silent films: by dividing the action with titles, he cued the viewer through signs that the scene and action had shifted through time and space. Doing so granted him, as it allowed silent film masters, the ability to jump from one scene to another, plausibly and without any explanation of how or why. As for silence, before the advent of sound, films may have lacked a soundtrack, but they were often accompanied by music that reflected, anticipated, and enhanced the mood of the scene playing on the screen. Kubrick also uses music in this fashion, as a kind of counterpoint to the action, and his choices have been much noted and often discussed. So, for example, he uses Richard Strauss's *Also Sprach Zarathustra* to accompany the beginning of man's evolutionary ascent. The bone/weapon tossed by Moon-Watcher into the air and then transformed into a shot of an armed space ship circling the Earth is perhaps the most famous cinematic element of the film (figures 3 and 4). And this is accompanied by the transition from Strauss to Strauss, from Richard to Johann, Jr., from the rising, majestic chords of the famous tone poem, to the banal oom-pah-pah of *The Blue Danube*. In the "Dawn of Man" sequence, the music lends mystery, tension, and brilliance to the action; in the second, the waltz reduces the technological miracle of space travel to the ordinary—which is exactly how the humans in the film react to it. Further on, Kubrick uses the eerie voice and orchestra pieces by György Ligeti (*The Requiem*, *Lux aeterna*, and *Atmospheres*) with their religious and mystical overtones to suggest the mythical dimensions of the voyage of the *Discovery 1*.[20]

Reaching back into the history of cinema is only one way that Kubrick reinforces and highlights the symbolic and metaphoric gravity of the film.

He also engages in a long-running dialogue with the genre characteristics of science fiction films, in effect, arguing against their conventions in order to distinguish his work from the hugely popular and often trite plot lines and conventions of the form. At the same time, he remains within the form in certain key respects, capitalizing on the expectations of an audience that had been well trained in what to expect from other depictions of technology gone berserk or the encounter with ETs.

With the exception of a few science fiction films that owed their plots to literature (like *Fahrenheit 451*, *War of the Worlds*, or even *A Clockwork Orange*), most of them repeated a clearly identifiable set of characteristics. It can be argued that *2001* is an argument against the conventions of science fiction as much as it is a representative of that genre. Sometimes Kubrick intentionally introduced extraneous elements into the general format, even as he satirized others as if to call attention to his understanding and contempt for the platitudes of the genre.

Kubrick's ambiguous relationship to the standard format of science fiction films can be grouped around four general themes: depicting aliens, scientific verisimilitude, the ironic denouement, and humor. Susan Sontag's famous essay "The Imagination of Disaster," written in 1965, outlined the principal elements of the genre for her time. Taking the Hollywood monster invasion films as her model, she suggested that audiences responded to "the fantasy of living through one's own death and more, the death of cities, the destruction of humanity itself." Dehumanization and the threat of being "taken over" by alien forces of some kind demonstrate, she suggests, "the depersonalizing of modern urban life." Ambivalence toward science, she continued, is another hallmark of these films. In effect, they constitute a record of fears, disappointments, and apprehension about the future, metaphorically reproduced and dramatized through the imagination. They emerge, she says, from the present condition of society. Arthur Clarke himself said something similar of ordinary science fiction literature:

> The majority of authors who have called up science and fiction, with a characteristic lack of imagination have only seen in these monsters (other forms of intelligence in the solar system) a pretext to describe the conflicts and acts of violence just like those that sully the pages of our own history.[21]

In other words, science fiction is the displaced, disguised drama of our own nightmares, set in an alien atmosphere, but like the dreams they resemble, only thinly disguise the disturbingly familiar dread of loss of self-control, invasion, and death.

Kubrick's *2001* includes many of these generic elements. There is the director's much-publicized belief in intelligent aliens, even superior aliens. There is his well-known hostility toward technocracy and the destructive effects of a technology devoid of any human control or empathy. There is an evil monster: HAL, the computer turned murderer. There is the loss of control and personal invasion. There are aliens. There is space and time travel. Indeed, almost all of the principal elements that constitute the classic science fiction film are in *2001*.

At the same time, Kubrick appears to enjoy playing against stereotype and the expected. Compare his work, for example, with *Planet of the Apes*, also released in 1968 and the film that won the Academy Award that Kubrick thought should be his. *Planet of the Apes*, like many previous science fiction films, is a morality play whose ending is an ironic commentary and sudden explanation of everything that has preceded it in the film. Like many other examples of this genre, it employs the distance of science fiction to depict (and disguise) a contemporary social question—for example, racism. Kubrick certainly includes social commentary in his portrayal of the dangers of technology. And yet the director undercuts the very elements he invokes so seriously, like his distrust of technology. For example, the "monster" HAL, albeit a murderer, dies an almost comic death. When Bowman destroys his intellectual capacity piece by piece, he pathetically sings the chorus from the old song "A Bicycle Built for Two."

In what is perhaps their wisest move, Kubrick and Clarke, unlike almost any other sci-fi makers, resisted the temptation to embody the aliens. Instead, geometric monoliths represent them rather than, as Clarke put it, "some pathetic papier-mâché monster." And the geometric slab, which only symbolizes the aliens is, itself, suggestive of a variety of other mythic or psychological meanings. While the two creators debated the ending of the film for months, considering all manner of possibilities, such as strange new cities or alien creatures, they chose to picture the death and rebirth of Bowman through the psychedelic sequence, the surrealistic scene set in the Louis XVI room, and the final birth of the star child, contemplating Earth and an unknown future. In one sense, Kubrick here is playing with the expectations of the audience, who had been trained to expect a final unveiling of the aliens and a specific explanation of their motives.[22]

Kubrick also confronts three clichés common to many other films, all of them based upon a misapprehension of the dynamics of space travel. His rocket ship makes no noise in the vacuum of space, for example. There is no visible plume of exhaust. And, when a meteor tumbles perilously near the *Discovery 1*, in a scene with no other purpose than to demonstrate his technological knowledge, it makes no *swoosh*.

Together with such obvious moments when he is having fun with the form, the director was meticulous in his research into anthropology for the section on "The Dawn of Man" and in visualizing the various other effects of space travel. Scientists like Carl Sagan and Ordway, among others, were consultants, and an original, ten-minute prologue of interviews with scientists and theologians about the possibilities of alien existence was filmed, although it was cut from the final version. As David Stork has noted, the depiction of space travel was so accurate that portions of the film were used in training

NASA astronauts. Kubrick also consulted corporations like IBM and Boeing to make sure that he got his hardware and software right. To some observers, this was not necessarily a positive. As physicist Freeman Dyson of the Institute for Advanced Study at Princeton observed, "When I saw Kubrick at work on *Space Odyssey* in London, I was immediately struck by the fact that he was interested in gadgetry rather than in the people." Or as Renate Adler put it in her famous hostile review for the *New York Times*, "The movie is so completely absorbed in its own problems, its use of color and space, its fanatical devotion to science-detail, that it is somewhere between hypnotic and immensely boring."[23]

Kubrick's commitment to scientific plausibility further differentiated his work from most science fiction films, especially in its conclusion. The stock sci-fi film ordinarily ended with a preposterous but easy to grasp explanation, for example, that radiation had caused a mutant monster, or that man's aggrandizing soul had ironically tempted him to commit harmful mistakes. Kubrick had little use for this ironic interplay between human aspiration and failure. Kubrick's film, rather than returning to the human condition and the comforting *status quo ante*, self-consciously breaks through to rebirth and regeneration. Thus it is open-ended and speculative, where most other science fiction films circle back upon themselves in asserting the moral limitations of humanity. Where most science fiction returns to a kind of stasis, delivering the audience back to the world of mundane reality, *2001* ends with an opening to the future.

Finally, and perhaps most dramatically, Kubrick challenges the science fiction genre through the use of humor. This occurs in many guises and several places, but perhaps most notably in the initial sequence in part 2, the section dealing with the alien monolith discovered on the moon. Even some of Kubrick's most perceptive critics, in their undivided attention to the brilliant jump cut from Moon-Watcher's bone to the encircling nuclear warheads, have missed his follow-up comic gesture. From the orbiting bombs, he segues to the approaching space ship, and finally, inside, to Heywood Floyd's floating pen (the same shape as the bone and the rocket ship; figure 5). What follows are a number of verbal and visual jokes about eating (bad airline food), airplane bathrooms, and telephones in space, replete with a stewardess in a tacky airline uniform. The end of this sequence is the almost ludicrous and uninformative briefing given by Floyd to scientists working on the moon discovery. And over all of it are the bouncy chords of *The Blue Danube*—one of the most decidedly non–science fiction sounds in the universe. Although there are other moments of humor sprinkled throughout the film, none is so pointed or extensive as these. But they all serve to differentiate his work from the deadly serious plots of most other science fiction films.

At the same time, Kubrick raises serious issues that he does not resolve but that other films might have fully engaged. For example, there is a slightly ominous discussion with Russian scientists about the moon slab, which the Americans are keeping a secret under the cover story of a quarantine. Floyd pointedly warns that disclosing the existence of the slab might cause panic and fear throughout the world. Yet Kubrick declines any follow-up to these ideas of nuclear competition and worldwide alarm at the discovery of alien intelligence, just raising and dropping them as if to say, "I could have gone in this direction, but I chose not to."

Perhaps only Kubrick was sure-footed enough to be playful and even misleading where other directors feared to break the continuity of mood and verisimilitude. Yet, nothing about these numerous encounters with the platitudes of science fiction in any way diminishes the serious intent of *2001*. Instead, like everything else in the film, these moments call attention to the director, the choices he makes, and his sometimes obscure purposes.

To understand why there is this constant reminder of the mechanics of movie making, we must return to the beginning, to the fundamental question of what sort of story Kubrick is telling. In confronting and combining the two grand narratives of the origin and fate of man in the universe, of creation and evolution, of religion and science, where does he stand, finally? The answer, insofar as there is one, is suggested by Kubrick's incessant depiction of the eye. There are eyes and cameras everywhere, and HAL's "seeing" is, in fact, a form of camera work. Whether it be in the guise of the sun rising over the first monolith (like the Masonic symbol on the dollar bill), the eyes of the ape-men, the eyes of the tiger, HAL's computer camera-eye, or finally, the distended eye of the star child, this is a shifting, significant symbol (figures 13, 14, 31–35).[24] Seeing is conflated with the camera and then, again, with Kubrick's camera, which is present at every moment. This witness indicates that the most important presence in the film is finally not HAL or Bowman or Moon-Watcher or the star child—not the hero of the Odyssey, but the poet of the drama, like Homer or the singer of the psalms, or the auteur himself. In this respect, the auteur as creator takes on a new meaning. In the end, the only one, finally, who knows the meaning of the mythic story in *2001* is Kubrick himself. And like other great creators of myths about human origins and fate, he has invented a story that is filled with possibilities, which he may or may not have intended. Thus it is left, finally, for the viewer to decide whether this new myth is religion or science or some personal combination of the two—and whether it merits a place among the other important stories of origin and fate.

Notes

1. Quoted in Stephanie Schwam, ed., *The Making of* 2001 (New York: Modern Library, 2000), 265.

2. Quoted in ibid., 163.

3. Vincent LoBrutto, *Stanley Kubrick: A Biography* (London: Fine, 1997), 313.

4. Lynn Spigel, "From Domestic Space to Outer Space: The 1960s Fantastic Family Sit-Com," in *Close Encounters: Film, Feminism, and Science Fiction*, ed. Constance Penley et al. (Minneapolis: University of Minnesota Press, 1991), 205–35. Spigel notes

that critics deplored the boring, unpoetic, vulgar, "oh boy!" tone of the Apollo 11 mission (229).

5. John C. Whitcombe, Jr., and Henry M. Morris, *The Genesis Flood: The Biblical Record and Its Scientific Implications* (Philadelphia: Presbyterian and Reformed Publishing, 1962), xx. If this biblical tract shares some generic characteristics with science fiction (in its use of scientific arguments to validate an imaginative narrative), Tim La Haye's enormously popular *Left Behind* series goes one step further in imagining the end of the world. Both *Genesis Flood* and *Left Behind* exhibit some of the key characteristics of science fiction typology outlined by Susan Sontag in "The Imagination of Disaster," in *Against Interpretation* (New York: Farrar, Straus, and Giroux, 1966), 209–25.

6. See Stephen Jay Gould and N. Eldredge, "Punctuated Equilibria: The Tempo and Mode of Evolution Reconsidered," *Paleobiology* 3 (1977): 115–51.

7. Thomas Allen Nelson, *Kubrick: Inside a Film Artist's Maze* (Bloomington: Indiana University Press, 2000), 5.

8. Alexander Walker, *Stanley Kubrick, Director* (New York: Norton, 1999), 173. On other possible allegories and myths, see Leonard F. Wheat, *Kubrick's 2001: A Triple Allegory* (Lanham, MD: Scarecrow, 2000), 2–10.

9. Sontag, "Imagination of Disaster."

10. David G. Hock, "Mythic Patterns in *2001: A Space Odyssey*," *Journal of Popular Culture* 4 (Spring 1991): 961–64; Michael Herr, *Kubrick* (New York: Grove, 2000), 13; Carolyn Geduld, *Filmguide to* 2001: A Space Odyssey (Bloomington: Indiana University Press, 1973), 62, 67–68.

11. Gene Youngblood, "Interview with Arthur Clarke," in *Expanded Cinema* (New York: Dutton, 1970), 147.

12. Neil McAleer, *Odyssey: The Authorized Biography of Arthur C. Clarke* (London: Gollancz, 1992), 194; Charles Kohler, "Stanley Kubrick Raps," *East Village Eye*, in Schwam, *Making of* 2001, 246. See also Gene D. Phillips, Rodney Hill, et al., *Encyclopedia of Stanley Kubrick* (New York: Facts on File, 2002), xx.

13. "Stanley Kubrick: *Playboy* Interview," in Schwam, *Making of* 2001, 275.

14. LoBrutto, *Stanley Kubrick*, 266; Herr, *Kubrick*, 13.

15. Schwam, *Making of* 2001, 272.

16. Norman Kagan, *The Cinema of Stanley Kubrick* (New York: Continuum, 2000), 146. Since the 1990s, there has been an extraordinary surge of writing about Kubrick and his films, including several biographies. In addition to the other works cited, see John Baxter, *Stanley Kubrick: A Biography* (New York: Carroll & Graf, 1997); James Howard, *Stanley Kubrick Companion* (London: Batsford, 1999); David Hughes, *The Complete Kubrick* (London, Virgin, 2001); Piers Bizony, 2001*: Filming the Future* (London: Aurum, 1994); Jerome Agel, *The Making of Kubrick's* 2001 (New York: New American Library, 1970); David G. Stork, ed., *HAL's Legacy: 2001's Computer as Dream and Reality* (Cambridge, Mass.: MIT Press, 1997); Gene D. Phillips, *Stanley Kubrick Interviews* (Jackson: University of Mississippi Press, 2001); Michel Chion, *Kubrick's Cinema Odyssey* (London: British Film Institute, 2001); Mario Falsetto, *Stanley Kubrick: A Narrative and Stylistic Analysis* (Westport, Conn.: Praeger, 2001); Michel Ciment, *Kubrick* (Paris: Calmann-Levy, 1987); and Robert Kolker, *A Cinema of Loneliness* (New York: Oxford University Press, 2000).

17. Frederick I. Ordway, "Testimonies," in Schwam, *Making of* 2001, 126–28; and Chion, *Kubrick's Cinema Odyssey*, 9.

18. Arthur Clarke, *2001: A Space Odyssey* (New York: New American Library, 1968), 21, 25. Clarke explained in detail how the aliens transformed the ape-men and why.

19. Thomas Nelson suggests that Kubrick was influenced by V. I. Pudovkin's concept of films laid out in his book *Film Technique* (London: Newnes, 1933). See Harry M. Geduld, "Return to Méliès: Reflections on the Science-Fiction Film," *Humanist* 28 (November–December 1968): 23. See also Bizony, 2001: Kubrick, he wrote, "was happy to draw inspiration from the brilliant back-yard magic of George[s] Méliès and his *Voyage to the Moon* (1902)" (144). Also see McAleer, *Odyssey*, 217.

20. As Richard Strauss wrote of *Zarathustra*: "I mean to convey in music an idea of the evolution of the human race from its origin, through the various phases of development, religious as well as scientific, up to Nietzsche's idea of the *Ubermensch*." Phillips et al., *Encyclopedia*, 12.

21. Sontag, "Imagination of Disaster," 212–13, 216–17, 222–23. Arthur Clarke quoted in F. Hoda, "Éprouvante et Science Fiction dans le Cinéma américain actuel," *Positif* 2 (November–December 1954): 16.

22. Clarke, *Lost Worlds of* 2001*: Science Fiction* (London: Sidgwick & Jackson, 1972), 189; Fred Chappell, "The Science Fiction Film Image: *A Trip to the Moon* to *2001: A Space Odyssey*," in *Science Fiction Films*, ed. Thomas R. Atkins (New York: Monarch, 1976), 33–45.

23. Geduld, *Filmguide to* 2001, 33–34; David Stork, "The Best-Informed Dream: HAL and the Vision of *2001*," in Stork, *HAL's Legacy*, 133–34, 147.

24. W. R. Robinson and Mary McDermott, "*2001* and the Literary Sensibility," *Georgia Review* 26 (Spring 1972): 26.

3

The Gravity of *2001: A Space Odyssey*

J. P. TELOTTE

Stanley Kubrick's *2001: A Space Odyssey* has provided us with one of the most frequently noted transitions in film history, the match cut that takes viewers from "The Dawn of Man," as the film's first sequence is titled, to the year 2001 (figures 3 and 4). That cut matches a bone cast into the air by a shrieking hominid, one of those on which the opening sequence focuses, to a space station, similarly thrust into space by the modern humans who dominate the succeeding sequences. It is a wonderfully ironic piece of editing, suggesting how, for all of our technological advances—advances attested to by the complexity of the space station, the other satellites we glimpse, and the civilized strains of a Strauss waltz that accompany this shift—we have fundamentally progressed very little. We continue to fling our bits of technology into the air, higher and faster, of course, but with a similar sort of exultation, of self-conscious pride, as we strive to overcome one of the fundamental laws that weighs us down, governs human life, and constrains our ambitions: gravity. It is on gravity that this chapter focuses, in part because the film itself, perhaps simply with a desire to be faithful to the scientific laws governing space travel—which are often selectively ignored by earlier science fiction films—frequently reminds us of its operation and emphasizes how in various ways it impinges on us. But gravity also becomes something more than just a scientific context for this narrative; it opens onto a larger *gravitas*, or seriousness of purpose of *2001*, a seriousness that has at times gone unappreciated because of our focus on the film's painstaking efforts at scientific accuracy.

One hallmark of the initial response to *2001* was precisely an appreciation for its unusually rigorous attention to scientific detail, a rigor that had pointedly been missing both from the "space operas" of the serials and early science fiction television and from the mutation and alien invasion films that had largely dominated the genre during the previous decade. Yet it was an appreciation that curiously suggested very different attitudes toward the film. On the one hand, critics repeatedly underscored its technical accuracy as the surest sign of the film's achievement, almost as if that were its point. As one reviewer offered, "[T]he detail . . . is immense and unimpeachable, I'm sure. This must be the best-informed dream ever."[1] And Kubrick's frequent praise for his "staff of scientific advisors," including Marvin Minsky of MIT, one of the leading authorities on artificial intelligence, certainly encouraged this approach.[2] Yet on the other hand, a number of critics complained about that very emphasis. One claimed that the film demonstrates "a kind of fanaticism about . . . authenticity" that results in a story "somewhere between hypnotic and immensely boring."[3] Prior to *2001*'s appearance, the science fiction narrative had largely become a platform for speculation not so much on how our science and resultant technology might allow us to accomplish things, but on the dramatic and usually fearful consequences of those developments. The landmark science fiction films of early cinema, *Metropolis* (1926) and *Things to Come* (1936), were both heavily melodramatic and highly stylized dystopic visions, while the flood of such films that appeared in the 1950s and early 1960s had become, as Susan Sontag famously noted, a kind of cultural "imagination of disaster," one in which our technological developments simply "stand for different values," as the narrative itself becomes an almost moralistic "allegory."[4]

In marked contrast, *2001*, with its careful attention to detail, its scrupulous accounting for the various laws of nature and the physics of space flight, and its expert-driven extrapolation from current science and technology,[5] seemed to stake out a different trajectory. As Edward James offers in his history of the genre, Kubrick's film, because of its realistic texture and aura of scientific authority, "did as much as Apollo to make space flight both real and even banal" for audiences of the era.[6] He suggests that its main effect was to prepare us for the real thing. And indeed, in some ways, it recalls the near-documentary nature of such rare earlier efforts as *Destination Moon* (1950) and *The Conquest of Space* (1955; figures 1 and 2), both of which employed the leading rocket experts of the day as technical consultants in attempts to realistically forecast how mankind would take its first halting steps into space. However, both of those movies, because of their B-film budgets and B-film imaginations, failed to marshal the sort of special effects or dramatic visions that would make their versions of space travel either convincing or compelling. In *2001*, though, the real, even in its sometimes banal or mundane forms, is central to the film's—and the filmmaker's—imagination.

Certainly, one of Kubrick's strengths, as demonstrated in his previous films, was his scrupulous—if not quite fanatical—attention to detail and especially to scientific and historical accuracy. An earlier film, *The Killing* (1956), with its characters who minutely plot out the elements of a race track heist and their planned escape, points toward the director's meticulousness, as well as his fascination with human efforts at fashioning and living by a thoroughly rational world view. As Kubrick noted, his approach to each project he undertook was to "totally immerse" himself in it, reading and researching exhaustively in an effort to achieve a level of total verisimilitude.[7] Beyond achieving a simple realism, though, that attention to detail consistently served a larger film aesthetic for Kubrick, his belief that filmmaking is "dealing in a primarily visual experience, and telling a story through the eyes."[8] If his painstaking efforts helped to create the vision of a scientifically true and believable experience of space and space travel in *2001*, then they also point toward something more, his sense that film conveys its most important messages—"complex concepts and abstractions"—most directly by exploiting the intricate texture of the world we see around us, forcing us to use our eyes to see it clearly and better understand it, and thereby, as he says, "short-circuiting the rigid surface cultural blocks that shackle our consciousness to narrowly limited areas of experience."[9] In short, the real—including a rigid scientific accuracy—was the essential path to increased understanding.

One of those complex concepts is bound up in that famous match cut—which Annette Michelson has justly termed "the most spectacular ellipsis in cinematic history"[10]—and particularly in what it realistically visualizes and anticipates. Tossed bones, of course, inevitably fall back down to Earth, thanks to the law of gravity. Good science simply anticipates that something thrown into the sky will eventually arc downward. Yet that hominid's exuberant effort to defy gravity, an effort celebrated by the images of satellites and other space probes that we then glimpse as the narrative bursts through the boundaries of the past and moves to the year 2001, is a signpost for a most momentous development for humankind, which justifies the narrative's radical jump in time and space. As Paul Virilio explains, the relatively "recent acquisition of the speed of liberation from gravity" constitutes a feat of "historic importance," comparable to the development of "the absolute speed of our modern *real-time* transmission tools," enabling us "to escape the *real space* of our planet and so to 'fall upwards.'" Yet that new trajectory—or different sort of "fall"—ultimately means little, he offers, unless it also spurs us to move beyond a certain way of thinking, the influence of "the stability of gravitational space that has always oriented man's habitual activities" and left him clinging to a stable yet staid, even stultifying mode of thought.[11] It is this subtler, yet ultimately stronger force of stability and complacency which *2001* and its meditations on gravity eventually bring into focus.

To further tease out that image on which we have initially focused, we might again note that thrown objects never continue along their original vectors for long. Bent by the force of gravitational space, they tend to curve back, in much the same way that human thought, grounded in custom, seeks out a point of stability. Thomas Kuhn has offered one of the most noteworthy explanations of this pattern, or what he terms the scientific "problem of progress."[12] As he offers, the scientific breakthrough that powers technological advances also tends to become the confining paradigm that stands in the way of further advances; the insight which once effectively "transformed the scientific imagination," arcing out beyond the status quo, eventually becomes a way of thinking which patterns all that follows, or what Kuhn labels the "tradition of normal science."[13] In terms of *2001*'s pattern of visual design, we might simply say that the vector warps into a curved shape or, given a bit more force, produces a circular pattern, that described by the typical orbital body, such as a satellite or, more pointedly, the shape and motion of the space station that introduces the second major sequence of *2001*.

In fact, it is this space station, itself circular and inducing a spinning motion to the shuttles that want to dock there, that provides us with another sort of paradigm for the narrative that follows. The shuttle carrying Heywood Floyd to the station, we might note, repeatedly foregrounds the power of gravity, in part by frequently underscoring its absence—through Floyd's floating pen (figure 5), retrieved by a passing stewardess; his arms that undulate as he sleeps, as if he were floating in water; and the lingering close-up of the stewardess's special gravity shoes, which allow her to perform normally if rather awkwardly in the zero-gravity conditions of space[14] These details, precisely the sort upon which most reviewers quickly seized, not only illustrate the weightless state attained on this flight, but also point up the human effort at countering this state, at constructing gravity where it is not natural. Thus, as the shuttle approaches the circular space station, which is rotating in order to generate its own gravity, it too begins to spin, as if engaged in a dance with the station to the tune of the Strauss waltz on the soundtrack. The music and movement together suggest a kind of harmony here, although they also hark back to an earlier state—to the romantic era and to the gravity of Earth. No longer falling upward, as Virilio puts it, the space travelers on board the station have reconstructed their customary stability, translating the exploratory vector of space flight into a *stationary* circularity and hinting of a larger tendency here, even as humanity moves into the unknown, to compromise exploration, to control or even cover up discoveries, to cling to the ruling paradigms. We might think of it as a kind of fear of falling—upward.

On board the space station too we see underscored the problems of that gravitational and intellectual stability, at least in its cultural manifestations. Here Heywood Floyd encounters his Soviet counterparts, and their polite banter eventually gives way to pointed questions and even warnings about strained relations between the Russian and American moon colonies. With this encounter, Kubrick suggests that there is to be no falling away from Cold

War realities, no end in sight to—or hope for progress beyond—the confrontation between East and West that he had so bleakly satirized in his previous film *Dr. Strangelove* (1964). This potentially destructive stability would apparently continue far into humanity's future. At the same time, it inscribes another sort of narrative circularity, by reframing the opening sequence and the hominid conflict that eventuated in violence, killing, and a bloody bone tossed into the air. Here, of course, a civilized humanity puts a polite cover on its violent potential, its bloody bones, but the veiled threats of the Russians and Floyd's transparent misrepresentations remind us how, even as we seem ready to break free of the past or fall upward, humanity appears almost gravitationally bound to replicating its earlier, violent history, to continuing along the dominant cultural paradigm.[15]

During Floyd's journey from the space station to the Clavius moon colony, we encounter at almost every turn the human difficulties involved in functioning in this new, gravity-free environment—difficulties that help to underscore Michelson's precise assessment of *2001* as a "film of dis-orientation."[16] Eating in zero gravity means sucking liquefied food through a straw, and when Heywood Floyd momentarily lets go of his food tray, it quickly begins to float away. The stewardess must awkwardly cope with a constantly shifting interior horizon, as we see when she tries to serve the ship's pilots and seems to walk around the circular wall of the ship and exit upside down (figure 6). And in one of the film's infrequent light moments, we see Floyd in close-up as he stands bemused, staring at the elaborate instructions attached to the "zero gravity toilet," complete with an ominous caution that "Passengers are advised to read instructions before use" (figure 26). Each example reminds us—and in the case of the stewardess's gravity-defying movements, almost literally—of the fundamental ways in which we rely on that customary pull of gravity and easily become disoriented in its absence. And the visualization of these effects only serves to prepare for that far more unsettling effect that has instigated Floyd's trip, his effort to investigate and maintain a cover for the discovery at Clavius of the mysterious black monolith, an artifact that, he assures his colleagues, must be kept secret because of its enormous potential "for cultural shock and social disorientation."

Tellingly, the subsequent sequence, titled "Jupiter Mission—Eighteen Months Later," quickly returns to this emphasis on disorientation, keyed to the problem of weightlessness. For while it begins with a slow and deliberate tracking shot of the spaceship *Discovery*—a shot that makes maximum use of the Super Panavision aspect ratio to underscore the ship's linear trajectory in space[17]—it leads to a pointedly unsettling image, that of Frank Poole jogging on a seemingly vertical track within the ship. As the camera tracks along with his movement, we recognize that our sense of disorientation, the visual challenge to our normal sense of "up" and "down," results from the movement of a portion of the ship; the living quarters of *Discovery* are housed in a centrifuge that rotates in order to produce its own artificial gravity, thereby allowing Poole to seemingly run upside down (figure 18). To further emphasize this effect, the subsequent scene in which Poole and his fellow crewman Dave Bowman eat and watch a BBC interview is constructed of shots that show the two astronauts seated but place them on a horizontal axis, as if their backs were to the floor (figure 7). While Alexander Walker has called attention to the repetition of these "bizarre 'irrational' angles possible in this 'squirrel's cage' environment," he passes them off as simply a matter of style, of Kubrick trying "to pull off some spectacular effects."[18] But more than simply an effect, these images link both simple and complex elements of the narrative: the human effort to create an artificial gravity and the larger consequences of that constructed orientation. Those strange angles do, of course, make the astronauts' positioning in screen space repeatedly seem awkward and unnatural, in the process hinting of how unready they are for the task of "discovery," which will ultimately render a conventional, Earth-centered, and gravity-determined orientation irrelevant.

Those same bizarre angles also help to prepare us for the narrative's eventual trajectory: a movement away from this sort of conventional orientation and from the psychic gravity that has so bound humanity to Earth, to certain modes of Earth-oriented behavior, and to particular paradigms of thought. For an announcement by the HAL 9000 computer, which keys the principal action in this sequence—that part of the ship's communication equipment will fail within seventy-two hours—quickly focuses the narrative on issues of stability and orientation. Throughout the following scenes, HAL's red, staring eye becomes an unmoving—and unblinking—presence, representing the electronic intelligence that controls all functions, including life support, on board *Discovery* and carefully monitoring the behavior of the two astronauts in case they too become in some way unstable and pose a threat to the mission (figure 13). In marked contrast, we see Dave and Frank being forced out of their comfort zone, that is, the artificial gravity of the centrifuge. First, Dave and Frank, in a section of the ship lacking that gravity, are depicted at an unsettling 90-degree angle from each other as they run a check on HAL's calculations, and then Frank floats in space while replacing the AE35 part that has been predicted to fail. The visual contrast between the constantly oriented eye and the physically disoriented astronauts—disoriented both in space and in terms of their newfound uncertainty about HAL's own reliability—foreshadows the coming conflict, as HAL returns to the violent ways of the hominids, killing Frank and sending him floating off into space,[19] and then locking Dave out of the *Discovery*, and thus out of the artificial environment on which he has come to rely.

Suggesting both desperation and a kind of imaginative growth, Dave's response points to the sort of momentous human development that Virilio has described, to our new ability to "fall upwards." Shut out of the *Discovery* and lacking a helmet that might allow him to move around safely in space, Dave essentially gives birth to a new attitude, positioning the pod, as if it were a kind of womb, opposite the emergency entry (a long corridor suggesting the birth canal) and squatting in a fetal position behind the pod's door, which he then blows open, exposing himself briefly to a most unstable environment—cold, airless, and certainly weightless. Blown out with the door, he does seem to fall upward, and even as he is sucked back toward the pod, to space, and possibly to death, in a sort of inevitable complement to that explosive trajectory, he manages to shut the emergency hatch so that he can begin his new life (figure 8). It is one in which we no longer see him in the grip of gravity; rather, he moves at odd angles and even floats through portions of the ship as he deactivates HAL: disengaging portions of the computer's memory which, appropriately, float out from the mainframe, and in the process disengaging himself from the sort of conventional stability and rational limits that HAL and the control section of the *Discovery* have come to represent (figures 14 and 22).

It seems fitting that only with this move, with the shutting off of the computer (and of conventional logic) and in a completely weightless state, does Dave finally confront the problem of "disorientation" and learn of his purpose—to investigate the source of that black monolith whose "origin and purpose [are] still a total mystery" on Earth. For the subsequent wordless sequence, as Dave emerges from the *Discovery* to pursue a monolith apparently floating among the moons of Jupiter, involves him in a new sort of exploration, one beyond gravity, beyond conventional orientation, in a visionary experience that critics at the time quite rightly described as a kind of "light show." In the course of this scene, there is no stability, no easy orientation, only the sense of constant movement through space and eventually across a landscape that looks remarkably like that of Earth in the opening sequence, yet outlandishly colored to suggest its different nature, to emphasize that Dave has not simply fallen or followed a circular trajectory back to Earth. Here, it is his eye—in contrast to HAL's—that becomes the narrative ground, as the film cross-cuts between the landscape over which we rapidly move and close-ups of his eye, blinking and straining to take in these scenes while deprived of the sort of stability and orientation to which earthmen are accustomed (figures 33 and 34).

To underscore the importance of these images, we might recall Kubrick's next effort, *A Clockwork Orange* (1971), in which the protagonist Alex wears a set of cufflinks styled like bloody eyeballs (figure 9). Given the decaying, crime-ridden, and futureless world that Alex and his "droogs," or companions, inhabit, those cufflinks immediately suggest the violent nature of his environment, but they also point beyond it, hinting at a way out of a decadent dead end for humanity. What they point to is a new mode of seeing, a vantage that has been literally, even violently ripped from its normal orientation, freed from its common limits, although here mainly to function as decor, as a symbol of the sort of different perspective for which Alex and his companions subliminally long and which their world so sorely needs if it is to pass beyond this manifestly dead cultural end. However, for various reasons—political, cultural, perhaps even genetic—no one here seems able to achieve that new sort of vision, to cut the ties to the violent human past, to progress much beyond the lingering influence of those hominid ancestors who, in *2001*, toss the bloody bone/club skyward in a gesture of transcendence. Style notwithstanding, their vision is simply gravitationally bound to an earlier way of life. But in *2001*, seeing in a new way is a key part of what is accomplished: seeing liberated from HAL's restrictive vantage, from the *Discovery*'s artificial environment, from an earthly perspective.

For Virilio, as we have noted, that new human capacity to fall upward, to escape from the limiting forces and mindset of our world, is simply one sign of a much larger shift in human orientation, as we enter an environment in which speed and movement, as defined by "the cosmological constant of the speed of light,"[20] becomes a key dimension of human development. It is in this context that we might read the film's final sequence, which finds Dave Bowman, along with the pod that has transported him, in a mysterious, classically decorated suite, wherein he undergoes a series of transformations—transformations that defy the normal paradigms of human thought and that effectively warp our normal sense of space and time. Within this strange environment, described by some as a kind of human zoo, Bowman experiences a series of rapid changes. Starting from his position as an astronaut within his pod, Bowman looks out, and his vantage ultimately produces an image of himself, outside the pod. Each look thereafter produces not the simple and expected glance-object relationship typical of classical film editing, but rather an image of himself in another position, even at a later age, as if the look itself were now enough to rapidly propel the self through space and time, to give birth to a later version of the self (figure 15). Perhaps paradoxically, gravity still operates in this unnatural circumstance, as the falling of a glass from a table underscores. But it is as if it were simply part of the furnishings here, recreated from the storehouse of Bowman's personal and cultural memory, and something that momentarily catches his attention, as if he were suddenly reminded of how it functions. But it is also readily suspended, as we then see when an aged Bowman, lying in bed, extends his hand and points to a monolith (figure 23), now floating in front of him, and when, in another reverse angle shot, we see the embryonic star child suspended above the bed in Bowman's previous position. One of the points implicit in this concluding sequence is that gravity—and even space and time, which, we know, are warped by gravity—finally matters very little. It is something to which we are accustomed, a convention of our lives, one of the old laws that bind us to a status quo, that keep us from achieving the sort of escape velocity that, as a species, humanity needs to attain in order to evolve further, to be something other than highly rational and inevitably violent ape-men.

The film's final scene precisely illustrates this situation, as it offers us two symmetrical images floating as if side by side in space. One is recognizably the Earth, the starting point for the trajectory of the spaceship *Discovery* as well as the film's trajectory of discovery. The other is the star child that Dave Bowman has become, as he too completes his trajectory and comes back to Earth. Recalling the bone earlier tossed into the sky, momentarily defying gravity and through a sharp break in narrative time avoiding falling back to Earth and instead magically turning into a kind of satellite, Bowman[21] as the star child seems suspended in space, free from the physical laws that bind the planet to which he has arced back, but also a companion to and model for that planet, his birth/rebirth the start of a new round of human evolution (figure 35). As Virilio offers, "beyond earth's pull, there is no space worthy of the name, but only time,"[22] and here time seems ready to produce a transformation every bit as significant as that from hominid to human, from bone to satellite.

In this ultimate ability to defy gravity, we can locate at least a portion of the real *gravitas* or seriousness of purpose that marks *2001*. For this final image emphasizes that humanity will not be bound by the conventional laws of science, by the paradigms that seem to insist on a limited human trajectory, and that once the journey of discovery begins, we need not be drawn back to or fall into a primitive condition. When questioned about that kind of human destiny, about our place in the cosmos, Kubrick has been emphatic on this point. Even with his manifest fascination for scientific detail and the careful attention he gives to it in *2001* and elsewhere, he has also professed his skepticism toward the state of scientific knowledge and what the scientific community often regards, despite Kuhn's caution, as absolutes. As Kubrick has offered, "I find it difficult to believe that we have penetrated to the ultimate depths of knowledge about the physical laws of the universe. . . . I'm suspicious of dogmatic scientific rules; they tend to have a rather short life span."[23] The result with *2001* is a film that astonishes with its scientific accuracy and yet also pulls viewers up short with its profound skepticism about the rational world view from which our science operates.

Of course, as we earlier noted, with its unprecedented focus on scientific detail—on the laws that govern us and the technologies we have crafted in line with those laws—*2001* originally asserted its difference from the long tradition of popular science fiction films and suggested its quite serious intent. Kubrick produced one of the most compelling versions of space travel ever put on film, convincingly described the sort of ships and structures that would be needed to colonize space, and effectively suggested our increasing reliance on the computer for the command and control functions of space flight. Yet that very texture, as the ruminations on gravity here suggest, also serves to challenge one sort of paradigm. It can help us to consider the role of science and technology in shaping our future and particularly the ways in which a kind of thinking associated with science can both open onto and, if we are not careful, draw us back from, almost gravitationally, the full potential of that future, a future in which we might evolutionally become more than we are. In his study of paradigmatic thought in the sciences, Kuhn offers a similar caveat, noting that "scientists should behave" in a constantly skeptical way "if their enterprise is to succeed."[24] While thoroughly scientific, Kubrick's film seems skeptical in very much this way. It offers us a glimpse of our potential, as it suggests that if the very human "enterprise is to succeed," if we are ever to "fall" in the right direction, we shall need to overcome the pull of the physical and even cultural gravity that holds us, that stays the ultimate human odyssey.

Notes

1. Charles Champlin, review of *2001*, in *The Making of Kubrick's* 2001, ed. Jerome Agel (New York: New American Library, 1970), 213.

2. Jeremy Bernstein, "Profile: Stanley Kubrick," in *Stanley Kubrick: Interviews*, ed. Gene D. Phillips (Jackson: University Press of Mississippi, 2001), 36.

3. Renata Adler, "We'll Get This Info to You Just as Soon as We Work It Out," in Agel, *Making of Kubrick's* 2001, 208.

4. Susan Sontag, "The Imagination of Disaster," in her *Against Interpretation* (New York: Dell, 1966), 218, 226.

5. A noteworthy contribution to that expert-driven attention to detail came from Frederick I. Ordway, one of America's foremost rocket and space experts. A former member of Wernher von Braun's rocket team at the NASA Marshall Space Flight Center and author of numerous books and articles on rocketry and space flight, he served as scientific and technical consultant on the film for eighteen months and subsequently offered a number of postproduction suggestions on the shape of the narrative. For Ordway's description of his involvement in the film, see his account in Agel's *Making of Kubrick's* 2001, 193–98.

6. Edward James, *Science Fiction in the Twentieth Century* (Oxford: Oxford University Press, 1994), 191.

7. Joseph Gelmis, *The Film Director as Superstar* (New York: Doubleday, 1970), 298.

8. Ibid., 300.

9. Ibid., 302.

10. Annette Michelson, "Bodies in Space: Film as Carnal Knowledge," in *The Making of* 2001: A Space Odyssey, ed. Stephanie Schwam (New York: Random House, 2000), 198.

11. Paul Virilio, *Open Sky*, trans. Julie Rose (London: Verso, 1997), 2.

12. Thomas Kuhn, *The Structure of Scientific Revolutions*, 3d ed. (Chicago: University of Chicago Press, 1996), 170.

13. Ibid., 6, 144.

14. In an interview with Jeremy Bernstein, Kubrick indicates that even the flightwear for his space stewardesses was designed with gravity in mind: "the hats have padding in them to cushion any collisions with the ceiling that weightlessness might cause." See his "Profile: Stanley Kubrick," 35.

15. We might note how the film links cultural modes of thought with the trope of gravity here, as the polite encounter between Floyd and the Soviet scientists begins with a gravitationally oriented query, about the direction in which each group is heading: "up" or "down." In space, of course, and even more so within a spinning and orbiting space station, their finger pointings in one direction or another are essentially meaningless, what we might term a gravitational anachronism.

16. Michelson, "Bodies in Space," 208.

17. Super Panavision was a wide-screen format developed by MGM that used 65mm or 70mm film. It allowed for a much higher quality image than was achieved by the most popular widescreen process, CinemaScope, without relying on an anamorphic

lens. It typically produced an aspect ratio of 2.2:1, although when reprocessed for anamorphic projection, it could be projected in a wider format, simulating the Cinerama process. For a discussion of Super Panavision and its applications, see John Belton's *Widescreen Cinema* (Cambridge, Mass.: Harvard University Press, 1992), 178, 182.

18. Alexander Walker, with Sybil Taylor and Ulrich Ruchti, *Stanley Kubrick, Director* (New York: Norton, 1999), 185.

19. Suggesting a link between HAL and the hominids of the narrative's first sequence is the way that Frank is effectively hurled into space by the pod under HAL's control. He becomes a sign of that aggressive violence just as did the bone cast into the air by the hominid at the end of the opening sequence.

20. Virilio, *Open Sky*, 13.

21. Bowman's name, of course, precisely suggests the human ability to use our rather primitive technology to send things arcing into space, to defy the limiting law of gravity.

22. Virilio, *Open Sky*, 3.

23. Eric Nordern, "*Playboy* Interview: Stanley Kubrick," in *Stanley Kubrick: Interviews* (Jackson: University Press of Mississippi, 2001), 59.

24. Kuhn, *Structure of Scientific Revolutions*, 207.

4

Kubrick in Space

STEPHEN MAMBER

The pretentiousness of *2001: A Space Odyssey* has been a considerable obstacle to appreciating its status as masterpiece. The collaboration with Arthur C. Clarke and Kubrick's own statements about the film have obviously obscured how deeply it connects to the rest of his work. The diversion provided by the film's technologies that has led to enjoyable but incidental books like *HAL's Legacy* makes it too easily the Kubrick movie to talk about by people who don't know much about movies.[1] Pondering such issues as the meaning of the monolith, whether HAL is really IBM a letter-back-each, or Bowman's journey to star child has kept *2001* criticism in an interpretive dead end for a long time.

Happily, since the 1990s, we have seen great breakthroughs in Kubrick analysis, putting *2001* in its rightful place in close relation to his other films. Most particularly, the stellar work by a pair of Michels, Ciment on *2001* and *The Shining* and Chion on *2001* and *Eyes Wide Shut*, has convincingly demonstrated how valuable *2001* is as a major manifestation of Kubrick styles and obsessions.[2]

Continuing from their inspiration, I want to consider the idea of space in Kubrick. *2001: A Space Odyssey*, as its title indicates directly, is a journey through Space, with a capital *S*, but like all Kubrick films, it explores space in other significant ways. I recognize that this is but one way to consider the film, but I'm very much of the Chion point of view that "a book of a thousand pages could not begin to do justice to all the dimensions of *2001*."[3] So this is no more than an attempt to do partial justice to a great film and to an important aspect of Kubrick's artistry.

Looking at Space

Some aspects of Kubrick's space seem almost obvious, and it may appear that we are moving into generally observed aspects of his work by foregrounding this concern, particularly such matters as decor and traveling shots, which have generated much discussion. But around such subjects, an awareness that larger questions of space were lurking has been suggested by others, even if they haven't followed through on the implications. Alexander Walker, for instance, echoing E. M. Forster on *War and Peace*, says, "Space is also the lord of Kubrick's film."[4] Walker and his collaborators are very good on issues of space, especially about confinement and tracking shots, and a statement like this is fair justification for considering the subject further. When Ciment considers "the confined space which Kubrick's camera endeavors to pulverize," he's also working along the same lines, as he does when referring to a reverse tracking shot in a narrow corridor as "both mastering the space and conveying a sense of confinement within it."[5] Chion aptly sums up Kubrick's work as "an art of space," and it is these aspects of space that I will be attempting to clarify and expand upon.[6]

As space itself overlaps, so shall my areas of exploration—categories with fluid boundaries but useful as ways to start thinking about Kubrickian space. These forms are

1. institutional-official space
2. ritual-game-war space
3. parody space
4. dream space
5. alien space
6. geometrical space
7. ubiquitous space

Institutional-Official Space

In *2001*, institutional-official space is best represented by all things manmade. The space station waiting rooms, the meeting rooms of Dr. Floyd and his colleagues, the working areas of the *Discovery*—all reflect a manufactured, sanctioned, government-like space (figure 10). Even the Louis XVI–style bedroom in which Bowman lives and ages before his transformation into the "star child" has been recognized as possibly either a constructed-by-aliens observation zoo-like room, a space of confinement, or as a dreamlike vision of a regal deathbed. All suggest familiar Kubrick concerns: banality, repressed violence, a stark contrast between the natural and the manmade, and too much regularity and bureaucratic sensibility to reflect well upon those who constructed these spaces.

This might seem like an extremely unlikely comparison, but the nonfiction films of Frederick Wiseman, many filmed in public institutions, share roughly analogous spatial characteristics (and other qualities as well) with Kubrick's films. The famous impersonality of the *Discovery* crew (one of whom, HAL, is often identified as the most human figure in the film) is partly a function of their being subordinated to their institutional space. Beyond actors dominated by decor and costume, they are integrated into the space which surrounds them to the point of being stripped of most individual identity. Like their hibernating colleagues, Poole and Bowman are contained by their functions, in spaces designed for them to perform as required. We shouldn't ignore that many Kubrick characters are government employees—soldiers, scientists, social workers, politicians, astronauts—and one could say of Kubrick as well as of Frederick Wiseman that both regularly present quasi-scientific, military, and technological environments in which individuals function in their institutional roles. Wiseman's *Primate* (1974) and *Missile* (1987), particularly, are probably most analogous to *2001*, but there are also Wiseman's military films (*Basic Training I* [1971], *Maneuver* [1979], *Sinai Field Mission* [1978]) which match up nicely to *Paths of Glory* (1957) and *Full Metal Jacket* (1987). And *High School*, released the same year as *2001*, shows students engaging in a mock shuttle mission, visible at first only inside their helmeted spacesuits; in both films, they are "bodies doing a job" (figure 11).

One aspect of institutional space is the office, and Kubrick always excelled at presenting the work space in all of its ironic, oppressive ordinariness. Ullman's office in *The Shining* (1980), site of Jack's interview, with its tiny ax clearly visible in his pencil holder, has to be close to the top of this list, but nearly all Kubrick films have some form of getting down to work in spaces which define the enterprise more than the individuals, who are often left to perform repetitive, mechanical activities. General Mireau, in *Paths of Glory*, trudging through the trenches like it's another day at the office; Kong in the cockpit of his military B-52; Ripper's office at the air base, its bank of computers just outside the front door (*Dr. Strangelove* [1964] is entirely made up of institutional spaces); Lady Lyndon, in *Barry Lyndon* (1975), signing check after check like an automaton; all work and no play making Jack a dull boy—all of these instances point us back to the *Discovery* crew, mixing work and play in the same spaces. Chess playing with HAL is first a recreational game and then a deadly one, played out in the same space (figure 24). Kubrick presents the spaceship as work space, making it more ordinary and more fantastic at the same time.

The attention to work decor and office embellishment becomes a sign of underlying human traits that are subordinated to (or repressed by) the space which envelops them. People will be dominated, controlled, made to look small by the strongly prevailing institutional environments. The house, the room, the office will win.

Ritual-Game-War Space

The role of the game, especially chess, has been widely recognized, but perhaps the construction of the game space hasn't. We can find ample evidence that Kubrick's films construct this space and that not only is there a game space, there are games of space.

Consider the game aspect to camera movement. The justly famous circular tracking shots when we first see the interior of the *Discovery* are game-like on so many levels—they seem a magic trick and an example of the pleasure of technical prowess that recalls Orson Welles's comment that a film studio was "the biggest electric train set a boy ever had." This is clearly not accomplished by digital effects or compositing. Because we go full circle without a cut, we can't help but wonder how it's done, and the general elaborateness to Kubrick's tracking shots induce this wonder of how has he pulled it off?—as do so many other camera movements throughout his films (recall the opening credit sequence of *The Shining* when the camera continues into space when we thought we were earthbound). The first level of game space is the game of movement—rigid yet free, constricted yet brilliantly daring.

Camera movements representing game moves, chesslike and authorial, are a component of Kubrick game space too. The game is in the calculation, the awareness that the movement is planned, though the characters being filmed don't know it. "Caught in a maze" is a spatial condition and an oft-used description of the plight of Kubrick's characters, for whom, of course, wrong moves abound.

Game space is repeatable: we can return and play again, perhaps with new contestants or the same ones again. *The Shining* is the ultimate repeatable game space, but the narrative repetition, the circularity, of Kubrick films has always emphasized the sense that playing games, repeating duels, fighting battles, is all that people do. The returns of the monolith or the cut from bone to space station are not just narrative repetitions—they signal that the game is about to start over, just as General Turgidson, in *Dr. Strangelove*, is planning how to start over as soon as survivors can leave the mine shafts after impending nuclear annihilation.

Chion in his book about *Eyes Wide Shut* introduces another inviting element to the tracking-shot space, which he says "often seems to mean: there is no living space for two men. I appropriate the space I cross: I clear the space before me."[7] A characteristic Kubrick tracking shot is of a character appearing to play in a violent way or practicing for a bout—the shadowboxing of Poole in the first interior tracking shots on the *Discovery*, for example—and these shots are repeated in some form across most Kubrick films. Shadowboxing can be taken almost literally—mock punching inner demons, past and future selves, and attempting to escape the captivity of the shot by rebelling against it. From Kubrick's first films about boxing (the early short film *Day of the Fight* [1951] and his second feature, *Killer's Kiss* [1955]), this punching has been a sign of imprisonment (figure 18).

Traveling through space in this manner ritualizes it and creates repetitive cycles—the characters have been there before, or they are replacing those who did the same, or they are giving way to future versions of themselves. (One witty and easily overlooked version of this is our first tracking-shot view of Poole, already horizontal and shown with his three hibernating colleagues. All four will, of course, soon be dead.) Soldiers in sing-song chants in *Full Metal Jacket*, gangsters heading to place bets in *The Killing*, Jack pondering his "all work and no play" novel in *The Shining*—all move forward through tracking-shot space, making these time-traveling movements equivalent to moving through life and into death itself.

Games, of course, turn violent and deadly, but so does game space. Ping-Pong in *Lolita* (1962) turns to gun play, the Korova Milkbar in *A Clockwork Orange* is both preparation for violence and later a site of violence itself, as are numerous other resplendent recreational spaces. The bar/ballroom of *The Shining*, the orgy house of *Eyes Wide Shut*, the casino/game room/castle spaces of *Barry Lyndon* are gloriously beautiful and terrifyingly base, tipping from fun to horror at any moment. From recreation to being trapped or engaged in struggle is a small trip, and let's not forget the War Room in *Strangelove* ("you can't fight in here, this is the War Room"), which, together with *2001*'s *Discovery*, wins the prize for the most elaborately beautiful space in which to die, with perhaps an escapee or two to survive and replay the scene.

Parody Space

Elements of parody figure largely in Kubrick's work, and that space would be treated in this manner makes sense. Starting with decor again, there is a too-muchness, an obsessiveness, that makes spaces seem extreme, not just beautiful and repellent (though certainly those), but also ironic, comic, and exaggerations of more ordinary spaces.[8] For all of the praise of its realism which *2001* has received over the years, we should recognize its spatial construction goes well beyond anything we might call cinematic "realism." Some characteristic ways this is expressed are in the overly symmetrical compositions, the somewhat too-smooth camera movements, the overcleanliness of spaces, and one wants to add overspatiality itself, in the sense that awareness of space is hyped up by the sense of there being so much of it, so very visible. We can see space—not just outer space, but the space of a room, the space the camera moves through, the space of space, as it were. In *2001*, it is the largeness of the universe, the size and emptiness of space, which presents the paradox of parody space—there's more and less of it at the same time. As Ciment says, despite "a desire to open up his sets as far as possible . . . they nevertheless remain prisons."[9]

There are many scenes in Kubrick's films played out in bathrooms (*Full Metal Jacket* and *The Shining* are among the major examples), and *2001* provides written instructions for how one uses a toilet in space (figures 26–30). Here the reference to the toilet plays against the sanitized, antiseptic, white spaces that make up the decor of much of the film. Being too clean as a way to hide the dirty business really going on is a parodic use of space, the contradiction of clean and dirty one of the structured paradoxes (Susan White expands on this in her chapter in this collection). Clean and dirty, bright and dark, the edginess of Poole's death in the silence of space and HAL's silent killing of the hibernating astronauts are parts of the same contradiction. Here, what should be loud is quiet, and Kubrick pushes the opposites of sound and space to a parodic extreme. In a similar vein is the exaggerated use of signs, evident in *Dr. Strangelove* and most obvious in the "Life Functions Terminated" graph, when HAL kills the astronauts, and the "Explosive Bolts" sign, which points to Bowman's salvation in allowing him to return to the ship to destroy HAL (figure 12). Again these act as extreme, almost parodic images that in fact point to serious, even deadly events.

In Tuan's *Space and Place*, he says, "Freedom implies space," and it is this implication which suggests how parody space is constructed in Kubrick—but *implies* doesn't mean *creates*, so the distance between the two becomes an element of parody.[10] The implication of freedom not allowed leaves a comic tension. Those who express power by constructing or inhabiting large, ornate, beautiful spaces don't operate freely within them: they are constrained by everything, including the baseness of their own impulses, the camera movements which entrap them, and technology beyond their control. This is both horrible and funny.

The humor of *2001*, often lost sight of, is many times a humor of parody space. A circular interior spaceship path that can be traversed in a single shot, space that can be turned upside down, the hugeness and strangeness of the monolith appearances and the portentous manner in which they're photographed—the bizarre nature of these spaces is a quality of their parodic nature. Even the bone that becomes a space station in the film's (and cinema's) most famous edit, is as humorous as it is portentous (figures 3 and 4).

Kubrick's self-references to *2001* in subsequent films are self-parody of a subtle sort. The appearance of the *2001* album cover in *A Clockwork Orange* is parody enough, but it comes at the conclusion of an elaborate tracking shot of Alex's entrance to the music store, which has the humorous trademark quality which harks back, fanfare music included, to the movie it is referencing. And the monolith speakers rolled in at the end of the same film, symmetrically placed, are a spatial visual joke and a parodic self-reference.

As Tuan says, "The world feels spacious and friendly when it accommodates our desires, and cramped when it frustrates them."[11] Kubrick stretches this notion further by frustrating desires in open spaces and accommodating them in cramped spaces—variations on our earlier take on dirty and clean. Maybe the parody versions of the *Discovery* spaceship in films like *Alien* and *Dark Star* were made possible because *2001* leaves itself, in its parodic extreme, so ripe for further development, the qualities of being excessive, imitative, and slightly in bad taste ready to be taken a few steps further along.

Dream Space

2001 is literally unworldly and, especially by the time of the "Stargate" sequence, can leave a viewer to wonder how much of the film represents itself as if in a dream. Whether dream or nightmare, the sense of a shift into subjectivity characterizes a construction of space. It is not so important from a narrative sense, I would say, whether certain sequences may be read as dreamlike, as it is significant that a dream space, unlike a "real" or "physical" space, characterizes the Kubrick world. It is also possible to see these as hypothetical or proposed spaces, or spaces as seen by disembodied narrative positions.

My favorite argument that alludes to this is by Chion, who presents a compelling case that *Eyes Wide Shut* is an "imaginary sequel to *2001*" and that the film is a vision of another star child, "the child about to be born at the conclusion of the film."[12] *The Shining*, from its opening fly-over credits, also presents this kind of somebody's-point-of-view-but-whose quality. While we might want to read these weird spatial manipulations as authorial (or third person), they may also be as subjective as Kubrick ever gets. Kubrick is not a director who uses conventional point-of-view shots, therefore, the suggestion of point of view through other means, other eyes, gives the impression of a dream. We see as if we're participating in some sort of hallucination. Bowman's return through the airlock is not simply nightmarish as an event—the silence and then the breathing, coupled with just enough visual subjectivity, makes the scene primal, birthlike, and hallucinatory, as of course is the "Stargate" sequence. No more hallucinatory and dreamlike a segment has ever appeared in a mainstream film. *2001*'s early reputation as a "trip" movie was not entirely undeserved.

Dream space in Kubrick also extends to the too-slow sense of movement, the disembodied quality of frequent stillness. The hibernating astronauts, whom HAL will kill, expressionless and never moving, are akin to the frozen death moments of Jack Torrance and Private Pyle—dead but somehow still haunting those living. Jack alive before and dead before, Pyle but one of the earliest dead, will come back again, as a presence in the second half of *Full Metal Jacket*, like the ghosts of the Overlook Hotel in *The Shining*. Rebirth and return imply a never-ending frozen dream state—ambiguous time returning as dream. Alex imagining himself a Roman soldier flogging Christ in *A Clockwork Orange* is analogous to the link between the apes and astronauts in *2001*. Chion argues that Bill Harford (Tom Cruise) in *Eyes Wide Shut* is being pushed out by the spirit of his yet unborn son (whom Chion suggests will be conceived just after the movie ends). There is even a suggestion in *The Shining*—at least in a scene cut from the film that shows Danny, after Jack's death, throwing a ball against a wall just as Jack did—that his son will continue in his path.

Substitution and replacement in Kubrick leave a trail of multiple personalities or repeated cycles—the same character reliving experiences or old spirits returning. Bowman seeing himself in the bedroom at the end of *2001* can be read literally, or as a dream, or as another kind of perception. Peter Sellers in *Lolita*, his multiple manifestations, perhaps all versions of Quilty or all visions of Humbert's, suggest what Chion calls in *2001* "replacements in space."[13] Replacements look like dreams, spirits, hallucinations, and although seemingly a realistic filmmaker (especially in the war and period films, as well as *2001*), Kubrick is far more a filmmaker of dream states—paranoia, fear, violent nightmares, and horror. The room of mannequins in *Killer's Kiss* is among his first dream spaces (figure 36). And the dream of movement through the streets, photographed in negative in that film, has also been noted as foreshadowing the "Stargate" sequence in *2001*—a confusion of the human and the hallucinatory mechanical which extends all the way to the costumed, masked orgy participants in his last film. Identities shift, characters merge, we're not sure when we're awake or sleeping, alive or dead. Dark empty space will lead to death and/or rebirth.

Alien Space

Otherworldliness may appear dreamlike, but it can also be taken literally. Kubrick can make the earth alien or the edges of space routinely banal and earthly. It is particularly the alien landscape, or the earth as planet-like-many-others which he has expressed many times.

Gliding rapidly over barren ground suggests primordial Earth, or Earth without humans, a planet like any other. Flying closely over Colorado at the start of *The Shining* or closely over Russia at the end of *Strangelove*, the landscapes are devoid of people, as it was before we were here, or as it might look when we're done destroying each other. And Randy Rasmussen has suggested that the "reworked terrestrial sequences" of the "Stargate" sequence "convey an alien planet."[14]

The magical alignment which begins *2001* treats the Earth as a planet, as one place among many, no more or less. The beautiful opening vistas of "The Dawn of Man" section subordinate the appearance of near-humans to the almost Mars-like (or at least non-Earth-like) terror of hostile environments, of isolated water pools and still-prehistoric predators. As triumphant as the moment of bone-tool wielding is, marking the significant early moment of the Kubrick chronicles of violence, it also signals the moment that we leave Earth. Certainly, in relation to humans, Earth is the dominant location. But often the connection of Kubrick's characters is with the solidity of being bound to Earth, whether it's Jack Torrance in his VW heading for the otherworldly Overlook Hotel, or Kong's lone plane moving over the Earth for a brief last time before it is destroyed. When we're told in *Barry Lyndon* that the battle we're witnessing was never recorded, the many soldiers about to die do so in a kind of historical silence akin to Poole's death in space—worlds go on as if they never existed.

In the war films (and, in a sense, most Kubrick films are war films), alien landscapes abound. Looking up the periscope in *Paths of Glory*, a hostile and empty terrain could as well be any time and most any planet. When snow engulfs the space around the Overlook and Jack freezes (again), it seems as though the world returns to the way it was before humans attempted a foothold; and the mushroom cloud coda to *Strangelove*, however ironic the song over it may be in suggesting cyclical repetition, also signals the return to an uninhabited planet, back to something like where it started. The star child is no less otherworldly and alien. It's not an Earth child, is it? And it has the promise of rebirth, not the actualization, as does Alice Harford's final pronouncement at the end of *Eyes Wide Shut*, suggesting that they engage in the activity that will lead to birth. Babies hold promise, but when babies grow up, they become Alex, Johnny Clay, General Ripper, Jack Torrance, etc., etc.—all temporary inhabitants of worlds which will be there when they're not, worlds populated by their perpetual replacements.

Geometrical Space

The geometry of Kubrick is generally straight lines and right angles—the geometry of the hotel corridor and the labyrinth. Visual symmetry marks off a walled, enclosed space, confined and made even more geometrical by the limits of the frame. Chion correctly labels space in Kubrick as *centripetal*, "attracting attention to what is at its center," rather than *centrifugal* as in the work of directors like Alfred Hitchcock and Robert Bresson, who direct interest beyond the frame.[15] This force to the center also serves to create geometrical space—space which is laid out in an orderly, arranged fashion. While the occasional hand-held shots, generally during violence (e.g., the Cat Lady scene in *A Clockwork Orange*), can introduce a bit of nongeometric chaos, these are very much the exceptions. Instead, the perfect straight-line movement out from Alex's face at the start of *Clockwork* is itself as regular as clockwork, as geometrical in laying out the space of the Korova Milkbar, the movement and the room matching each other for symmetry. The Torrance family's incredible straight-line walk through the lobby of the Overlook is first of all geometrical in its precise straight movement, and it is reinforced by the geometry of the Indian-influenced patterns as they march past.

A labyrinth is as geometrical as a space can be. It exaggerates and complicates the line. Many have suggested that all of Kubrick's films are labyrinthine in structure, and, in *The Shining*, he uses a literal labyrinth, exaggerating it further, emphasizing its organization, first by showing us an impossible shot of the Overlook's labyrinth from Jack's point of view, and then by trapping Jack himself in its impossible lines.

In *2001*, Kubrick makes the circle a straight line through the magic of weightlessness, a circular walk laid out linearly without interruption. Geometrical space is everywhere, to the depths of HAL's memory core. Kubrick's beautiful space vehicles are impositions of geometry in space, just as the alignments of stars, planets, and moons suggest geometry on as grand a scale as there is, a cosmic spatial organization.

There is a geometry as well to Kubrick's regular structure of replacement, perhaps a narrative and temporal geometry (like his inclination toward three-part narrative structures) that has a spatial dimension as well as superimposition. Chion points out that Bowman and HAL are superimposed several times, either by reflecting Bowman's first appearance in what we come to learn is HAL's eye, or cutting from one to the other before their big battle (figures 13 and 14).[16] In battles of winners and losers, the equality Kubrick offers is regularly spatial. The amazing epilogue to *Barry Lyndon*, "they are all equal now," has visual expression in Kubrick: all are equal in their equivalent visual treatment, photographed the same way, so that one replaces or appears superimposed upon the other.

The symmetrical tracking shot is Kubrick at his (and cinema's) most geometrical, and the straight line of many of his tracking shots is unique to his spatial vision. Few directors, except perhaps Alain Resnais in *Last Year at Marienbad* (1961) or Tom Tykwer in *Run Lola Run* (1998), filmmakers who share Kubrick's serious penchant for movements and geometries of the straight line, can equal this geometric perfection. Kubrick can take tracking literally: movements seem anchored in a direct line, as if there were really a metal track on the floor. Maybe we'll turn a corner or change direction but, like Major Kong's plane switching targets in *Dr. Strangelove*, that will mean we are now only on another straight line. The trench and the hallway mark a movement that is inexorably straight. Unlike Max Ophuls (one of Kubrick's favorite directors), whose tracking shots are choreographed to look free and unpredictable—though they took great planning—Kubrick determinedly marches toward a likely destination, turning corners at right angles if necessary, and leading you just where you know you will go. The geometry is so stringent because the movement is almost always following a single character, who occupies a constant space in the arrangement of the frame. Danny on his tricycle, soldiers on the march, Johnny Clay at the racetrack, Kong in flight—all have their paths inscribed, the distances they must travel are determined.

The labyrinth is the model most often applied to Kubrick's camera and narrative movements, and anywhere his camera moves is turned into patterned, geometric spatial configurations.

Ubiquitous Space

There is geometrical space, a disembodied space, in Kubrick. When Chion describes HAL as "panoptic and invisible"—all seeing and barely seen—he links this to the multiple parts played by Peter Sellers in *Lolita* and *Strangelove*.[17] Calculation and arrangement (and therefore geometry) are behind ubiquity, and seeing the laying out of ubiquitous space as having strong connections to the daring behind multiple roles is an important insight. Multiple roles have long been viewed as a gimmick or parodic element, but Chion provides the key for seeing their function as so much larger and more significant. The multiple roles become another form of rebirth: replacement and linkage. More than just the reappearance of the actor, a "character" returns transformed and occupying usually a seemingly impossible space for the character to occupy. The reappearance needs explanation, and one such explanation is that the spaces of reappearance are part of the same space: ubiquitous space.

We can use time travel in *2001* as an entry point into the idea of ubiquitous space, especially in the penultimate sequence, in which Bowman sees himself in the bedroom. The actor Keir Dullea here plays multiple roles, his self aging before his eyes, multiplied again as he is mutated into the star child, another version, through rebirth, of the same character. (Bowman views himself from nearly his first appearance, so his multiple versions are at least as prevalent in the film as the superimpositions of Bowman and HAL, mentioned earlier.) This is not just Bowman everywhere at the same time; he is occupying positions impossibly simultaneous; ubiquity is no more conventionally physically possible than to "really" occupy dream space. Ubiquity and dreams collide, just as Kubrick's multiple uses of spaces can't be simply sorted out. Bowman looking at himself, transforming into his future self, the multiple spaces he occupies break down the limits of conventional space. This is its own kind of "shining": being able to reappear in different forms in different places, or simultaneously across time. Does Bowman see his older self (figure 15)? When Jack walks into the ballroom in *The Shining*, full of a ghostly party or laden with the bones of dead guests, it can be read as time travel, or alternatively it can be seen as a ubiquity of space, not just everywhere at the same time, but each place containing all of its own times within it.

We can also see ubiquitous space as reminders of other spaces, either the space we are currently occupying as it was or will be at another time (past or future), or the overlapping of this space with others. The jigsaw puzzle of *The Killing*, for example, would seem to suggest fragmented space; instead, it is very much ubiquitous space. We understand the space of the racetrack as no conventional rendering ever could allow us. Through his own kind of time travel, Kubrick's overlaps and repetitions perform a dense unpacking of space. The many things we see repeatedly (the start of the seventh race, money being thrown out a window, etc.) become extensions of conventional space. Going back isn't just (or quite) going backward in time. The direction of time is less important than the reconstituting of space. The returns signal a kind of go-anywhere, see-everything or, might we say, panoptic vision. A repeated event invokes an extension of space.

One form of bold space in *2001* is a consequence of its three-part structure and the repeated appearances of the monolith, which become a version of the repeated appearances of characters in different stages of their lives and afterlives. Is it the same thing back again, or another version "reborn" of the first? This is the same question we ask of Jack Torrance when we learn of Delbert Grady, and see him reappear in a time when he shouldn't belong. Jack, of course, *is* Delbert Grady, or Grady is Jack, and when we see Jack in the final photograph on the wall back in Grady's time, it is like a monolith's reappearance or another reincarnation of the same character. Kubrick's visual and narrative daring invites us to see these multiple appearances as a ubiquity of space. Returns of the same character or object break us out of conventional spatial perceptions.

The two films with Peter Sellers—*Dr. Strangelove* and *Lolita*—are versions of this same spatial daring. Especially amusing, I would say, are the near-quaint over-the-shoulder shots where a stand-in was used to allow multiple Sellers characters to appear in the same shot. Admirably and boldly, Kubrick doesn't resort to split-screen pastings together, as other multiple-role films do (even other Sellers films, like *The Mouse That Roared* [1959], go this route). In *Strangelove*, Sellers was to have played Major Kong too, so that he would have been in every narrative space, and one can imagine him not just playing three roles, but many more. Would we say Sellers is "reborn" in these other roles? We could as well say what we know, that it is the same person transformed and constructed into an "impossible" space where he can see himself.

In *Lolita*, Sellers's impersonations are initially read as disguised versions of his first character, Claire Quilty, who is killed through the painting in the opening scene and so is "reborn" in flashback in a series of alternate roles. Even the dapper Quilty at the school dance looks a different character than the toga-wearing, burned-out Quilty at the start. Characters in Kubrick films rarely change much over the course of a film. When they do, they do not so much change as transform, don a new guise (as happens regularly, say, in *Barry Lyndon*). So we may wonder, which is the "real" character? Lolita's last appearance as Mrs. Richard Haze is like a jump into a new time frame, and we can never be sure how much of the character Lolita we see throughout the film, like all of Quilty's roles, are imaginings or dreams of Humbert's. Humbert, Bowman, Jack, even Bill Harford in *Eyes Wide Shut* are all subject to these time-traveling, space-shifting, dream-affected reappearances of multiple selves.

Narrative gaps in Kubrick can also be seen as an overlaying of space—spaces made extensions of each other through an otherwise drastic break of time. Clearly, the "Dawn of Man" bone-to-spaceship does this—linking prehistoric Earth to future space travel. Another bold cut in a Kubrick film is the break between the two parts of *Full Metal Jacket*, from death at the training camp to Vietnam. The cut performs a similar function as in *2001*: it ties the spaces together and essentially makes them one space; the raw recruits are also reborn as soldiers. In *Strangelove*, too, we might start by thinking that the three locations—the war room, B-52 bomber, and Burpelson Air Force Base (and the characters contained in each)—are very different, and surely by the end, despite many elliptical cuts between narratives, the equivalencies among the three spaces are far more significant than their differences. We might say as well that in *Eyes Wide Shut* the fantasy/dream space and "real" space by the end of the film are no longer sharply divided.

It is ubiquitous space in *2001* that takes us ever farther from Earth, but, like a Möbius strip, it seems to turn back on itself and return us to where we began. Like HAL recapitulating his beginnings at the moment of his demise, death and rebirth are contained in each other, just as are spaces and characters. So whether the dead seem to live on, or the living make way for their replacements (as in *2001* and, as Chion suggests, in *Eyes Wide Shut*), for Kubrick it is the spaces (and Space) that will always be there, asserting their presence as a powerful force unto themselves.

Concluding Space

Kubrick's conception of space is complex and distinctive. We might start to understand his films by noticing visual characteristics, such as tracking shots and symmetries, but the visual style is only a first indication that deeper ideas are at work. Equivalencies and reappearances of characters, patterns of rebirth, parodies of conventional movie genres, and other by-now familiar Kubrick characteristics also have significant spatial consequences. Michel Ciment, talking about tracking shots, for example, argues that their use "adds further to the sense of implacable logic and an almost mathematical progression, and hopefully we have seen this to be the case."[18] The most distinctive Kubrick devices share this trait, for behind them is the force of an implacable logic, with larger consequences than the devices themselves.

One of the great pleasures of *2001* is the inevitability of the struggle between HAL and Bowman, with the very future of humanity seeming to be at stake. Bowman's determination to wrest power back from HAL is a kind of "tunnel vision" that seems at odds with HAL's ability to see and understand everything. But the conflicting visions collapse upon themselves: HAL wasn't so smart after all, and Bowman's determination to destroy HAL leads to the Infinite and to rebirth. Even though we love this struggle, its grand designs are so beyond a simple winning or losing as to make individual outcomes largely beside the point. Like Dax at the end of *Paths of Glory*, or virtually the end of any Kubrick film, there is the pattern repeating, the returning to battle, the ending that is the starting over.

Space, in this sense, is also a great reward that one can take from Kubrick. The spaces he created are stylized, otherworldly, strange, ironic, and often terrifying—not just in terms of visual design, but for the ability they have to convey larger feelings and ideas. He created spaces that contain time and its repetitions and that express grand visions of humanity and its movement through that time. Maybe the pretentiousness of *2001: A Space Odyssey* isn't such a bad thing after all.

Notes

1. David G. Stork, ed., *HAL's Legacy: 2001's Computer as Dream and Reality* (Cambridge, Mass.: MIT Press, 1997).
2. Michel Ciment, *Kubrick: The Definitive Edition*, trans. Gilbert Adair (New York: Faber and Faber, 1999); Michel Chion, *Kubrick's Cinema Odyssey*, trans. Claudia Gorbman (London: BFI, 2001).
3. Chion, *Kubrick's Cinema Odyssey*, vi.
4. Alexander Walker, *Stanley Kubrick, Director* (New York: Norton, 1999), 172.
5. Ciment, *Kubrick*, 75, 114.
6. Chion, *Kubrick's Cinema Odyssey*, 130.
7. Michel Chion, *Eyes Wide Shut*, trans. Trista Selous (London: BFI, 2002), 66.
8. For more on parody in Kubrick, see Stephen Mamber, "In Search of Radical Metacinema," in *Cinema/Comedy/Theory*, ed. Andrew Horton (Berkeley: University of California Press, 1991), 79–90.
9. Ciment, *Kubrick*, 75.
10. Yi-Fu Tuan, *Space and Place* (Minneapolis: University of Minnesota Press, 2003), 52.
11. Ibid., 65.
12. Chion, *Eyes Wide Shut*, 167.
13. Chion, *Kubrick's Cinema Odyssey*, 171.
14. Randy Rasmussen, *Stanley Kubrick: Seven Films Analyzed* (Jefferson, N.C.: McFarland, 2001), 104.
15. Chion, 78.
16. Ibid., 86.
17. Ibid., 83.
18. Ciment, *Kubrick*, 136.

5

Of Men and Monoliths

Science Fiction, Gender, and *2001: A Space Odyssey*

BARRY KEITH GRANT

The general impression that viewers tend to bring away from Stanley Kubrick's *2001: A Space Odyssey* (1968) is an overall feeling of "coldness," not just the physical cold of outer space, but of the film's sense of humanity. As has often been observed, the computer HAL seems a more complex character with greater emotional depth than any of the people in the film. And while the computer's death is a scene of wrenching pathos, the three hibernating scientists expire in what is perhaps the most antiseptic depiction of death in all of cinema, a bland-looking monitor indicating "Life Functions Terminated." *2001*'s relative dearth of dialogue, wooden characters, slow pace, and sleek production design, which depicts the environments of space travel as thoroughly antiseptic and ordinary, all contribute to the film's cold tone.

These aspects of *2001* have been much commented upon by other critics, sometimes positively, sometimes not, but what has gone largely unnoticed is how many of the film's stylistic elements work in relation to one of its primary themes, the gendered implications of space exploration. The coldness of the film's characters, most of whom are men, is part of the film's overall view of the relationships among science, technology, violence, and patriarchal masculinity, a view consistent with other Kubrick films. This perspective is surprisingly similar to that of feminist philosophers of science, who have critiqued traditional science as informed by a masculinist bias at least since Francis Bacon employed metaphors of rape and seduction to describe men's mastery over a feminized Nature.[1] Baconian science, based on rational empiricism, induction, and a masculine culture of objectivity and nonsensuality, is "a science leading to the sovereignty, dominion, and mastery of man over nature,"[2] as Evelyn Fox Keller puts it. I want to suggest that this sensibility of masculine mastery, as conveyed in popular culture's representations of space travel, is purposefully undermined by *2001*. That is to say, Kubrick's space epic explores a discursive space as much as physical space in that it seeks for a stylistic alternative to the science fiction film's conventional depiction of space exploration as an act of phallic masculinity, of penetration and possession—or, to borrow the title of one of the first Hollywood movies on the subject, *The Conquest of Space* (1955; figure 1).

2001 makes clear immediately in the opening section, entitled "The Dawn of Man," that it will explore these issues. Kubrick depicts the landscape here as harsh and hostile, a man's world where only the fittest survive. Warring bands of apes contest with each other and with animals for control of the crucial natural resource, a waterhole; the blanched skeletons of dead apes mingle with the rocks and dust, a reminder of the stakes of survival. The balance of power tips decidedly when one ape (Moon-Watcher in the script) takes the human race's first technological step by turning a bone into both a tool for killing prey and a weapon for bludgeoning enemies. Only now do the apes seem to walk more upright for, the film suggests, it is the very point when men begin to harness technology for the purposes of extending their inherent aggression that they truly become men. This opening section of *2001* plays out in brief this theme, which preoccupied Kubrick over the course of his career even as it is central to the science fiction genre.

According to science fiction writer and critic Damon Knight, the genre's appeal resides in what he calls "a sense of wonder." As Knight explains:

> [S]ome widening of the mind's horizons, no matter in what direction—the landscape of another planet, or a corpuscle's eye-view of an artery, or what it feels like to be in rapport with a cat . . . any new sensory experience, impossible to the reader in his [*sic*] own person, is grist for the mill, and what the activity of science fiction writing is all about.[3]

Science fiction offers us worlds clearly discontinuous from our own, fantastic worlds that inevitably return us to the known world for comparison.[4] If this dynamic of "cognitive estrangement"[5] is central to science fiction, then theoretically it is an ideal genre for exploring the ideology of gender, for questioning our culture's rigid, constrained thinking regarding gender. Yet science fiction, both in literature and film, has been overwhelmingly masculine and patriarchal, and truly alternate visions of gender have been few.

Mary Shelley's *Frankenstein*, published in 1816 and generally considered to be the first true science fiction novel, offered a critique of masculine scientific presumption in its story of a masturbatory male scientist who chooses to create life on his own rather than with his new bride.[6] Yet by the time of Jules Verne fifty years later, the genre was taken over and shaped by men, and women writers retreated from the expansive vistas of science fiction to the more domestic spaces of Gothic melodrama and the novel of manners. Nathaniel Hawthorne, himself a writer of science fiction tales in the 1840s, famously dismissed women writers as "d——d female scribblers."[7] Verne's popular *voyages extraordinaires*, such as *Journey to the Center of the Earth* (1864), *From the Earth to the Moon* (1865), and *20,000 Leagues under the Sea* (1870), are colonialist tales about male explorers going where no man had gone before, adventure stories wherein, in the words of Robert Scholes, "boyish men played with new toys created by science."[8] At the turn of the twentieth century, H. G. Wells became the founder of modern science fiction with his series of "scientific romances" beginning with *The Time Machine* in 1895. Wells himself was a champion of women's rights, among other social causes, but his novels are "romances" only in the literary sense—that is, as a fictional mode. In fact, Wells's major science fiction novels contain no significant female characters, with the one possible exception of Weena, the childlike, helpless woman in the distant future of *The Time Machine*. But she is less a rounded character than a tabula rasa on which Wells's heroic but patriarchal Time Traveller, retreating from the rapid social changes at the dawn of the twentieth century, including the growing independence of women, can reinscribe his Victorian values.

Several decades later, during the so-called golden age of science fiction literature of the 1930s through the 1950s, the popular pulp magazines assumed a male readership with their typical stories of BEMs (bug-eyed monsters) to be destroyed and BBBs (big-breasted babes) to be enjoyed. The promise of both pleasures often was featured prominently in their sensational cover illustrations. These images carried over into science fiction film in the 1950s, when the abrupt arrival of the atomic era suddenly made the genre one of the most popular. *Gog* (1954), for example, is atypical only to the degree to which its imagery is embarrassingly explicit in linking masculinity with power, potency, and technology, all coming to a head, so to speak, in the deliriously libidinous climax wherein the scientist hero (the staunchly reassuring Richard Egan) asserts his phallic dominance by destroying rampaging robots that have been sabotaged from a Soviet ship in space. The robots are themselves excessively phallicized, their defeat by the hero indicating that American science is more potent than that of godless communists. Amply demonstrating his masculine potency, the hero wins the hand (and presumably the body) of the sexualized woman scientist, a damsel in distress dressed in a provocatively tight lab suit and high heels.

The rationale behind *Gog*'s typical conflation of space exploration as masculine potency and Cold War propaganda (the "space race") is emphatically clear in the scientist's explanation in *Invaders from Mars* (1953), another science fiction movie of the period, for why conquering space is so important: "If anybody dared attack us, we could push a few buttons and destroy them in a matter of minutes." *Destination Moon* (1950), the film that launched the decade's spate of science fiction movies, takes the position, as one of the characters explains, that "whoever controls the moon will control the Earth." When the astronauts land on the lunar surface, they claim the moon "by the grace of God" and (adeptly anticipating Neil Armstrong) "for the benefit of mankind" in the name of the United States.

The intertwined issues of technology and patriarchal masculinity are central to stories of space travel, which constitute such a significant part of science fiction that they have their own subgeneric designation—the space opera (a type, we might note, to which *2001*, with its soundtrack of classical music by Johann and Richard Strauss rather than the more typical Theramin-inspired electronic score, has a special relation). Space stories usually involve an emphasis on technology and gadgetry since both elements are required by the premise of interstellar travel. Outer space, like the frontier in the western genre, is a dangerous place that requires the fortitude of men to traverse it.[9] (It is worth noting that, according to the generic discourse of science fiction and mirroring the operative distinction in the real sciences, stories of space are deemed, appropriately, "hard" SF, as opposed to stories more concerned with social extrapolation, which are called "soft" SF.) Space stories have conventionally depicted interstellar travel as the penetration by men of the dark, womblike vastness of space in phallic-shaped rockets. In the standard iconography of the genre, while aliens frequently float in rounded spacecraft (UFOs, flying saucers), earthlings tend to take their giant steps for mankind in protruding, pointed ships.

Once rocket technology became imaginable in the early twentieth century, science fiction literature quickly dispensed with such patently impractical means of interstellar travel as Cyrano de Bergerac's bottles of dew, Poe's balloon, Verne's giant gun, and Edgar Rice Burroughs's astral projection, and seized upon spaceships, which were quickly streamlined and masculinized. The hyperbolic covers of the pulps typically emphasized the piercing and penetrating power of human spacecraft through such graphic techniques as the exaggerated foreshortening of rocket nose cones. With the aim of settling other worlds, astronauts often are depicted as piercing and impregnating the universe, spreading the seed of human civilization. In movies, the phallic power of human spaceships was emphasized with the first science fiction movie ever made, *Une Voyage dans la lune* (*A Trip to the Moon*, 1902), in which French filmmaker Georges Méliès envisioned a giant cannon that discharges a space capsule moonward with an eruptive force powerful enough to achieve escape velocity. As if to demonstrate the masculine triumph of this technology, the cannon ejaculates to the incongruous accompaniment of a group of dancing women—in effect, the first chorus line of "Rockettes"—in the mise-en-scène literally below the powerful phallus (figure 16). Méliès borrowed the idea of a giant space gun from Verne's *From the Earth to the Moon*, in which the cannon is erected by the members of the all-male Baltimore Gun Club, and it appears again as late as 1936 in *Things to Come*, where it sticks out, so to speak, as a strikingly unscientific anomaly in H. G. Wells's tale of the future, which otherwise strives for scientific accuracy.

Polish SF writer Stanislaw Lem parodies the phallic discourse of space fiction in his 1961 novel *Solaris* (an element entirely missing from both film adaptations). The novel opens with Lem's narrator, a male scientist named Kelvin, describing his journey through space in a small rocket shell:

> My body rigid, sealed in its pneumatic envelope, I was knifing through space with the impression of standing still in the void, my only distraction the steadily mounting heat. . . . The capsule was shaken by a sudden jolt, then another. The whole vehicle began to vibrate. Filtered through the insulating layers of the outer skins, penetrating my pneumatic cocoon, the vibration reached me, and ran through my entire body. The image of the dial shivered and multiplied, and its phosphorescence spread out in all directions. I felt no fear. I had not undertaken this long voyage only to overshoot my target!
>
> . . . A sharp jolt, and the capsule righted itself. Through the porthole, I could see the ocean once more, the waves like crests of glittering quicksilver. The hoops of the parachute, their cords snapped, flapped furiously over the waves, carried on the wind. The capsule gently descended. . . .
>
> With the clang of steel rebounding against steel, the capsule came to a stop. A hatch opened, and with a long, harsh sigh, the metal shell which imprisoned me reached the end of its voyage.[10]

Kelvin has traveled through space to investigate a distant planet that is one large sentient ocean. Earth scientists have been studying this ocean planet for generations, producing exhaustive volumes of data and theoretical tomes about it, but thus far have been unsuccessful in the attempt to make contact with it. In his opening description of Kelvin's space flight, Lem establishes his character's phallic stance toward the universe while, in contrast, the ocean planet represents a kind of feminine mystery, pliant yet impenetrable in its difference, seemingly beyond the scientific comprehension of men.

While the planet Solaris may never explain itself, in the 1970s feminist voices in science fiction began to speak, to venture into public space, beginning with the publication of Ursula K. LeGuin's *The Left Hand of Darkness* in 1969, just one year after *2001*. Earlier, a few women writers had ventured into the masculine territory of space fiction: including Thea von Harbou, who wrote the screenplay for her husband, Fritz Lang's *Metropolis* (1927) and *Frau im mond* (*Woman in the Moon*, 1929), which introduced the concept of the countdown adapted by NASA; and Kate Wilhelm, whose 1961 story "The Ship Who Sang" is about a physically deformed girl who is hardwired into a spaceship as its computer. But LeGuin's novel opened the stargates for women to write about space travel. Described by science fiction critic Carl Freedman as "the book with which sf most decisively lost its innocence on matters of sex and gender,"[11] *The Left Hand of Darkness* imagines an alien race, the Gethenians, who are normally genderless except during the fertility season, known as kemmer, when they may become either male or female depending partly upon the gender of others near them. The plot isolates a Gethenian politician and a human male ambassador from the planetary federation on an epic adventure, like Hawkeye and Chingachgook, Ishmael and Queequeg, or Captain Kirk and Mr. Spock. But while the classic American fiction of Cooper, Melville, and Twain, as Leslie Fiedler and D. H. Lawrence have pointed out, represses the dread of femininity and homoerotic desire within stories of male adventure,[12] LeGuin foregrounds these tensions with a character who is at once both genders and neither. As the two protagonists, initially alien to each other, begin to overcome their distrust and become intimate friends on their arduous journey together, the earthman, like the terrestrial reader, is prompted to rethink his rigidly conceived, heterosexist categories of gender and sexuality.

The influence of LeGuin's novel was enormous, and on its heels came a wave of feminist science fiction from such writers as Joanna Russ, Marge Piercy, Pamela Sargent, Connie Willis, Kit Reed, and Octavia Butler. Sargent's three anthologies of feminist science fiction, the *Women of Wonder* series, published between 1974 and 1978, provided solid evidence of a feminist "movement" within the genre. Earlier, women science fiction writers such as C. L. Moore (Catherine Moore), Idis Seabright (Margaret St. Clair), and James Tiptree, Jr. (Alice Sheldon), used masculine or gender-indeterminate noms de plume in order to get published, to "pass" with editors and readers. But by the 1970s, women science fiction writers could boldly go where few had before, announcing their gender difference and writing science fiction that in various ways challenged the genre's traditionally masculinist bias. Novels such as Russ's *The Female Man* (1974) and Piercy's *Woman on the Edge of Time* (1976) targeted the very language of science fiction as a masculine discourse, not only by featuring female protagonists, but also by experimenting with unconventional narrative structures and multiple points of view in order to provide alternatives to the masculine way of looking at things. These works provided science fiction's sense of wonder, but one consciously rooted in gender difference.

To take a particularly relevant example, Tiptree's story "The Women Men Don't See" (published in 1973, four years before the author revealed herself as a woman) deconstructs the masculinist assumptions and ideology of male adventure fiction by undermining the misogynist clichés of the genre's characteristic hard-boiled style. The story involves a stereotypical macho adventurer, Don Fenton, who becomes stranded with two women when the small charter plane on which the three are passengers crashes in an isolated, rugged part of Mexico. Fenton promptly takes charge, assuming the responsibility of providing for the women's survival and seeking a way of making contact with the outside world while, at the same time, the women stumble upon and make contact with aliens who have landed in the seclusion of the jungle for a quick pit stop. In the end, the women decide to leave Earth with the aliens rather than stay with the intolerably sexist Fenton, who would kill the aliens in order to "protect" the women, which he assumes without question is his masculine duty. The narrative is told from Fenton's decidedly male point of view, and although he uses all of the stereotypical clichés of male adventure fiction in his narrow attempt to understand the women, Tiptree makes clear that they are more complex people who could never be fixed by Fenton's formulaic phrases. Ultimately, the two women are as alien to Fenton as the undulating extraterrestrials he automatically fears, while the women are so alien-ated by Fenton's patriarchal limitations that they would just as soon pull up terrestrial stakes and, like so many male adventurers before them, light out for the territory. Trying to explain their decision to Fenton, one of the women tells him that Earth is a patriarchal world and that women are like opossums: "What women do," she says, "is survive. We live by ones and twos in the chinks of your world-machine."[13] The story's prose style, which appropriates but subverts the masculine hard-boiled style typical of its genre, is itself an example of a guerrilla aesthetic striking a blow at the patriarchal world machine.

In film, however, the genre has advanced little since the 1950s, when male anxieties about women's postwar independence were given expression in the form, on the one hand, of monstrous wasp women, she-creatures, and fifty-foot-tall dominatrixes, and on the other hand, of passive lab assistants and scientists' virginal daughters, who must be rescued by men, as in *Gog*. A few later science fiction films, such as the *Terminator* and *Lara Croft* movies, switch the gender of the traditional male hero, but this is an illusory form of "empowerment" that simply reinscribes rather than questions the patriarchal values of such narratives. Apart from only two films, Rachel Talaley's *Tank Girl* (1995) and Kathryn Bigelow's *Strange Days* (1995)—both of which critique masculinity and the pleasures of masculinist representations, and both of which, not coincidentally, were box-office failures—science fiction films have held onto the conventions of cinematic style and representation that have characterized popular cinema generally.

Laura Mulvey and other feminist film scholars have argued that one of the defining qualities of mainstream narrative cinema is that the gaze of the camera tends to be gendered as masculine. According to Mulvey, classical film construction positions male characters as subjects, as the bearers of the camera's gaze, authorizing its look, while women are consequently rendered as objects, possessed and fetishized by the camera.[14] In science fiction, the patriarchal gaze and objectification of the female body is clearest in campy space operas like *Fire Maidens of Outer Space* (1955) or *Barbarella* (made the same year as *2001*), but other movies are only slightly more subtle. *Alien*, for example, is progressive in its representation of gender insofar as it shows female characters working alongside men in space and as it makes one of them, Ripley, its hero, in fact, the only crew member of the *Nostromo* to survive and defeat the eponymous extraterrestrial. Yet precisely when Ripley is at her most heroic, the film stylistically reinscribes a masculine perspective during the climactic battle between Ripley and the creature by displaying her as an erotic sight, the object of masculine desire. The camera's position and angle emphasize Ripley's gender in a provocative "crotch shot," a shot motivated not by the requirements of the story but by the apparent necessity of reminding viewers of her gender difference.[15] Thus, if science fiction films like *Alien* present a more active and heroic female protagonist, on the discursive level they tend to remain traditional in their gender politics by containing women within a sexualized and controlling masculine gaze.

Given this generic context, *2001: A Space Odyssey* may be seen as especially progressive and innovative in ways far more profound than simply its convincing, then state-of-the-art special effects, although these elements of the film certainly contribute to its wider rewriting of the science fiction genre. In taking science fiction in new directions, in truly unexplored territory (to "Jupiter and beyond the infinite"), *2001* anticipated the wave of revisionist genre movies that characterized the New Hollywood of the 1970s. The way in which *2001* treats science fiction's depiction of space exploration turns the genre on its ear, like Kubrick's depiction of zero gravity in the film, and aims, as John Cawelti said, to "set the elements of a conventional popular genre in an altered context, thereby making us perceive these traditional forms and images in a new way."[16] Instead of rewriting the myths of the Western frontier as did films like *Little Big Man* (1970) and *McCabe and Mrs. Miller* (1971), *2001* deconstructs the myths of the final frontier.

An avid reader, Stanley Kubrick professed a particular fondness for science fiction. Three of the director's thirteen films—*Dr. Strangelove* (1964), *2001*, and *A Clockwork Orange* (1971)—are generally recognized as important contributions to the genre. The fact that Kubrick made three science fiction films in a row indicates the extent to which he was interested in the genre. (A fourth science fiction film, *A.I.*, was begun by Kubrick but completed by Steven Spielberg in, appropriately enough, 2001.) Indeed, Kubrick claimed that by the time he began work on *2001*, the middle film of the series, he had seen virtually every science fiction film ever made.[17] Robert Kolker argues that *2001* differs from earlier science fiction movies by deliberately employing elements of the genre's conventional streamlined production design, which equates progress with orderliness, neatness, and efficiency—but not to celebrate these values so much as to question them by showing how such progress "equals emotional and intellectual death" in a world where "perfect order and perfect function decrease the need for human interference."[18] This is true enough, but the film also differs from most earlier science fiction films in its focus on masculinity and technology as major themes rather than simply containing these values as unexamined or naturalized ideology.

Kubrick was drawn to science fiction for the same reason he was attracted by the war film: both genres are fundamentally concerned with these themes, which were prominent in the director's work. Masculinity and violence are central to *The Shining* (1980), which chronicles the descent of a family patriarch into violent madness. In *Dr. Strangelove*, the nuclear apocalypse is initiated when General Jack D. Ripper (Sterling Hayden), satirizing the Cold War paranoia of the previous decade's science fiction films, overcompensates for his sexual impotence by talking loudly and carrying several big sticks: a cigar clamped in the side of his mouth, a machine gun at his hip, and a wing of nuclear bombers, which he unleashes on the Soviet Union to prevent the communists from sapping his "precious bodily fluids." The marine recruits in *Full Metal Jacket* (1987) are trained to think of their weapons as synonymous with their penises. One of the platoon's marching mantras, as they parade holding their rifles in one hand and their genitals in the other, is "this is my rifle, this is my gun / this is for fighting, this is for fun." Grammatically, the antecedents of the couplet's pronouns are ambiguous, so it's unclear which tool is for which job. The film's very title, slang for a rifle's loaded magazine, also evokes the image of the male body armed and armored against the world.

The aggressive power of the phallus in Kubrick's world is made literal when Major Kong (Slim Pickens) straddles the nuclear bomb he drops on a Russian target in *Dr. Strangelove*, and in *A Clockwork Orange* when droogie Alex (Malcolm McDowell) attacks the Cat Lady with a sculpture of a giant penis. Kubrick's adaptation of Anthony Burgess's novel about urban life in the near future shows that sexual aggression is an essential part of masculine identity because when Alex is conditioned to be sickened by violence, he becomes a whimpering, helpless victim of the violence inflicted on him by other men. Women in Kubrick's films tend to be dominated within a patriarchal world, as metaphorically visualized by the tables in the shape of nude women in the Korova Milkbar in *A Clockwork Orange*, or living in the cracks of the male world machine, like the female sniper in *Full Metal Jacket*. The masculine world machine in *Dr. Strangelove* is ultimately the Doomsday Machine, which at the film's end destroys all life on Earth. In *2001*, Kubrick's view of the destructive, phallic nature of technology is expressed beautifully in the celebrated cut from the ape's bone, at once man's first tool and first weapon, to a space station: in this one magnificent edit, Kubrick summarizes 4 million years of human history as a continuation of phallic territoriality and conquest (figures 3 and 4). This is perhaps the film's most memorable moment, but other aspects of *2001* also may be understood in relation to this critique of traditional masculinity.

Most obvious perhaps is the film's casting and detached treatment of its characters, to which I alluded at the outset. Accounts of classical film narrative argue that the reliance on heroic and virtuous characters with whom spectators can easily identify is the central device for involving viewers in the cinematic story.[19] But *2001* denies viewers any such easy figure of identification. William Sylvester gives a low-key performance as Dr. Heywood Floyd, who serves as the audience's escort to the moon and then disappears from the narrative except for the recorded message that plays when the *Discovery 1* ship reaches Jupiter. Both Gary Lockwood and Keir Dullea, who play astronauts Frank Poole and Dave Bowman, are inexpressive actors cast in similarly inexpressive roles. Lockwood had only a few undistinguished roles before *2001*—perhaps his most notable being, ironically, his appearance on the *Star Trek* episode "Where No Man Has Gone Before" in 1966, in which some crew members of the *Enterprise* develop powers of ESP when they journey to the edge of the galaxy. Dullea's previous credits included *David and Lisa* (1962), his debut, and *Bunny Lake Is Missing* (1965), two films in which he played psychologically disturbed characters repressing their real feelings.

Vivian Sobchack has noted that in science fiction movies the combination of rationality and strength needed to "conquer" space means that emotion and sexuality are displaced onto the iconography of space technology. Almost always at the helm, in control, are men, astronauts who are typically cool, rational, even sexless. In Sobchack's words, "whether named Buzz or Armstrong, Buck, Flash or Bowman," they are typically "as libidinally interesting as a Ken doll; like Barbie's companion, they are all jaw and no genitals."[20] Kubrick's astronauts in *2001* are perhaps the most sexless and undemonstrative of the lot, their libidinous impulses completely sublimated by the technology that envelops them. The images of the semi-nude yet laconic Lockwood supine on his tanning bed have nothing of the corporeal, eroticized charge of Sigourney Weaver in her improbably flimsy space underwear in *Alien*. After the star-studded casts of *Paths of Glory* (1957), *Lolita* (1962), and *Dr. Strangelove*, the avoidance of big-name actors in a blockbuster production like *2001* seems a deliberate attempt to avoid the larger-than-life quality of movie stars in deference to the grandness of the celestial stars. If *2001* has a "hero," it is, as in Olaf Stapledon's novel *Last and First Men* (1930) or Wells's *Things to Come*, other science fiction narratives with similarly epic scope, the human race itself, not a particular individual.

David Bordwell describes the classical narrative style as "an excessively obvious cinema" because it always aims at orientation, which he refers to as "a larger principle of 'perspective'": "not the adherence to a particular spatial composition but a general 'placing' of the spectator in an ideal position of intelligibility."[21] Yet *2001* consistently works to thwart or make problematic such a privileged spectatorial position. For example, the film's motif of spiraling imagery denotes the weightlessness and absence of directional orientation in space, but also refuses to orient spectators with fixed reference points, unlike classic narrative construction. Such images appear, for example, in the cockpit console of the shuttle to the Clavius moonbase, with its spinning telemetry; when the flight attendant on the shuttle turns "upside down" to enter the cockpit with refreshments (figure 6); and in the spinning cylindrical drum that Poole and Bowman enter before leaving the *Discovery 1* to repair the AE35 unit. When Dr. Floyd is in the Bell photophone booth at the space station talking to his daughter, through the window we see the Earth seeming to spin around outside the porthole ("Daddy's traveling," Floyd says tellingly to his daughter), a sight repeated during his discussion with the Russian scientists (figure 17). Although this use of sustained rotating imagery has since been absorbed into the mainstream, appearing, for example, in *Star Trek: The Motion Picture* (1979) and more recently in Brian de Palma's *Mission to Mars* (2000), the technique was radical when Kubrick introduced it in *2001*. Further, *2001* employs this imagery in more complex ways than these other films, playing off spectators' perceived spatial orientation with seemingly contradictory movement within the frame. So, for example, when Bowman is tumbling and spinning toward the *Discovery 1* from the repair pod—at the point, that is, when he is finally taking action, being most "heroic"—he looks upside down in the image. Back in the ship, as Bowman descends a ladder, he seems to be moving sideways within the frame, given the camera's position in relation to him. And when he proceeds with determination to disconnect HAL, Bowman goes up a ladder although in the shot it looks as if he is going down head first. A similar *trompe l'oeil* effect occurs while Bowman floats in HAL's memory logic center. The famous first shot inside the *Discovery 1* shows Frank Poole jogging in the rotating centrifuge, which immediately challenges our spatial orientation in the ship. As this is the first shot inside the *Discovery 1*, it is an ironic "establishing" shot because it establishes only our disorientation, an effect entirely apposite in the context of a journey into the unknown (figure 18).

According to Bordwell, classical mise-en-scène relies on balanced compositions and the centering of protagonists in individual shots.[22] But in *2001*, emphasizing the vastness of space and humanity's relatively humble place within it, Kubrick's characters are often depicted as tiny creatures in big widescreen images, often placed off to the side of the frame, as when Poole spins off into the void. The film's long takes use time to convey the immensity of space, as do the periods of silence on the soundtrack ("In space no one can hear you scream," as the advertising tag-line for *Alien* put it). While Dr. Floyd may be utterly certain of his central place in the universe ("moon/American/Floyd" is the way he identifies himself at the computerized security check), Kubrick's mise-en-scène in the space sequences undermines conventional ways of regarding the universe and our place in it.

The spatially disorienting images are echoed by the ambiguities Kubrick builds into the film even at the level of the soundtrack. Every time we see a monolith, it is accompanied on the soundtrack by the choral music of György Ligeti. But while Ligeti's music may sound, in the words of Norman Kagan, "like a frantic collage of all the religious themes in the world,"[23] its diegetic status, hence its meaning, is unclear. The apes do not seem to respond to the music, and the scientists looking at the monolith in the Tycho moon crater respond to its signal, not to the music. How, then, are we to understand the music? Are Ligeti's voices emanating from the monolith, the music of the spheres that modern man is incapable of hearing? Or is the music the stylistic embellishment of a filmmaker who is known for the careful and striking choices of music in his films?

Unlike classical film narrative, *2001* is excessively opaque rather than excessively obvious. Just as Stanislaw Lem wisely never reveals the motives or meanings for the humanoid manifestations created by the entity Solaris, so *2001* contains numerous enigmas that remain unresolved at the film's end. It is never clear, for example, whether the monoliths represent alien technology, a supernatural force, or the presence of God. Nor is it clear whether the monoliths actually determine human evolution and history, or merely inspire, or just observe us. And the film never explains what happens to Bowman once the *Discovery 1* reaches its destination and the final "Jupiter and Beyond the Infinite" sequence begins. Alexander Walker notes that when Bowman listens to Dr. Floyd's recorded message after disconnecting HAL—when, that is, the film is almost over—Floyd's comments are at once "the first audible and unmistakable clue to the audience of what the film is narratively 'about'" and, amazingly, "also the last utterance in the film."[24] And Floyd's brief briefing, which does not really explain very much (he notes in his recorded message that only HAL knows the details of their mission), is itself somewhat ambiguous. Is its playback, as would appear to be the case, pretimed to begin when the *Discovery* reaches Jupiter? Does the recorded message engage automatically when Bowman disconnects HAL? Or does HAL initialize it as his dying gesture? In the end, the film's story seems to remain a "total mystery," like the monoliths as described by Dr. Floyd in his recorded message. Just as we should not master the universe, we are unable to master this film's narrative.

What slim narrative *2001* possesses falls away completely when Bowman enters the Stargate where, along with the astronaut, we are showered with an awesome display of distorted landscapes and abstract, swirling colors, more like a nonrepresentational experimental film than a mainstream movie. The very length of the sequence seems motivated by a desire to immerse us in a visual experience rather than to convey narrative information and advance the story, the primary goal of classical narration. After the Stargate, Bowman appears in a room that looks at once old and new, a confusing combination of Louis XVI and modern styles, where the astronaut confusingly watches himself age and die (figure 15). It is never clear whether what we are seeing is a trip through outer space or the inner space of the astronaut's mind. In a detailed formalist analysis of this sequence, Mario Falsetto has shown how Kubrick's editing consistently subverts the viewer's understanding of narrative space and time by violating such normally inviolable techniques as the conventional shot/reaction shot in order to convey a sense of Bowman's transcendent experience.[25] Each time Bowman sees another, more-aged version of himself, we first see the new yet older Bowman from the physical point of view of the older but younger Bowman; but then the next shot reveals that the earlier Bowman is no longer there. Thus these apparent point-of-view shots cease to be point-of-view shots, and their perspective—and ours as viewers—becomes "disembodied," just as Bowman will lose his male body when he transforms into the star child.

As we travel through the Stargate, Kubrick inserts periodic close-ups of a human eye, presumably Bowman's, which each time it blinks changes to the same hues that color the Stargate images (figure 34). Whatever these images might "mean," we see them through Bowman's eyes, which begin to merge with what he beholds. This sense of extreme sensitivity to the point of merging with nature rather than conquering its secrets is what Evelyn Fox Keller describes as "a feeling for the organism" demonstrated by, for example, the intimate and empathic relationship that geneticist Barbara McClintock established with the maize seedlings with which she was working.[26]

In Kubrick's cinema, eyes figure prominently as images of vision and perception, or the lack of it. *A Clockwork Orange* features numerous close-ups of Alex's eye, first in his droogie garb with eye make-up and the eyeball cufflinks (figure 9), and later when his eyes are propped open during the Ludovico treatment. Kubrick's last film, completed just before his death, shows people blinded by the quotidian world, entrapped within the confines of their individual egos and living with their "eyes wide shut." But *2001* suggests that we learn to be more open to nature, to perceive beyond the armored confines of traditional masculinity. Significantly, the star child at the end of *2001* is not only naked, ungirded, vulnerable to the universe, but its eyes are already wide open, not shut. Orbiting the Earth in the film's last shot, the star child can see beyond our terrestrial limitations, perceiving with a new, widened consciousness even while still encapsulated within the enclosed but transparent cosmic womb (figure 35).

Twice we see close-ups of Bowman's face as he experiences the Stargate, bright colors reflecting off the glass visor of his helmet almost as if they were radiating from within. These shots recall the famous moment in experimental filmmaker Stan Brakhage's *Reflections on Black* (1955), in which Brakhage scratched the emulsion off the image of a man's eyes to suggest his metaphorical blindness. But where Brakhage's blindness is represented as a gaping absence within the image, Kubrick's astronaut experiences a transcendent vision which seems to flood his eyes with a riot of color. Brakhage was a filmmaker whose great subject was vision and the possibilities of expanding perception. He once challenged spectators to free their vision from the blinkered constraints of culture:

> Imagine an eye unruled by man-made laws of perspective, an eye unprejudiced by compositional logic, an eye which does not respond to the name of everything but which must know each object encountered in life through an adventure in perception.[27]

In *2001* Kubrick similarly asks us to look at the world out there in just this way, as an adventure in perception, as experience rather than expropriation. Kubrick himself refused to explain the ending of *2001*, saying that "its meaning has to be found on a sort of visceral, psychological level rather than in a specific literal explanation."[28]

Arthur C. Clarke's initial script for *2001* was based largely on his 1948 short story "The Sentinel," which concerns the future discovery of an alien artifact on the moon. The artifact, a crystal pyramid, acts as a beacon, presumably signaling its makers that the human race had, in Clarke's words, "proved our fitness to survive—by crossing space and escaping from the Earth, our cradle."[29] Although the conclusion of the story seems carefully constructed to avoid using any masculine terms, such as "mankind," after working with Kubrick on *2001* Clarke said that from the outset the director "had a very clear idea of his ultimate goal. . . . He wanted to make a movie about Man's relation to the universe."[30] His words are well chosen, for Kubrick was talking about exploring a perceptual space that has been left largely uncharted by men.

In Kubrick's 1960 epic, *Spartacus*, there is a telling scene in which Kirk Douglas as the rebellious slave, inspired by his sudden freedom, tells his love, Virinia (Jean Simmons), of the new horizons he envisions. Spartacus crouches on the ground, just as Kubrick's man-apes would do several years later in *2001*, and says he wants to know everything (including, significantly, where the sun goes at night and why the moon changes shape). When he concludes that as yet he knows nothing, Virinia responds by reminding him, and the audience, that in fact he knows important things, things that cannot be taught, deeper truths than mere scientific facts. Spartacus is a true hero for Kubrick because he seeks a higher wisdom, to understand without possessing, the very opposite of the decadent Romans in the film, who know only material wealth and power. Ina Rae Hark argues that in searching for a subjectivity other than the two choices offered to Spartacus, animal or Roman, *Spartacus* asks the question: "Is there a non-phallic human subjectivity?"[31] Within the context of science fiction rather than the biblical epic, *2001* asks the same question. In the film's final shots, the star child's gender is indeterminate: the first glimpse of it is a quick long shot which shows no visible genitalia, while subsequent shots do not show it below the chest. The star child is a new human who, in its openness to creation, has transcended patriarchy's characteristic binary thinking about gender. If Bowman begins his journey to Jupiter and beyond the infinite in a spermlike ship, one more astronaut out to conquer and impregnate the universe, he comes to possess nothing from his previous being but the spherical, womblike repair pod before he is reborn, the aspiring sire becoming the sired.

Kolker suggests that instead of regarding the monoliths as literal artifacts of a higher alien intelligence, they be read as metaphorical "markers of humanity's evolution," perhaps a symbolic "obstacle, a perceptual block that must be transcended."[32] This obstacle, I would suggest, is phallic masculinity. The monoliths have a firm and solid presence and are seemingly everywhere, like the Law of the Father. In "The Dawn of Man" section, when the first monolith appears, the apes gather around it, touching it provocatively, at once wary and worshipful. At the end of the film, the aged, dying Bowman also reaches for it, but his gesture, like so much else in the film, is ambiguous: is he reaching out, like Moon-Watcher in the opening sequence, to touch the monolith, or is he raising his arm in a gesture of farewell as he completes the process of dying to an old consciousness and being reborn into a new (figure 23)? The ending would seem to suggest the latter, for, as I have argued, *2001* seeks to restore to us a sense of wonder that modern man has forgotten in embracing a masculine quest for scientific mastery.

Of course, it might be argued that *2001*'s reliance on special effects is itself a fetishization of cinematic technology and a betrayal of its theme. Given the resources available for the film's production, one is reminded of the young Orson Welles's remark upon finding RKO's studio resources available to him for making *Citizen Kane* (1941), that he felt like a boy with the world's largest train set. Filmed in Super Panavision and presented during its first run in Cinerama, with state-of-the-art special effects costing more than half of the film's total budget of $10.5 million and all supervised or created personally by Kubrick, *2001* is a convincing display of technological mastery by a master director entirely in charge of his production. That majestic cut from the bone to the space station not only cuts to the bone of cinema's unique ability to conquer time and space through editing,[33] but also points to the pervasive and potent presence of the author.

There is no escaping the fact that the cinema is an inherently technological medium, and *2001* marshals cinema's technological possibilities to invite us to experience the world rather than to master it—not unlike Bowman, who needs technology to reach Jupiter, but who then abandons it to journey beyond the infinite. If the film's astronauts initially privilege the values of reason and control, in the end Bowman must turn off his ship's computer in order to let the Force be with him. But this is not to suggest that George Lucas's space opera is anything like *2001*, for the *Star Wars* saga is a juvenile Oedipal drama that embraces the very patriarchal myths of space adventure fiction ("I am your father," in the immortal words of Darth Vader) that Kubrick seeks to go beyond. Where Luke must grow up and take his place within the patriarchal order, Bowman grows into a new being with a new perspective.

2001: A Space Odyssey ends with the star child back in the view of Earth, not only looking at the Earth in a different way, but also rotating to face the camera, returning our gaze as spectators as if challenging us to meet it, that is, to see better, to attain its higher plane of being. Here Kubrick, usually regarded, and rightly so, as a pessimist and determinist, offers us a remarkable gesture of hope and faith for an artist who elsewhere sees violence and death. The kind of sensual, open spectators whom Kubrick's film encourages us to be recalls Stapledon's description of the sexual nature of the next human order in his similarly visionary *Last and First Men*:

> Around the ancient core of delight in physical and mental contact with the opposite sex there now appeared a kind of innately sublimated and no less poignant, appreciation of the unique physical and

mental forms of all kinds of live things. It is difficult for less ample natures to imagine this expansion of the innate sexual interest; for to them it is not apparent that the lusty admiration which at first directs itself solely on the opposite sex is the appropriate attitude to all the beauties of flesh and spirit in beast and bird and plant.[34]

Simultaneously one of the most scientific of science fiction films and an anti–science fiction film, *2001* suggests that with such an open, nonmasculinist perspective, we can leave the cradle and truly take a giant step for humankind.

Notes

1. See, for example, Evelyn Fox Keller, *Reflections on Gender and Science* (New Haven, Conn.: Yale University Press, 1985); Donna Haraway, *Simians, Cyborgs, and Women* (New York: Routledge, 1991); Judith Wajcman, *Feminism Confronts Technology* (University Park: Pennsylvania State University Press, 1991); and Lynn Hankinson Nelson and Jack Nelson, eds., *Feminism, Science, and the Philosophy of Science* (Boston: Kluwer Academic, 1996).

2. Fox Keller, *Reflections on Gender and Science*, 34.

3. Damon Knight, *In Search of Wonder: Essays on Modern Science Fiction*, rev. ed. (Chicago: Advent, 1967), 13.

4. Robert Scholes explains the special dynamic of such fiction this way: "In the worlds of SF, we are made to see the stoniness of a stone by watching it move and change in an accelerated time-scale, or by encountering an anti-stone with properties so unstony that we are forced to reinvestigate the true quality of stoniness." *Structural Fabulation: An Essay on Fiction of the Future* (Notre Dame, Ind.: University of Notre Dame Press, 1975), 46.

5. See Darko Suvin, *Metamorphosis of Science Fiction: On the Poetics and History of a Literary Genre* (New Haven, Conn.: Yale University Press, 1979), chap. 1.

6. For an overview of feminist criticism of *Frankenstein*, see Catherine Gallagher and Elizabeth Young, "Feminism and *Frankenstein*: A Short History of American Feminist Criticism," *Journal of Contemporary Thought* 1, no. 1 (1991): 97–109.

7. For a discussion of Hawthorne's science fiction, see H. Bruce Franklin, *Future Perfect: American Science Fiction of the Nineteenth Century* (New York: Oxford University Press, 1966), 3–64.

8. Scholes, *Structural Fabulation*, 15.

9. Hence the number of westerns that have been adapted as science fiction. For more on this, see Barry Keith Grant, "Strange Days: Gender and Ideology in New Genre Films," in *Ladies and Gentlemen, Boys and Girls: Gender in Film at the End of the Twentieth Century*, ed. Murray Pomerance (Albany: State University of New York Press, 2001), 186–88.

10. Stanislaw Lem, *Solaris* (New York: Berkley, 1971), 8–10.

11. Carl Freedman, "Science Fiction and the Triumph of Feminism: Barr's *Future Females, the Next Generation*," *Science Fiction Studies*, no. 81 (2000): 278.

12. Leslie Fiedler, *Love and Death in the American Novel* (New York: Delta, 1967); D. H. Lawrence, "Fenimore Cooper's Leatherstocking Novels," in *Studies in Classic American Literature* (New York: Penguin, 1977), 40–51.

13. James Tiptree, Jr., "The Women Men Don't See," in *The New Women of Wonder: Recent Science Fiction Stories by Women about Women*, ed. Pamela Sargent (New York: Vintage, 1977), 205.

14. Laura Mulvey, "Visual Pleasure and Narrative Cinema," *Screen* 16, no. 3 (1975): 6–18.

15. James Cameron's *True Lies* (1994) offers a more egregious example in the overlapping genre of the action film. While on the one hand the film allows the wife of the spy to become a partner in espionage, it includes a lengthy scene, again entirely gratuitous in relation to the plot, where the husband (Arnold Schwarzenegger) arranges for his wife (Jamie Lee Curtis) to perform a seductive striptease in a hotel room for a stranger. She remains unaware that the man watching in the shadows is in fact her husband, whose anonymous voyeurism in the dark becomes emblematic of the male spectator, for whom the camera obligingly emphasizes Curtis's curvaceous body.

16. John Cawelti, "*Chinatown* and Generic Transformation in Recent American Films," in *Film Genre Reader III*, ed. Barry Keith Grant (Austin: University of Texas Press, 2003), 251. The only film Cawelti discusses that pre-dates *2001* is Arthur Penn's *Bonnie and Clyde* (1967).

17. James Howard, *Stanley Kubrick Companion* (London: Batsford, 1999), 107.

18. Robert Kolker, *A Cinema of Loneliness: Penn, Stone, Kubrick, Scorsese, Spielberg, Altman*, 3d ed. (New York: Oxford University Press, 2000), 135.

19. David Bordwell, "Story Causality and Motivation," in *The Classic Hollywood Cinema: Film Style and Mode of Production to 1960*, ed. David Bordwell, Janet Staiger, and Kristin Thompson (New York: Columbia University Press, 1985), chap. 2.

20. Vivian Sobchack, "The Virginity of Astronauts: Sex and the Science Fiction Film," in *Alien Zone: Cultural Theory and Contemporary Science Fiction Cinema*, ed. Annette Kuhn (New York: Verso, 1990), 107.

21. Bordwell, "Space in the Classical Film," *Classic Hollywood Cinema*, 54.

22. Ibid., chap. 5.

23. Norman Kagan, *The Cinema of Stanley Kubrick* (New York: Grove, 1972), 150.

24. Alexander Walker, *Stanley Kubrick Directs*, rev. ed. (New York: Harcourt Brace Jovanovich, 1972), 259.

25. Mario Falsetto, *Stanley Kubrick: A Narrative and Stylistic Analysis* (Westport, Conn.: Praeger, 1984), 115–28.

26. Evelyn Fox Keller, *A Feeling for the Organism* (New York: Freeman, 1983). See also Nancy Tuana, "Revaluing Science: Starting from the Practices of Women," in Nelson and Nelson, *Feminism, Science, and the Philosophy of Science*, 22–31.

27. Stan Brakhage, "Metaphors on Vision," *Film Culture*, no. 30 (Fall 1963): n.p.

28. Stanley Kubrick, quoted in Howard, *Stanley Kubrick Companion*, 112.

29. Arthur C. Clarke, "The Sentinel," in Jerome Agel, ed., *The Making of Kubrick's* 2001 (New York: New American Library, 1970), 22.

30. Clarke quoted in Howard, *Stanley Kubrick Companion*, 104.

31. Ina Rae Hark, "Animals or Romans: Looking at Masculinity in *Spartacus*," in *Screening the Male: Exploring Masculinities in Hollywood Cinema*, ed. Steven Cohan and Ina Rae Hark (New York and London: Routledge, 1993), 163.

32. Kolker, *A Cinema of Loneliness*, 136–37.

33. H. G. Wells noted this distinctive ability of the new medium of cinema in his first novel, *The Time Machine*, published in 1895, the same year as the first public film screening, where he describes the experience of time traveling as being like watching a speeded-up film.

34. Olaf Stapledon, *Last and First Men: A Story of the Near and Far Future* (New York: Viking Penguin, 1987), 134. In his preface, Stapledon writes, "To romance of the far future, then, is to attempt to see the human race in its cosmic setting, and to mould our hearts to entertain new values" (11).

6

The Cinematographic Brain in *2001: A Space Odyssey*

MARCIA LANDY

> There is as much thought in the body as there is shock and violence in the brain. There is an equal amount of feeling in both of them. The brain gives orders to the body which is just an outgrowth of it, but the body also gives orders to the brain which is just a part of it.
>
> GILLES DELEUZE, *Cinema 2: The Time-Image*

2001: A Space Odyssey is an allegory of the evolution of human intelligence, deliberately appropriating the cinematic apparatus to embark on its philosophic journey, which is realized in its conception of the "cinematographic" brain. The film has a subversive agenda and a design on the spectator. Critical to its own journey, the *Odyssey* probes conceptions of the human brain: is it the rational center for and seat of knowledge about a constant and determined world, the embodiment of intelligence whose evolution began with the tool-wielding ape and culminated in the computer that never errs? Or is there more to understand about the history and trajectory of evolution? And how does the technology of space in conjunction with the cinematic apparatus enter into the film's allegory of perception, affect, and intelligence?

Stanley Kubrick pursues the enigma of intelligence by turning the Cartesian brain-body dualism on its head by invoking images of faces, eyes, interiority, and exteriority that place spectators outside the traditional anthropocentric context. He inverts and distorts the potential of the brain to "give orders to the body" and the body's ability "to give orders to the brain." As in Kubrick's other films, the intellectual journey is reliant on the meticulous figuration and questioning of bodies, images, sounds, and verbal language. The identity between the world and the brain involves a rethinking of the relations between mind and body, affect and thought, sight and sound. Describing the films of Stanley Kubrick as an "intellectual cinema," Gilles Deleuze wrote:

> If we look at Kubrick's work, we see the degree to which it is the brain, which is the *mis[e] en scène*. Attitudes of body achieve a maximum level of violence, but they depend on the brain. For in Kubrick, the world itself is a brain, there is identity of brain and world, as in the great circular and luminous table in *Dr. Strangelove*, the giant computer in *2001: A Space Odyssey*, the Overlook Hotel in *The Shining*. The black stone of *2001* presides over cosmic states and cerebral states: it is the soul of the three bodies, earth, sun, and moon. But also the seed of the three brains, animal, human, machine. Kubrick is renewing the theme of the initiatory journey because every journey in the world is an exploration of the brain.[1]

The challenge posed by Deleuze's comments on Kubrick's work is to think through the "identity of brain and world" in *2001*. The allegory that limns and unfolds this identity is not seamless, linear, and progressive in a conventional sense; it is discontinuous and fortuitous, dependent on flashes of selective memory: it creates unsettling associations between past and present. The film's allegory is an exploration of an "acentered system."[2] It explores the destructive consequences of a reductive and obsessive commitment to the primacy of either subjectivity or objectivity, body or mind. The film turns its investigation of consciousness into a simultaneous investigation of the history and character of cinema, a medium that has the potential to explore unexamined connections between forms of intelligence and representations of the world. Moreover, while some of the images in the film may seem dated to some critics,[3] the questions that the film raises about simulation, space, and time are timely given the astronomical growth of television, video, and computer technology and their relation to the technology of the cinema.

The worlds of *2001* are neither a celebration of the tools of technology nor their denigration. To interpret the allegory as moral parable, a commentary on the evils or blessings of technology, is to skew the work of the film *as* film and reduce it to a statement. The characters (apes, scientists, robotic HAL, and astronauts) are portrayed as automatons, sleepers and sleepwalkers, subject to forces that appear to emerge from outside themselves yet determine their interior states. The spectator becomes a seer or visionary who, instead of being placed in the familiar and repetitive position of having to "recall or reconsider the past," is invited to invent the future.[4] The film's reflexivity about its status as film enhances its investigation of the cinematographic brain, a brain that has the potential to generate incorporeal images of thought not present to the senses and productive of different and hitherto unperceived relations of time and hence existence.

Following Deleuze's provocative comments about an identity between world and brain, this chapter treats the film as an allegory that proffers a critical and historical treatment of intelligence that raises disturbing questions about the future and about human survival as well. At the core of the film is the unanswered question about the "purpose and meaning of human existence."[5] This allegory of the cinematographic brain implicates the spectator in the film through the film's investigation of "what is thinking?" This chapter tracks different configurations of the brain—animal, human, computer, and cinematographic—and probes the film's tactics for creating an experimental and philosophical narrative based primarily on visual and aural images with a minimum of verbal language.

The Animal Brain

The initial episode of the film, "The Dawn of Man," is proleptic, that is, anticipatory of events to come in the subsequent three episodes. Day and night herald the different temporal phases of the transformation of the man-apes from omnivores to carnivores and from cringing and threatened beasts to aggressive hunters. The visual and aural themes involve the accenting of sound in the animals' grunts and screaming and in the György Ligeti and Richard Strauss music associated with the appearance of a mysterious black object referred to in the novel as a monolith. This enigmatic object, which appears four times in the film, produces alterations in those who respond to its presence. However, the monolith remains a puzzle. Is it benevolent, malevolent, or neutral? How does its presence serve to alter the behavior of the ape-men and the subsequent direction of human life?

"The Dawn of Man" episode highlights the primacy of gesture. The mysterious (chance? predetermined?) arrival of the black object transforms the apes (and the viewer's) sense of movement and action. The random movements of the animals become focused as the apes' attention becomes directed toward the monolith. This unusual object with its impact on the ape-men projects the animal brain as connected to the body and to terrestrial space. The animal brain is sensory and physical; communication and decision making are expressed through the body, which conveys affects relating to fear, pain, threat, pleasure, and aggression. The animal brain constitutes one form of intelligence that is often regarded as inferior in comparison with the human brain. Yet *2001* does not fall prey to this judgment.

Initially, the perspective in this episode is that of the objective gaze of the camera, offering a perspective (alternating middle- and long-distance shots) on the static and barren landscape and on the monotonous and threatening world of the apes whose existence is devoted to foraging, survival, and defending their territory. Close-ups, especially of Moon-Watcher (the name in the script for the alpha male played by Daniel Richter), precede the apes' approach to the monolith. After the arrival of the monolith, the camera work and editing change, finally becoming expansive in relation to outer space. The apes' movement toward the monolith is accompanied by Ligeti's otherworldly music. The music increases in volume and in complexity as the apes approach and retreat from but finally return to the alien object. The suggestion of the ape-men's increasing mobility in this episode is enhanced by the passage of time, from night to day, from darkness to light, and from retreat and hiding to aggressive attack (figure 19).

The editing now consists of lengthier shots, now involving more agitated movement on the part of the apes that culminates in the touching of the monolith. Moon-Watcher's at first tentative, then more assured, wielding of the bone is accompanied by the renewed and jubilant sounds of Richard Strauss's *Thus Spake Zarathustra*. Further, the appearance of the image of the sun flaring at the top of the monolith enlarges the spectator's sense of space, as if signaling that the constraints of the apes' earlier existence in the African veldt has been overcome and anticipating the journey to outer space. From a tight framing of the landscape, which suggests the impossibility of visually contemplating the out-of-field, the episode has expanded its cinematic horizon. The odyssey to consciousness has begun. The movement climaxes in the spectacle of Moon-Watcher's exultant and victorious throwing of the bone into the air and the bone's transformation into a space ship that resembles the shape of the bone (figures 3 and 4). The Strauss music dramatically and effectively marks a transformation in the apes, producing a shocking caesura. Visually and aurally, this moment is characteristic of the film's allegorical treatment predicated on its dramatic yoking of an image from the past with one from the present.

This episode also is indicative of the film's mode of allegorizing by way of introducing a connection between vision and thought. The episode is remarkable for its emphasis on gesture. It becomes an investigation of gesture as a form of consciousness that recalls how the early, silent cinema was an instrument of perception and not merely a storytelling medium. Kubrick's insistence on the importance of affect is clearly conveyed in the focused and sensory-motor behavior of the apes, evident in their awakening as expressed in their killing of game and establishing their territorial dominance by means of the bone. If the early cinema was supreme in focusing on situation and action and relating them to modes of perception, these early moments of *2001* are for the spectator an invocation of the "dark dreams of the past" not as linear, immutable, and absolutely true but as exposing different presents and relations to the past, a past threatening ever to return.

The behavior of the ape-men is exemplary of what Giorgio Agamben has described as the politics of the gestural, the potential of the body for communicability as something other than a means to cultural, economic, and political control. This potential for communicability is what he describes as a means without end. Relying on music, dance, and display, the body communicates the power of the gesture, returning, in Agamben's language, "images back to the homeland of gesture," where life can once again become decipherable, breaking "with the false alternative between means and ends that paralyzes morality and presents."[6] In producing the gesture, "the duty of the director," Agamben further writes, is "to introduce into this dream the element of awakening"[7] and, if anything, to explore the potential of cinema to jar the spectator into wakefulness. In allegorical and proleptic fashion, the episode invites speculation on the question of technology as a problematic prosthesis, a means of survival at great intellectual and affective expense, but also a tool to think differently from prevailing conceptions of rationality and consciousness.

In heralding the transformation of the apes to "the status of a sapient subject,"[8] the film has not only posed the problem of knowledge and its effects but has confronted the viewer with the cinematic medium as a visual and auditory instrument for this cerebral examination. The dramatic visual transformation in the landscape and in the portrait of the ape-men connects the prehistory of humankind to the present of the spectator, but the episode has also offered a meditation on the history of cinema as more than a mere recording but as a medium capable of reflecting on its own uses of the technology of images in the sparse dialogue, valorization of music, and "abandonment of narration, emphasizing the sense of sight at the expense of language."[9] The technique in addition suggests an early form of filmmaking, where perception was communicated through sensory experience, gesture, and affect.

The Human Brain of the Scientist

As the ship, a craft that resembles the bone thrown in the air by the ape, floats through space in the next (untitled) episode to the music of *The Blue Danube Waltz*, the spectator is given a different perspective on the brain. The transition from the terrestrial world to that of space

> [i]nvolves a passage from a shot that has a certain subjective force, since the bone has been thrown by the ape and there is a relationship of contiguity between them, to a shot that is utterly external in its presentation. The view of the spaceship does not belong to any character and cannot be attributed to any contiguous person; and the following dance to "The Blue Danube Waltz" is meant to be enjoyed as a spectacle, not as the presentation of anybody's perception or subjectivity.[10]

If "The Dawn of Man" episode highlighted the solidity of the terrestrial terrain, the apes' physical proximity to each other, and the bodily movements of the proto-men in relation to the emergence of decision making, what is evident in this untitled segment is a loss of contact with the landscape and with the body expressed in the unsteady movement of humans and the restraints on communicability (particularly in the banality and duplicity of the verbal language that has replaced the vocalization of the apes).

Dr. Heywood Floyd (William Sylvester), on his way to investigate the presence of a disturbing object on the moon, is Moon-Watcher's replacement. Yet he appears only after an elaborate series of shots in space, highlighting the Hilton Space Station, the vehicle seeking entry to it, and views of the ship's controls and computer monitors as the ship is brought to a precise landing. The image of the pilots is impersonal; they are shot from the rear minus dialogue, and the first encounter with the scientist Floyd reveals him to be immobile as he sleeps and not in complete control of the milieu. A moving object, resembling a miniature spaceship (his pen), floats until seized by the flight attendant, who plants it in his pocket, her movements unsteady in her "grip shoes" (figures 5 and 6).

After landing at the space station, Floyd is greeted by the mission controller (Frank Miller). The interior is predominantly white with the exception of the pink-clothed attendants and the startlingly red modernistic chairs seemingly designed for appearance rather than comfort. Finally, the film provides dialogue in the banal and clichéd greetings of the mission controller and Floyd; in Floyd's telephone conversation to Earth with his daughter, Squirt, played by Vivian Kubrick, the director's daughter (figure 17); and in his interchange with the Russian scientists. Floyd is the antithesis of the ostensibly malevolent scientist of conventional science fiction who is passionately consumed with the quest for knowledge to effect the transformation of humanity into godlike or demonic creatures. Floyd as scientist is without affect, a sleepwalker, a transmitter of clichés, un-self-consciously imbued with a sense of superiority.

His gaze is belligerently opaque in his brief but low-key "fight" with Smyslov (Leonard Rossiter). Floyd is "consistently casual, affable, and bored, wearing the same pleasant managerial mask whether it confronts an actual stranger's face, the video image of his daughter's face, or that synthetic sandwich."[11] He is formed in the image of the mechanistic world he inhabits. Though identified with space travel, he is indifferent, if not inured, to the mysteries of outer apace. His affinity with the apes seems obscure. He is not a predator for food, and his territoriality is expressed through his reductive use of language to conceal his military objectives. He appears to be a creature of verbal language rather than of vocalization, but his use of words suggests, in Thomas Allen Nelson's terms, "an archaic and earthbound verbal baggage. Language has not kept pace with a technological entry into a universe far beyond the boundaries of Earth."[12] Floyd's speech and behavior are dissonant with the continuity, openness, and vastness of space.

Despite the elaborateness of the technology and the sophistication of the instrumentation, this episode shares with the postmonolith apes a preoccupation with territoriality (defending a claim to an occupied area), an assumption of the superiority of nation, science, and technology. If the apes do not communicate via words, ironically neither does Floyd. The episode with him portrays the brain of the scientist as consecrated to state power and hence to paranoia, secrecy, and deception. Language is his tool to mystify and conceal; briefings are cryptic and authoritarian; the conversation with the Russians is similarly aggressive and withholding: "language conspires with politics and a primitive social hierarchy to conceal the discovery of the monolith."[13]

Conspicuously, his limited and controlled body movements, verbal impoverishment, and confined sensory-motor capacity locate him in a world where intelligence is focused on suspicion, where the brain appears detached from the body, and where knowledge implies secrecy. In this episode, the body disappears; it does not make decisions. The brain gives orders; it is in command but, as portrayed through Floyd, the human brain has become specialized, capable of purposeful thinking in terms of means and ends, but woefully deficient in imagination, feeling, empathy, and creative activity.

The confrontation of Floyd and the other men with the monolith, which parallels that of the apes, obscures the men's bodies, giving them the impression of aliens, looking like the insectlike or robotic figures familiar in popular science fiction films. The doctor and his colleagues are helmeted and completely sheathed in their suits of synthetic material as they move toward the monolith and slowly surround it while the Ligeti music rises in intensity. Like Moon-Watcher, Floyd touches the black object, and the camera lingers on his hand in close-up as he runs it along the edge (figure 20). Attention is focused on the man with the camera, who organizes the others into a group in front of the monolith (incongruously like a tourist shot), but then something different occurs than had happened with the apes. Instead of the triumphant Richard Strauss music, the audience hears the Ligeti music culminating in an aversive screeching crescendo and ending in a squeal as the men, apparently in pain, raise their hands to their ears, which are covered by their space helmets, and the scene fades to black.

The distinction between the earlier, prehistorical episode and this cerebral journey resides in the human loss of bodily, sensory-motor connections to the world. What is operative here is the transformation from the actual to the virtual, from the real to its simulacrum. The cinematographic brain is reduced to images on a monitor: the sumo wrestling observed on the TV by the attendant, the information shown on the screen that enables the pilots to land the spacecraft, and even window shots of the Earth and moon that are like cinematic stills from the interior of the ship. The disturbing shriek emanating from the monolith can be construed as a massive reproach to the indifferent men who surround it, taking its picture and robbing it of its power and magic. Perhaps this is the film's conception of popular cinematic technology where the visual images appear to have no links to the outside world, where the alienated brain has no connection to an exterior world: it is disjoined from the body, which is an encumbrance rather than a source of knowledge.

This episode is an investigation of vision. The viewer is everywhere confronted with instruments of visual technology: the information on the video monitors, the telephone-video image, and the surveillance technology that separates friend from foe. This visual cornucopia invokes, as in *Dr. Strangelove*, a world where vision does not equate with seeing and critical comprehension. Visual and verbal information are exchanged among the men, but it is very clear (as in the encounters among the scientists) that knowledge is withheld. The understated style of these encounters, the implied stylistic differences between this film and popular cinema suggest that the film is also an exploration of spectatorship and a critique of conventional forms of cinema technology (e.g., the genres of science fiction).

Perhaps the last moment of this episode with its discordant sound is further a major strategy for jarring the spectator into wakefulness. The sound disrupts and possibly diverts the spectator from the forgetfulness engendered by conventional cinematic forms. The satiric allegory can be compared to the exploration of language and silence and their relation to scientific conditioning dramatized in *A Clockwork Orange* (1971). In its critique of the scientific brain, *2001* has trod the path of other science fiction narratives. However, in its allegorical treatment, its daring tampering with narrativity, its eschewing of dialogue, character, and psychology, its introduction of critical questions derived from social science and film theory, the film has challenged the clichés about the brain and consciousness dominating the literature, science, and popular writings on the brain.

The Computer Brain

The action now shifts to the spaceship *Discovery* where three characters—two astronauts, Dave Bowman (Keir Dullea) and Frank Poole (Gary Lockwood), and the computer, HAL (given a human voice by Douglas Rain)—become melodramatically involved in a life-and-death struggle. The satiric dimensions of the previous episodes become elegiac (reinforced by the music of Aram Khatchaturian): "The mood now becomes deeply melancholy—a pair identical and yet dissociated, like a man and his reflection—eat and sleep and exercise in absolute apartness, both from one another and from all humankind."[14] The astronauts' passive reliance on and complacency about the computer's brain turn into suspicion and alarm after HAL's expression of concern about "extremely odd things about the mission" that are linked to the strange story of "something being dug up on the moon" and the "melodramatic touches" of bringing on board three men in hibernation. Indeed, the struggle between man and computer begins to unfold when HAL characterizes his own unease as "silly" moments before reporting a prospective failure in his AE35 unit.

The *Discovery* episode contrasts with other science fiction films in its uses of melodrama, its injection of the politics of sexuality in a cybernetic milieu, its reflexive focus on vision, and its transforming of the usually grotesque alien figurations of the extraterrestrial regime into men and their technology. The helmets of Bowman and Poole with their shimmering surfaces are shot at a distance or from above, concealing the astronauts' faces and making them appear alien. Further, the spaceship appears to have anthropomorphic features, specifically heads with prominent eyes (figure 21).

The body seems to be most often reduced to an image of the head. Elements of the human face are prominent in images of the shuttles with their glowing eyes. Similarly, the cockpits of the ships appear as faces as does "the shape of the *Discovery* with its elongated round head."[15] The emphasis on images of the head underscores the film's investigation of the specialization of the brain—now, the computer brain—emphasizing disengagements between body and brain, feeling and rationality, childhood and adulthood. The episode's evoking of the imagery of birth and of phallic sexuality and its decidedly anthropomorphic presentation of technology reinforce the allegorical character of the filmic text as an exploration of "displaced eroticism and a mystification of modern technology"[16] that obscures distinctions between the human and the technological, the actual and the virtual. Kubrick's computer brain reproduces the customary tendency to think of technology in terms of received categories of human perception that rely on reason and affect in contrast to the latter-day technology of electronic images, which "are the object of a perpetual reorganization" and "no longer seem to refer to the human posture."[17] HAL's portrait seems to rely on a conception of technological power based on a mythology of decision making in the interests of establishing control from a central source. Power over others is legitimated by a long-standing myth about human progress: the possibility of producing a robotic intelligence, a machine free from miscalculation, blunders, and lapses.

HAL, the "personification" of the computer brain, is the latest model of the "9000 series," has never made a computational error and is described by his creators as being virtually incapable of error. As befitting the film's resistance to conventional science fiction imagery, HAL is not a formed robot. Rather, HAL's ubiquitous presence is conveyed through his voice, the recurrent image of his Cyclopean eye, and the memory modules stored in the brain room. Though ostensibly the "brain and nervous system of the ship," HAL has charisma and his candor exceeds that of the astronauts. Thus, the film raises the enigma of what goes wrong when HAL diagnoses an error in the AE35 radar unit with tragic effect. What accounts for HAL's rampage against the humans, for the struggle between the computer and the astronauts, and, finally, for Bowman's elimination of HAL's cerebral functions?

Cybernetic technology is implicated in knowledge and power, and HAL's brain is a "visually beautiful evocation of institutional order, in keeping with the sounds of HAL's voice, but at odds with his erratic behavior and the content of his speech."[18] The conflict between the human and the computer brains in this episode entails human emotion—anxiety, suspicion, rage, shock, and abjection. The agonistic encounter between HAL and the astronauts is not the conventional struggle between man and machine. It is the struggle of man against his own capacity for deceit.

The allegory does not lead in the direction of nostalgia for a prior state of primal innocence and a valorizing of physical life in the body. Rather, the allegory highlights the film's insistent critical concern with the human capacity for secrecy and deception in defense of territory, power, and position that ultimately leads to murderous aggression and death. The final termination involves Bowman's forceful reentry into HAL's body and the dramatic and speedy lobotomizing of HAL's computer brain (figure 22).

The character of HAL has understandably been the focus of much critical attention. HAL's programming to express emotions in order to facilitate communication is so successful that some writers find HAL's character more human than the depersonalized astronauts and the crew members in their hibernating chambers. Other critics find HAL sinister, identified with conspiracy and with the "machine mind" as being "more human than human, and thus doubly doomed to kill and be killed."[19] HAL's is a "queer voice" in the film, the carrier of the "odd, the uncanny, the undecidable."[20] The narrative further suggests a connection between paranoia and cinema linked to Kubrick's "queer musings on the future of sexuality."[21] Repressed desire can be read into the portrait of HAL, emblematized in ghostly voices and functioning "as a destabilizing force in the narrative"[22] capable of murdering four characters in his charge—the three hibernating men (appropriately identified as undergoing "life termination") and Frank (whose death is rationalized by HAL as an unfortunate "bad decision")—and attempting to murder a fifth.

HAL's role as a malevolent instigator of violence certainly speaks to the "human" character of his make-up. Ultimately, HAL's actions mime human limitations in relation to thinking and decision making. His vulnerability to emotion in his expression of anxiety about the "strangeness of the mission" or his expression of fear in the face of his "death" qualifies him to be regarded as human as does his ability to kill mechanically, to rationalize his actions, and, when apprehended, to express remorse and promise to make "better decisions" in the future. Thus, HAL is not a flawless expression of a new and higher form of thinking but a reminder of humans' evolutionary limitations in relation to thinking and action. Once again and with greater detail and complexity, the film probes the unresolved tensions between the actual and the virtual.

This melodrama is enhanced by vivid contrasts between sound and silence—the silence of space and the eroticized sounds of the astronauts breathing in their spacesuits—through understatement, the dearth of verbal language, HAL's disembodied voice, and the reiterated images of the computer's eye. Indeed, Poole's death becomes melodramatic not through gory images of an imploded corpse or inflated affective language, but through nuanced images of the receding spacesuit, and the hibernating astronauts' deaths are recorded on monitors in machine-generated words while otherwise passing in silence.

The critical moment in this melodrama is Dave's systematic dismantling of HAL's memory modules, rendering the affective part of the computer brain defunct. HAL's "demise" is conveyed through the film's tampering with conventional cinematic language, not in vivid and excessive images of mutilation, but in the lowering of HAL's voice's pitch and speed as Dave systematically dismantles HAL's functional memory and ability to perform independent behavior. Dave's "surgery" or HAL's "lobotomy" is, in the context of the allegory of the brain, a shocking action, but the event eschews a binary between good and evil. Dave's "neutralizing" of HAL would seem motivated by Dave's reasonable assumption that HAL poses a continuing threat, but the precipitousness of Dave's action suggests that his motives are tinged with vengefulness. The computer brain may be superior to the human brain in its speed of computation, accuracy, and logical thinking, but HAL's coexistence with human beings also made him vulnerable to human error. What is presented is not a simplistic binary vision of the war of man against the machine but a profound interrogation of man's wisdom in dominating the computer brain.

HAL's earlier assessment of the failure of the AE35 radar unit introduces a philosophic and political issue, namely, the human (and melodramatic) tendency to attribute aggression and violence reductively to an "error," to "bad decisions" stemming from faulty calculations, to find a psychological explanation for one's "mistakes," and hence to confess and expect absolution. However, finally, the central critical dilemma is not error but the character of the human creators of a machine that is made in their image and is at war with their bodies: "the men become (at least in fantasy) like HAL in that they no longer seem to require a body, sex, life support, or contact with earth."[23]

The disembodiment of the humans is further developed in the film's treatment of femininity. While portrayals of women are minimal throughout the film (they appear as hostesses and conventional maternal figures), conceptions of femininity are not absent but invoked in the somewhat effeminate voice of HAL and in his "maternal" care-taking of the astronauts (his attentiveness to their needs, playing chess, validating Dave's creativity, and sharing his feelings). Like children, Poole and Bowman are similarly dependent for their life functions on HAL. The two astronauts are infantilized; the hibernating men sleep like babies, their life systems sustained completely by HAL. The absence of women underscores poignantly the fantasy of a male universe, controlled technologically by thinking machines that can also feel, as personified by HAL, and by humans who are stunted in their affect. Yet both the men and the computer are compelled to respond with secrecy, deceit, and aggression to their paranoia about threats to their privilege, dominance, and domain. Ultimately the alienation of the men from their bodies reinforces the contiguity not the difference between the humans and the machines they have created. In contrast to celebratory versions of computer technology, the film's perspective appears to be a morose and critical treatment of humans, who can only create a computer brain that mirrors their aggressiveness and territorial ambition. However, are there other ways to understand Kubrick's treatment of cinema and technology and their relation to the history of thought in film?

The Cinematographic Brain

HAL's computer brain would seem to be cross-linked at several points to Kubrick's "cinematic brain." HAL's red eye with its yellow pupil is reminiscent of a camera lens, and his ubiquitous presence, monitoring, recording, and controlling the movements of men, elevates HAL to directorial status (figure 13). His studio/body is the *Discovery* itself, and the battle between HAL and the men for dominance turns on HAL's ability to see them even when they think they have escaped his surveillance. The agonistic encounter between men and machine, leading to the deaths of four men, the rape-like destruction of the sexually and affectively indeterminate computer brain, and Dave's survival present a critical "history of consciousness."[24] In the words of Gilles Deleuze: "Our lived relationship with the brain becomes increasingly fragile, less and less 'Euclidean' and goes through little cerebral deaths. The brain becomes our problem or our illness, our passion, rather than our mastery, our solution or decision."[25] Thus, Kubrick's treatment of the brain constitutes a formal strategy for the representation of the film's thematic and diegetic material.

The cinematographic brain is the film, underscored in the *Space Odyssey*'s last episode, "Jupiter and Beyond the Infinite." Here, the *Odyssey*'s confrontation with radically different conceptions of the brain reaches its apotheosis. Instead of the animal brain advancing inexorably toward domination, the human brain moving relentlessly toward deception, and HAL, the computer made in the likeness of man, dramatizing the failure of both animal and human strategies—unable to command human life without destroying it—the cinematic brain is the creation of media that have the potential to create a different and critical sense of reality.

"Jupiter and Beyond the Infinite" begins with psychedelic images of the astronaut's rush through space, intercut with a dizzying montage of lines and colors and close-up images of changing colors in Dave's eyes, and culminates in the Louis XVI bedroom, Dave's own aging and death, and the appearance of the monolith and then of the futuristic fetus. This episode recapitulates images and motifs from the previous episodes.[26] The emphasis is on the vastness of the universe, the role of the human traveler now swept up in space and time by forces over which he has no control, and the doubling of images, mirror images, and splitting between objects and their reflections. Doubling as a distancing device was conspicuous earlier in the film: the doubling of Moon-Watcher and Dr. Floyd; the twinlike appearance of the astronauts Dave and

Frank; the parallel computers on Earth and aboard *Discovery*; and, of course, the four identical black monoliths. The astronauts' images are also doubled in the video transmission from Earth and in the close-ups of their faces as they observe themselves (and as HAL observes them) on the monitors. More doubling is evident in Dave's two journeys in the pod, first to replace the AE35, then to retrieve Frank.

In the final episode, Dave sees himself in a mirror and over his own shoulder. Aging, freed from his astronaut's artificial skin, he observes himself as an older man sitting at a table. Dave observes himself on a bed as an even more aged human being (figure 15). With his final transformation into a fetus, the human form of the astronaut disappears. Camera consciousness presents a direct image of time that presumes a different order of thought, a different conception of the brain, one that is freed from the tyranny of clichés, from identity thinking, and from repetition without difference: "At the end of *Space Odyssey*, it is in consequence of a fourth dimension, that the sphere of the foetus and the sphere of the earth have a chance of entering into a new, incommensurable, unknown relation, which would convert death into life."[27]

Similar to the first episode in the film, there are no monitors in this epilogue, and the pod disappears to give way to the monolith, and the monolith gives way to the star child. While Moon-Watcher and Floyd had touched the black object, the dying Bowman can only point to its presence for the spectator to see (figure 23). The mirror and the early presence of Dave in his spacesuit are reminders of vision but, in contrast to the earlier episodes that prominently featured media, the emphasis on vision and sound is directed largely toward the point of view of the aging Dave and ultimately toward the film spectator, thus suspending the possibility of clarifying the point of view and passing on the burden of thinking to the viewer. If the ending alters the highly technological images of the previous episodes and downplays the multiple registers of vision, it also reiterates, albeit with a difference, the limitations of verbalization, "the tyranny of words,"[28] by returning to the techniques of the overture, the images of the ape-men, and the appearance of the monolith.

The reiteration of the images of birth and death is linked to the previous episodes, to the ape-man's birth of consciousness and his acquisition of power over life and death, to the world of the disembodied scientist whose intelligence is single-mindedly focused on an exercise of state power, to the fetal character of life aboard the spaceship *Discovery* (exemplified in the sleeping state of the three men and in the passive, childlike images of the astronauts' existence until they rebelled against their mechanical brain, HAL), and finally to the death of Bowman and the appearance of the star child (figure 35). In an economic display of images, the epilogue captures how life has passed through different phases in the history of human intelligence, the last being indeterminate in relation to the meaning of life and death. Bowman the astronaut is the last human, and his metamorphosis introduces ambiguous questions of the future, not the past. Is the star child a harbinger of the post-human brain, a trope for moribund humanity, or an expression of the coming of different life forms and forms of intelligence?

The cerebral journey has culminated in an indeterminate ending, suggesting in satiric and elegiac fashion that existing conceptions of the brain and forms of knowledge are as inadequate as cinematic technology has become in the post–World War Two world. The shattered crystal wine glass (the glass ball in *Citizen Kane*?) is a reminder of irreversible time, of the movement-image contrasted to a different conception of space and time through the crystalline time-image. In Nelson's words, "2001 brings the human race to the limits of its growth, where, like the bone, it is converted into an artifact that turns to crystal and shatters from the weight of evolutionary gravity. . . . The mirror world has been broken, and beyond its reflexivity awaits the unknown and unexplored."[29] Accordingly, the allegory confronts the medium in which it is expressed, which involves the history of cinema and, further, the history of consciousness, inviting the spectator to contemplate the cinema and the world as a brain. The viewer is presented with different relations between the brain and the world where "a reconciliation is carried out in another dimension [a fourth dimension], a regeneration of the membrane which would pacify the outside [the cosmos] and the inside [the brain], and recreate a world-brain as a whole in the harmony of the spheres."[30]

"Jupiter and Beyond the Infinite" confounds conceptions of the real that rely on a split between inside and outside, mind and body, cinema and "life." The film's self-reflexive treatment of technology and the medium of cinema is an instrument for sharing with the spectator a critique of spectacle. The fracture between subjectivity and objectivity, the privileging of vision and knowledge is misguided in "attempts to know the world by seeing the world."[31] As the final episode develops, the conflict between HAL and the humans recedes before technological pyrotechnics, and confusion between the human and the cybernetic brain reigns. The relationships between humans and their creations metamorphose into self-division and ambivalence.

The episode resolves in a cinematic alternative to anthropomorphic spectacles. The visual and aural images, expressed by the cinematographic brain, belong to the regime of what Deleuze has termed the "time-image" in contrast to the "movement-image," which is characterized by an identity of image and movement and a sensory-motor relationship among human beings, their milieu, and action. According to Deleuze, "[T]he optical and sound situations of neo-realism contrast with the strong sensory-motor situations of traditional realism,"[32] which rely on distinctions between subjective and objective perception and action within a milieu.

The movement-image is, in its varying forms, linked to the animal, human, and even computer brains, while the time-image is the cinematographic brain. In the time-image, the identity between movement and image has been sundered and a different relation to space and time has emerged, particularly associated with experimental and avant-garde, post–World War

Two cinema and art cinema. Neorealism carried the crisis of the movement-image further with "its slackening of sensori-motor connections." The regime of the time-image presupposes different conceptions of narration, character, and reception. In neorealism, as an instantiation of the time-image, "the character has become a kind of viewer. He shifts, runs and becomes animated in vain, the situation he is in outstrips his motor capacities on all sides. . . . He records rather then reacts."[33] The characters in the cinematic regime that Deleuze terms the time-image are, if not children, somnambulists, visionaries, and counterfeiters. The narratives blur lines between the everyday and the exceptional, the real and the imaginary, the physical and the mental, and the films are replete with empty spaces and idle periods of time. The "limit situations" in which the characters find themselves extend to the "dehumanized landscapes" where the spectator comes face to face with time. From the cinematic to the digital image, the technology question and its relation to thought has become increasingly complex, raising the issue of the possibility of intelligence and thinking in the face of man's substitution by the machine.[34]

Ultimately, indeterminacy is the guiding principle to the cinematic brain in Kubrick's film. The spectator, like the characters, is treated as a complex field of forces where the "distinction between subjective and objective . . . tends to lose its importance, to the extent that the optical situation or visual description replaces the motor action."[35] This indeterminacy is especially characteristic of electronic media and cybernetics. A generator of new forms of information and knowledge about causality, identity, perception, and materiality, cybernetics is a medium of power and control (technical, biological, and social) in ways still to be understood. The cinema has increasingly been allied to the production of electronic images that

> no longer have any outside (out-of-field) any more than they are internalized as a whole; rather, they have a right side and a reverse, reversible and non-superimposable, like a power to turn back on themselves. They are the object of a perpetual reorganization, in which the new image can arise from any point whatever of the preceding image. The organization of space here loses its privileged directions.[36]

Rather than reveling in or despairing about technology, Kubrick's film undertakes a cinematic odyssey that unhinges conceptions of space and time in the interests of exploring the fate of knowledge in the age of advanced mechanical reproduction, calling into question existing conceptions of the brain in terms that are temporal rather than spatial, open rather than closed. Particularly, by means of its allegory, the film questions conceptions of technology based on a reductive conception of and a belief in the "perfection" of the animal, human, cybernetic, and cinematographic. The film has offered the spectator a version of cinematography as an instrument for reflecting on consciousness.

Notes

1. Gilles Deleuze, *Cinema 2: The Time-Image*, trans. Hugh Tomlinson and Robert Galeta (Minneapolis: University of Minnesota Press, 2001), 205–6.

2. Ibid., 211.

3. Mark Crispin Miller, "A Cold Ascent," *Sight and Sound* 4, no. 1 (June 1994): 18–26.

4. D. N. Rodowick, *Gilles Deleuze's Time Machine* (Durham, N.C.: Duke University Press, 1997), 202.

5. Arthur C. Clarke, *The Lost Worlds of* 2001 (New York: New American Library, 1972), 271.

6. Giorgio Agamben, *Means without End*, trans. Vincenzo Binetti and Cesare Casarino (Minneapolis: University of Minnesota Press, 2000), 56.

7. Ibid., 55.

8. Robert Burgoyne, "Narrative Overture and Closure in *2001: A Space Odyssey*," *Enclitic* 5, no. 2 (Fall–Spring 1981–1982): 173.

9. Mario Falsetto, ed., "Introduction," *Perspectives on Stanley Kubrick* (New York: Hall, 1996), 11.

10. Luis M. García Mainar, *Narrative and Stylistic Patterns in the Films of Stanley Kubrick* (Rochester, N.Y.: Camden House, 1999), 30.

11. Miller, "A Cold Ascent," 20.

12. Thomas Allen Nelson, *Kubrick: Inside a Film Artist's Maze* (Bloomington: University of Indiana Press, 2000), 113.

13. Ibid., 114.

14. Miller, "A Cold Ascent," 24.

15. Randy Rasmussen, *Stanley Kubrick: Seven Films Analyzed* (Jefferson, N.C.: McFarland, 2001), 75.

16. Ellis Hanson, "Technology, Paranoia, and the Queer Voice," *Screen* 34, no. 2 (Summer 1993): 144.

17. Deleuze, *Cinema 2: The Time-Image*, 265.

18. Rasmussen, *Stanley Kubrick: Seven Films Analyzed*, 97.

19. Piers Bizony, 2001: *Filming the Future* (London: Aurum, 1994), 18.

20. Hanson, "Technology, Paranoia, and the Queer Voice," 137.

21. Ibid., 138.

22. Ibid., 140.

23. Ibid., 121.

24. Burgoyne, "Narrative Overture and Closure in *2001: A Space Odyssey*," 174.

25. Deleuze, *Cinema 2: The Time-Image*, 212.

26. Carolyn Geduld, *Filmguide to* 2001: A Space Odyssey (Bloomington: Indiana University Press, 1973), 60.

27. Ibid., 206.

28. Nelson, *Kubrick*, 115.

29. Ibid., 135.

30. Deleuze, *Cinema 2: The Time-Image*, 206.

31. Burgoyne, "Narrative Overture and Closure in *2001: A Space Odyssey*," 176.

32. Deleuze, *Cinema 2: The Time Image*, 5.

33. Ibid., 3.

34. Michel Ciment, *Kubrick: The Definitive Edition*, trans. Gilbert Adair (New York: Faber and Faber, 2001), 126.

35. Deleuze, *Cinema 2: The Time-Image*, 7.

36. Ibid., 265.

Bibliography

Agamben, Giorgio. *Means without End*, trans. Vincenzo Binetti and Cesare Casarino. Minneapolis: University of Minnesota Press, 2000.

Ansell Pearson, K. *Philosophy and the Adventure of the Virtual*. London: Routledge, 2002.

Benjamin, Walter. *The Origin of German Tragic Drama*, trans. John Osborne. London: Verso, 1996.

Bizony, Piers. 2001*: Filming the Future*. London: Aurum, 1994.

Burgoyne, Robert. "Narrative Overture and Closure in *2001: A Space Odyssey*," *Enclitic* 5, no. 2 (Fall–Spring 1981–1982): 172–180.

Charlot, John. "From Ape-Man to Space-Baby: An Interpretation," *East-West Film Journal* 1, no. 1 (December 1986): 84–90.

Chion, Michel. "*2001: l'Odyssée de l'espace*: Stanley Kubrick, les yeux grands ouverts," *Positif* 439 (August 1997): 82–87.

Ciment, Michel. *Kubrick: The Definitive Edition*, trans. Gilbert Adair. New York: Faber and Faber, 2001.

Ciment, Michel, ed. "Stanley Kubrick, les yeux grands ouverts," *Positif* 439 (August 1997): 66–102.

Clarke, Arthur C. *Greetings, Carbon-Based Bipeds! Collected Essays 1934–1998*. New York: St. Martin's, 1999.

Clarke, Arthur C. *The Lost Worlds of* 2001. New York: New American Library, 1972.

Deleuze, Gilles. *Cinema 1: The Movement-Image*, trans. Hugh Tomlinson and Barbara Habberjam. Minneapolis: University of Minnesota Press, 2001.

Deleuze, Gilles. *Cinema 2: The Time*-Image, trans. Hugh Tomlinson and Robert Galeta. Minneapolis: University of Minnesota Press, 2001.

Dumont, J. P., and J. Monod. "Beyond the Infinite: A Structural Analysis of *2001: A Space Odyssey*," *Quarterly Review of Film Studies* 3, no. 3 (Summer 1978): 297–317.

Ede, François. "De la terre à la lune," *Cahiers du cinéma*, no. 503 (June 1996): 76.

Elmsholz, Jean-Marc. "*2001: l'Odyssée de l'espace*: Stanley Kubrick, les yeux grands ouverts," *Positif* 439 (August 1997): 87–89.

Falsetto, Mario. *Stanley Kubrick: A Narrative and Stylistic Analysis*. Westport, Conn.: Praeger, 2001.

Falsetto, Mario, ed. "Introduction." *Perspectives on Stanley Kubrick*. New York: Hall, 1996.

Feldmann, Hans. "Kubrick and His Discontents," *Film Quarterly* 30, no. 1 (Fall 1976): 12–19.

Geduld, Carolyn. *Filmguide to* 2001: A Space Odyssey. Bloomington: Indiana University Press, 1973.

Gelmis, Joseph. "Stanley Kubrick: Une film doit être une illumination," *Positif* 464 (October 1999): 11–22.

Hanson, Ellis. "Technology, Paranoia, and the Queer Voice," *Screen* 34, no. 2 (Summer 1993): 137–62.

Howard, James. *Stanley Kubrick Companion*. London: Batsford, 1999.

Kagan, Norman. *The Cinema of Stanley Kubrick*. New York: Continuum, 2000.

Kolker, Robert Phillip. *A Cinema of Loneliness: Penn, Kubrick, Scorsese, Spielberg, Altman*, 3d ed. New York: Oxford University Press, 2000.

Krukowski, Damon. "Damon Krukowski Listens to *2001: A Space Odyssey*," *Film Comment* 38 (January–February 2002): 16.

Lucy, Niall. "Total Eclipse of the Heart: Thinking through Technology," *Senses of Cinema: An Online Journal Devoted to the Serious and Eclectic Discussion of Cinema* 7 (June 2000): 1–7. Available. Online: www.sensesofcinema.com/contents/00/7/technology.html.

Mainar, Luis M. García. *Narrative and Stylistic Patterns in the Films of Stanley Kubrick*. Rochester, N.Y.: Camden House, 1999.

Miller, Mark Crispin. "A Cold Ascent," *Sight and Sound* 4, no. 1 (June 1994): 18–26.

Nelson, Thomas Allen. *Kubrick: Inside a Film Artist's Maze*. Bloomington: University of Indiana Press, 2000.

Rasmussen, Randy. *Stanley Kubrick: Seven Films Analyzed*. Jefferson, N.C.: McFarland, 2001.

Rodowick, D. N. *Gilles Deleuze's Time Machine*. Durham, N.C.: Duke University Press, 1997.

FIGURES 1, 2
The changing details of the cinematic imagination. Rocket ship and space station in *The Conquest of Space* (George Pal and Byron Haskin, 1955) and *2001: A Space Odyssey*.

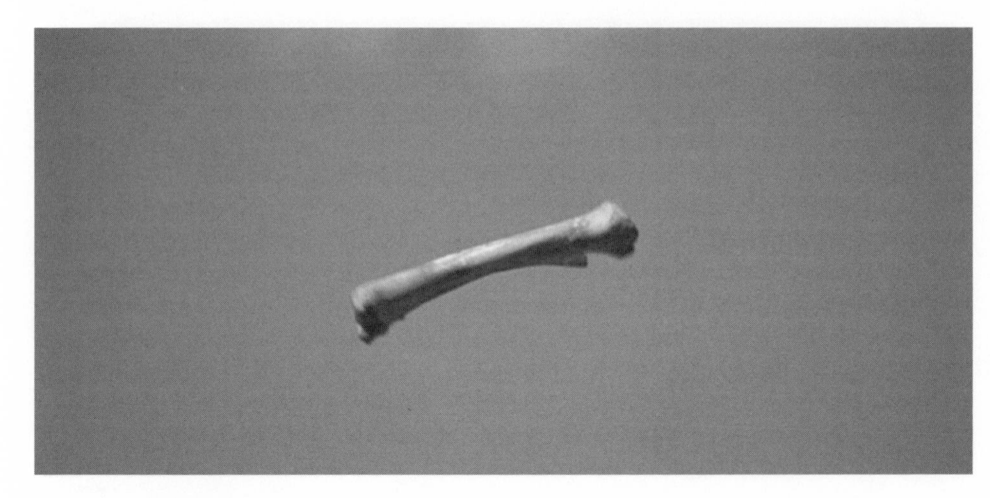

FIGURES 3, 4
Perhaps the most famous edit in contemporary film: the cut from bone . . .

. . . to spaceship.

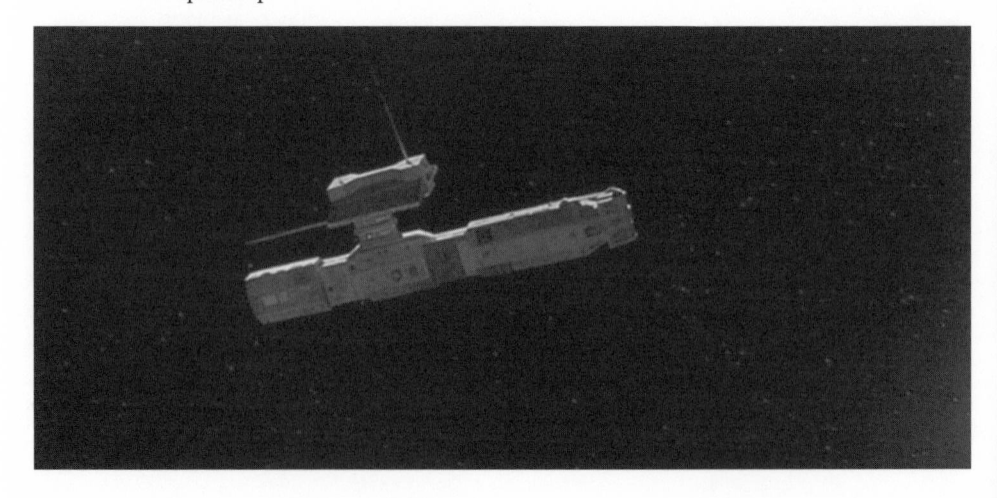

FIGURE 5
The floating pen.

FIGURE 6
Without gravity
and upside down.

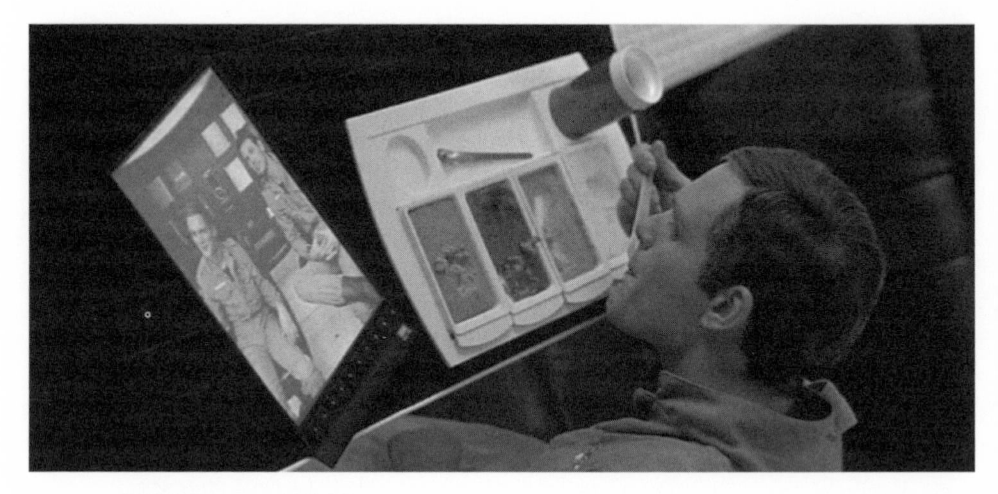

FIGURE 7

The "irrational angle." Aboard the *Discovery*, Dave watches himself and Frank interviewed by the BBC.

FIGURE 8

Bowman "reborn" as he reenters the *Discovery*.

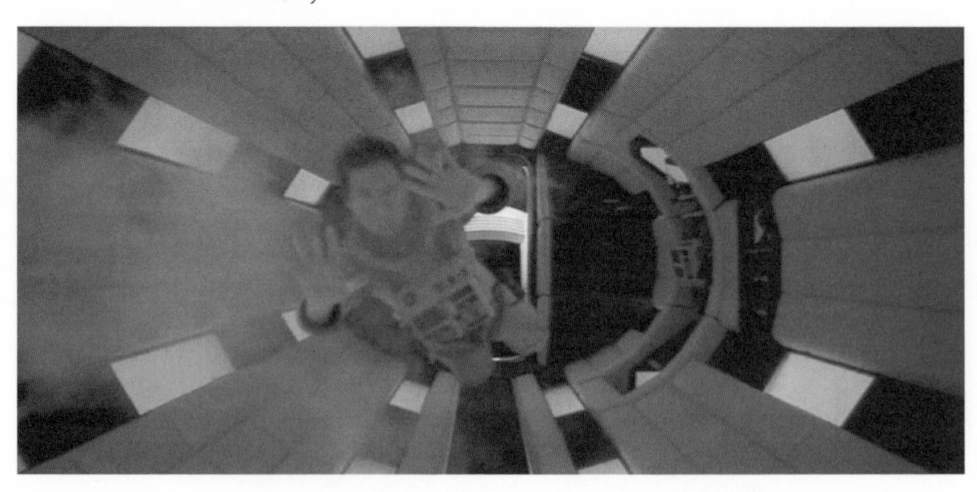

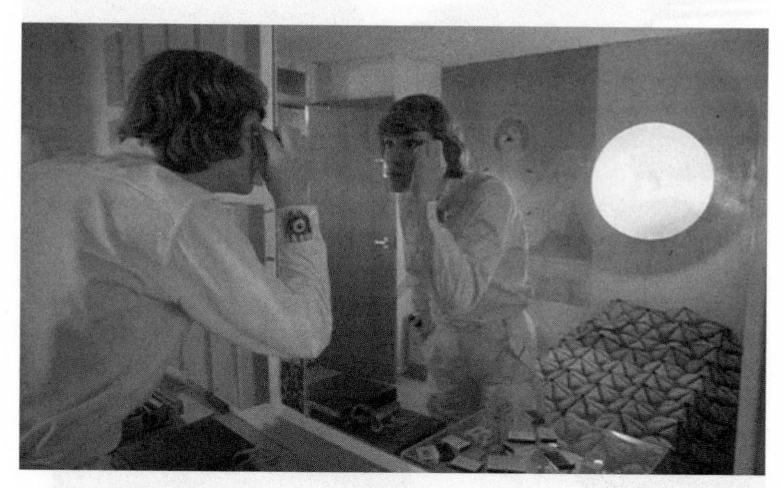

FIGURE 9
Alex's eyeball cufflink. Note that, as further emphasis on the eye, Alex is removing his false eyelash, which is part of his costume (*A Clockwork Orange*, 1971).

FIGURE 10
Institutional-official space: Dr. Floyd at lectern on Clavius. Even this space is made strange: it is both distorted and symmetrical.

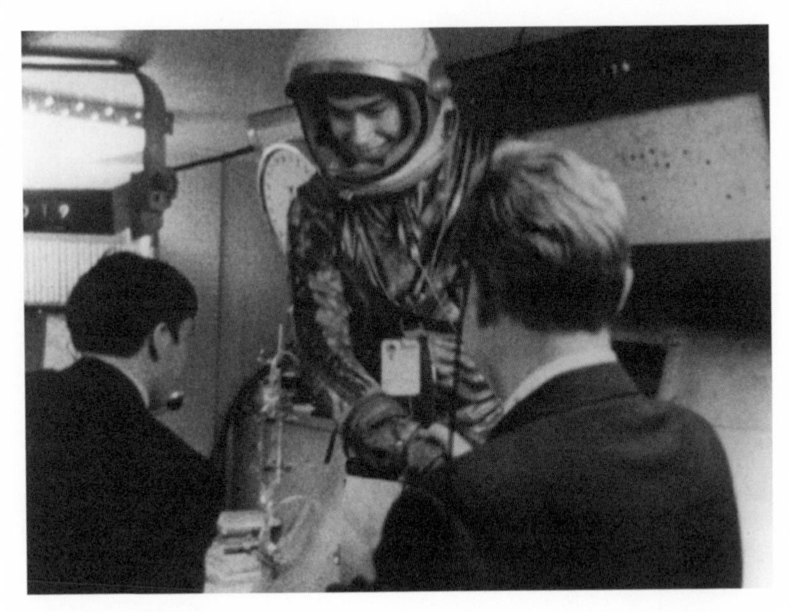

FIGURE 11
Student astronauts in Frederick Wiseman's *High School*. © 1968 Frederick Wiseman. All rights reserved.

FIGURE 12
Explosive bolts.

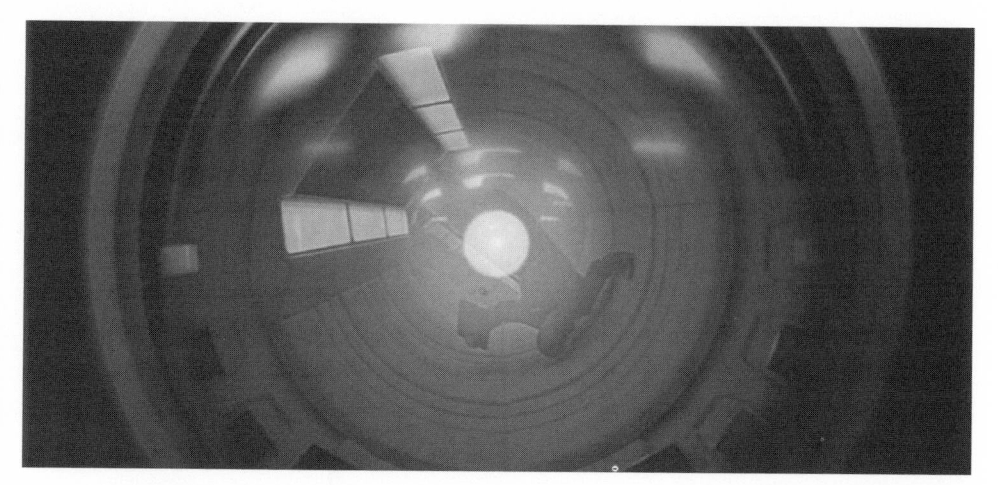

FIGURE 13
First shot of HAL's omniscient eye. This is also the first shot of Bowman, who is seen in reflection.

FIGURE 14
Dave's eyes—from HAL's point of view during their final confrontation.

FIGURE 15
An over-the-shoulder shot of Bowman occupying impossibly simultaneous positions.

FIGURE 16
The phallic cannon and the "Rockettes" (Georges Méliès, *A Trip to the Moon,* 1902).

FIGURE 17
Floyd phones home.

FIGURE 18
"Normal" activity in the disorienting spaces of the *Discovery*.

FIGURE 19
The apes and
the monolith.

FIGURE 20
Floyd touches
the monolith.

FIGURE 21
The humanoid face of the *Discovery*.

FIGURE 22
HAL's lobotomy.

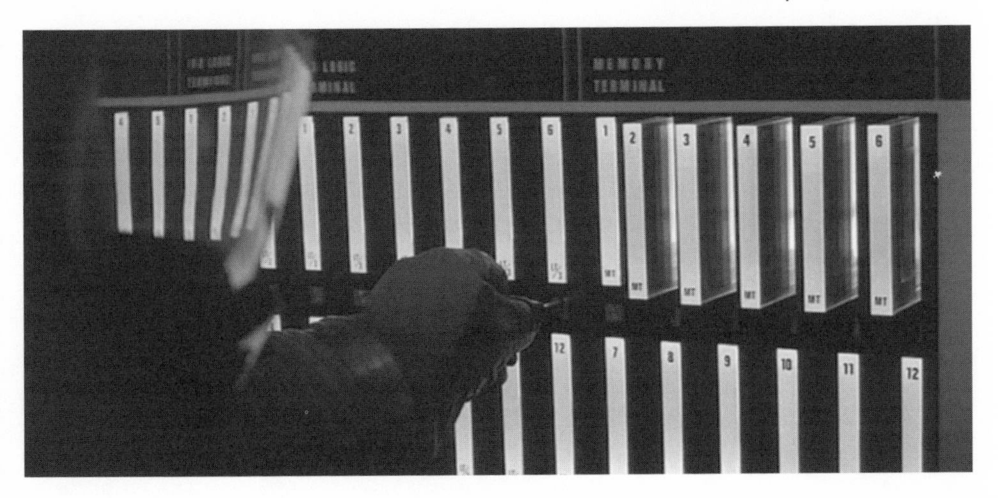

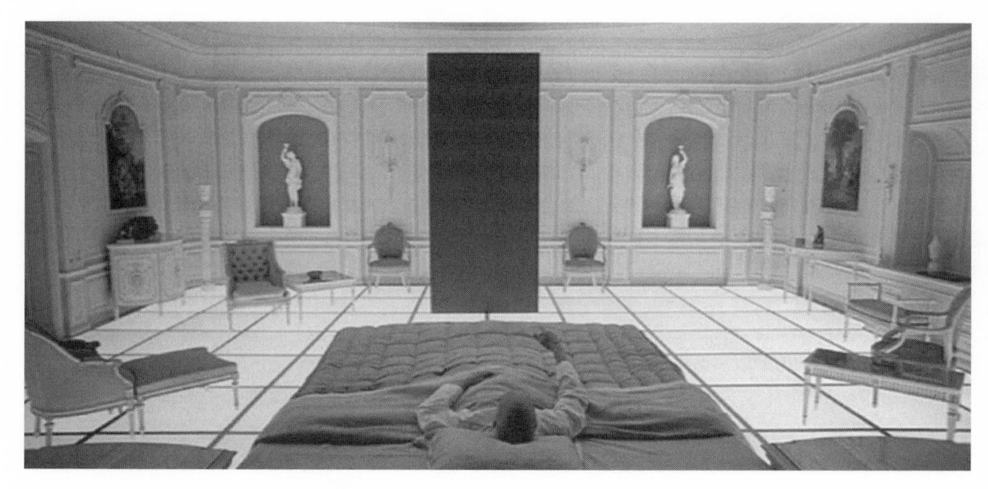

FIGURE 23
Dave, on the brink of his transformation, points to the monolith.

FIGURE 24
HAL and Frank play chess.

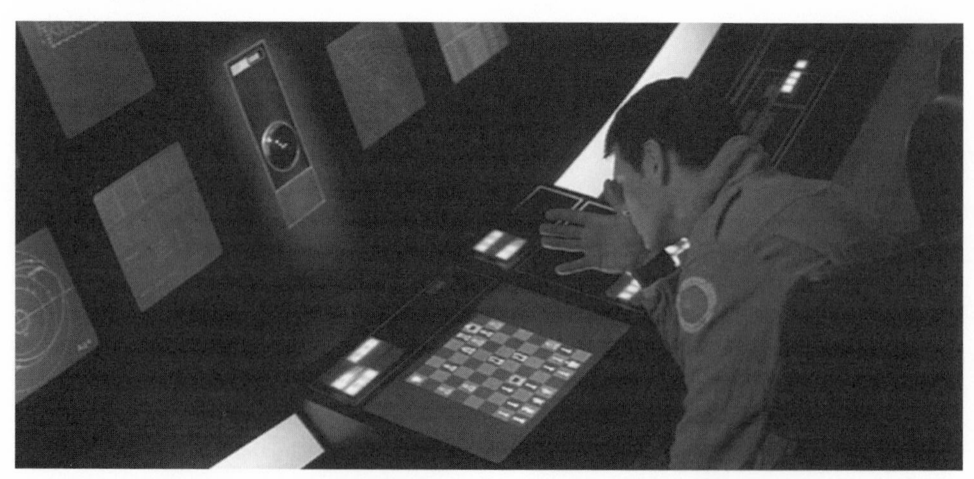

FIGURE 25
"Yes, it's puzzling. I don't think I've ever seen anything quite like this before." Frank and Dave from HAL's point of view.

The "obscene shadow": Kubrick's bathrooms (figures 26–30).

FIGURE 26
Toilet training (*2001: A Space Odyssey*).

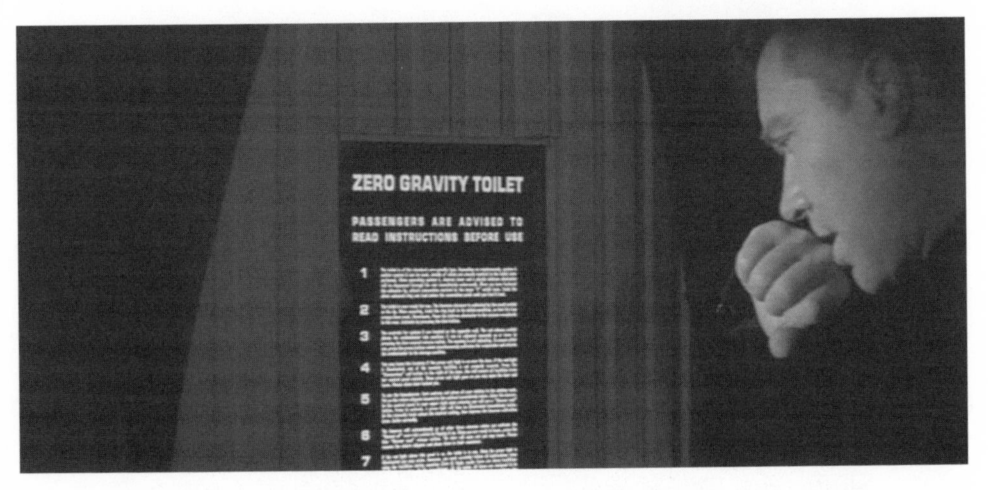

FIGURE 27
Bowman, newly arrived in the alien motel room, sees the bathroom reflected in the mirror (*2001: A Space Odyssey*).

FIGURE 28
Jack and Grady in the bathroom (*The Shining*, 1980).

FIGURE 29
Pyle's suicide
in the latrine
(*Full Metal Jacket*, 1987).

FIGURE 30
Kubrick's last and most
sumptuous bathroom
(*Eyes Wide Shut*, 1999).

FIGURE 31

The eyes of *2001* (figures 31–35 and see also figures 13 and 14).

FIGURE 32

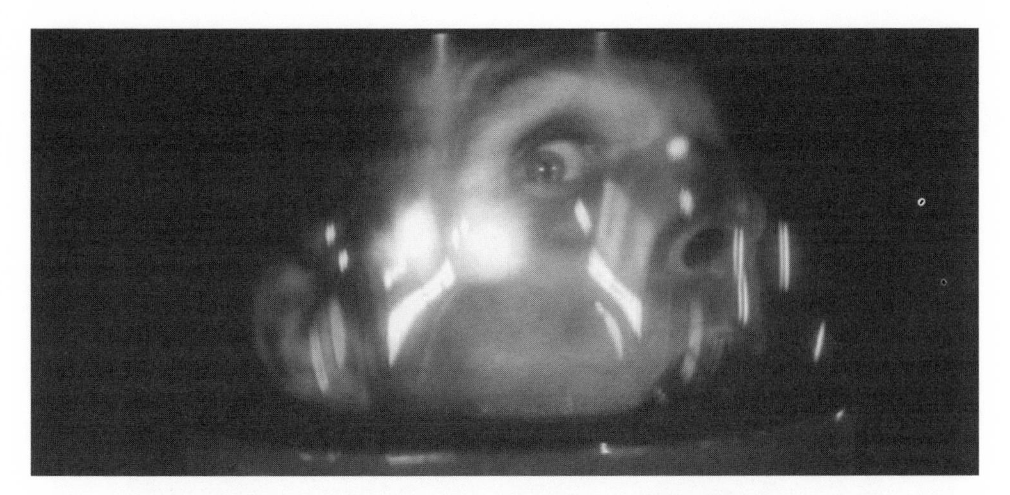

FIGURE 33

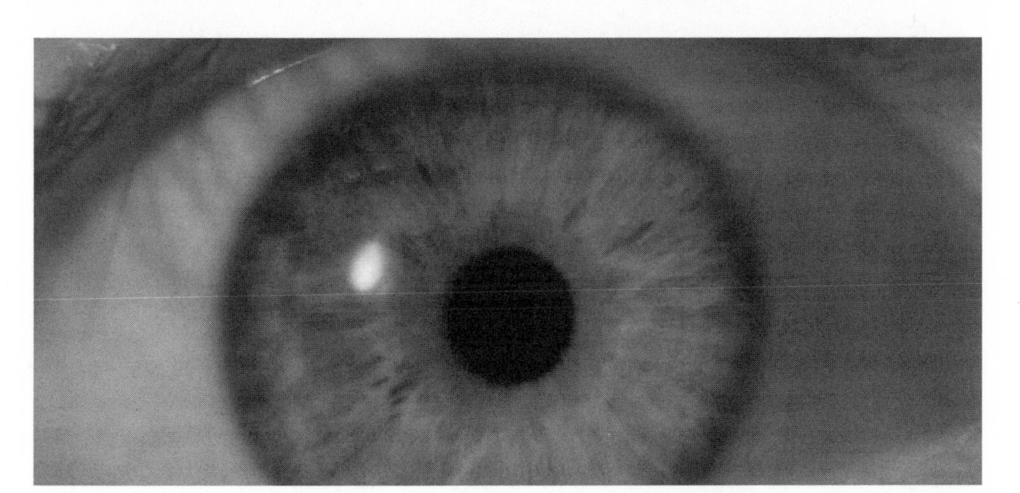

FIGURE 34

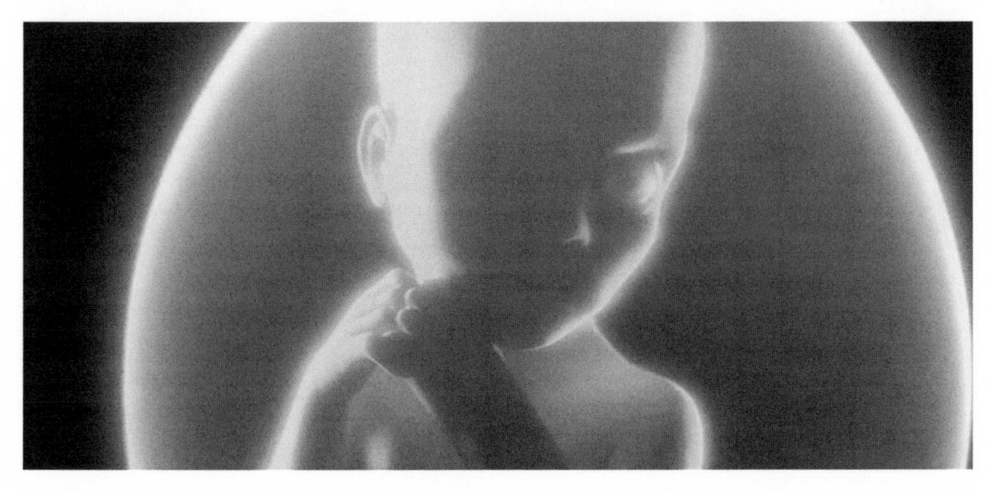

FIGURE 35

FIGURES 36, 37
The mannequins in Kubrick's *Killer's Kiss* (1955) and Spielberg's homage in *A.I.* (2001).

7

Reading HAL

Representation and Artificial Intelligence

MICHAEL MATEAS

In this chapter, I wish to focus on HAL 9000. Rather than reading HAL as a Frankensteinian cautionary tale, a representation of our disquiet over the cybernetic blurring of the human, of our fear of an evolutionary showdown with increasingly autonomous technologies, I'd like to read HAL as a representation of the goals, methodologies, and dreams of the field of Artificial Intelligence (AI). As a representation, HAL, and the role he plays within *2001*, both captures preexisting intellectual currents that were already operating within the field of AI and serves as an influential touchstone, which has had a profound impact on individual AI practitioners and on the aspirations of the field.

I come at this understanding of HAL from a disciplinary position that straddles the humanities, computer science, and digital art practice. While my degree is in computer science, specifically in AI, my research focus is on AI-based interactive art and entertainment. Consequently, my research agenda brings to bear new media studies and science studies, digital art practice, and technical research in AI. It is from this hybrid position, working in the context of a joint appointment in both the humanities and computer science, that I wish to read HAL as a representation of technical practice within AI.

In addition to a reading of HAL as a depiction of the disciplinary machinery of AI, HAL of course also functions as a character within the narrative machinery of *2001*, a character, as many have pointed out, with more emotional and psychological depth than any of the human characters. Once HAL is understood as a cinematic representation that simultaneously depicts specific agendas and assumptions within AI and performs an expressive function for an audience (i.e., serves as a character within a story), it is a small step to consider AI systems themselves as *procedural representations* that simultaneously encode agendas and assumptions and perform for an audience. The last section of this chapter will investigate Expressive AI, that is, AI considered explicitly as a *medium*.

HAL and AI

HAL was, and still is, a powerful inspiration for AI researchers. In *HAL's Legacy*,[1] prominent members of the AI research community describe both how HAL influenced their own work and the relationship between HAL and the current state of AI research. There have of course been many depictions of robots and intelligent computers in sci-fi films, but few of these representations have achieved, for AI researchers, HAL's emblematic status. Unlike other sci-fi representations of AI, HAL is special because of the way he connects to technical agendas within AI research.

HAL convincingly integrates many specific capabilities, such as computer vision, natural language processing, chess playing, etc., demonstrating the elusive generalized intelligence sought by AI researchers. Most filmic representations of AI act just like people, adding a few mechanical affectations to clearly human performances. There is no clear relationship between these filmic representations and current lines of research in AI. HAL, on the other hand, appears as a plausible extrapolation from current lines of work, serving as a visualization for the AI community of future AI systems.

Because achieving general intelligence is difficult to turn into a pragmatic research plan, AI research tends to proceed by attacking subproblems. The problem of creating an intelligent machine is either broken up into deep models of isolated capabilities (e.g., visually recognizing objects, creating plans of action in simplified domains) or broken up into systems that integrate a range of more shallow competencies (e.g., a robot that integrates simple sensing and planning in order to carry out a single task). In both cases, the systems lack general intelligence, the ability to integrate a broad range of knowledge and physical competencies, to apply knowledge from one domain to another, to handle unexpected and new situations. AI systems only perform intelligently on a single, narrow task or within a single, simplified domain.

HAL presents to researchers a powerful cinematic representation of AI precisely because he simultaneously demonstrates general intelligence while keeping visible the AI subproblems, roughly corresponding to different subfields within AI. Thus researchers can easily recognize AI specialties in HAL's individual capabilities, which makes HAL plausible, while seeing the individual capabilities integrated into a general intelligence, which makes HAL compelling. Marvin Minsky, one of the founders of AI, served as a technical consultant on the film; doubtless his contribution helped to establish the strong resonance between the depiction of HAL and subfields within AI, including language, commonsense reasoning, computer vision, game playing, and planning and problem solving.

Language is one of the hallmarks of intelligence; natural language processing has been part of the AI research agenda since the beginning of the field. HAL demonstrates a range of natural language competencies, including understanding (making sense of sentences and conversations), generation (producing responses), speech recognition, and speech generation. HAL is able to participate in conversations ranging from simple commands, such as Poole's commands to raise and lower his headrest and to display his parents' recorded birthday greeting in his room, to complex conversations where HAL expresses inner conflicts and tells sophisticated lies. In work on natural language processing, researchers quickly discovered that generalized natural language capabilities require commonsense reasoning, that is, a huge amount of knowledge about everyday objects, events, and situations. This background knowledge is needed not only to disambiguate meaning through context, but also to work out the ramifications of utterances: an utterance doesn't just have a denotative meaning, but also a complex halo of connotative meanings and implications for both the speaker and listener. The commonsense reasoning problem is enormous and unsolved. The problem with common sense is that it isn't really a subproblem of the sort that AI researchers typically tackle, but rather seems to be the whole of intelligence; if you have commonsense reasoning, you have general intelligence. For this reason, AI systems that use natural language only function within microdomains: specific, simplified domains of expertise. For example, research into dialogue systems (systems that are able to have an extended dialogue) generally takes place in task-based domains, such as travel planning,[2] where the system's creators are able to assume that all utterances relate directly to the task at hand and where connotative meaning is kept to a minimum.

HAL, on the other hand, demonstrates general language and commonsense reasoning capabilities. This is made plausible for an AI audience by sneaking this general competency in through the back door of an apparent microdomain. As the shipboard computer for the *Discovery*, HAL's primary function is to manage the ship and participate in the mission. Though HAL is certainly introduced as an extremely advanced AI system during the initial interview with the BBC reporter, this interview establishes HAL as a primarily functional, though advanced, onboard control system for the

Discovery. As the plot progresses, HAL gradually exhibits full-blown general language competency and commonsense reasoning from within this microdomain.

HAL's ability to see is emphasized throughout the film by frequent cuts to his camera eye and by occasionally giving the viewer a subjective view through HAL's cameras (figure 13). HAL demonstrates computer vision capabilities far more sophisticated than anything we're capable of today. His vision is fully integrated with the rest of his intelligence, allowing him, for example, to talk about what he sees (integrating natural language processing and vision) or to use his vision in pursuit of goals, as when he reads the astronauts' lips to stay ahead of his adversaries. Again, his visual capabilities are made plausible for an AI audience by demonstrating specific visual subproblems. For instance, when HAL asks to see Bowman's drawings, HAL is able to recognize the objects depicted in the drawings, including the face of one of the hibernating crewmen. Object and face recognition is one of the standard well-defined subproblems of computer vision; by giving the audience a view of the drawings through HAL's eye, the film emphasizes the specific object-recognition task in which HAL is engaged. However, within this same scene, HAL moves beyond mere object recognition by commenting on Bowman's drawing style and comparing his current drawings to previous ones. By framing this discussion of style within an implicit object-recognition task framework, the film presents reasoning about style and aesthetics as simple technical extensions of an understood AI research problem.

Game playing, and in particular chess, is one of the classic AI problems; early successes in chess playing were partly responsible for overly optimistic predictions made during the 1960s and 1970s for the achievement of general machine intelligence. Because chess is considered a difficult game, something that "intelligent people" do, it was assumed that if computers could play chess, then they must also be "intelligent." It turns out, however, that the really difficult tasks to make a computer do are generally not the tasks that humans consider to be difficult, such as chess playing, but everyday, "easy" activities, such as using language, seeing the world and understanding what you see, commonsense reasoning, and so forth. At the time that *2001* came out, AI was still in its early, optimistic phase, buoyed by successes on problems such as chess. The chess-playing scene therefore had special resonance for the AI audience: though HAL's chess performance may have been better than 1968-era chess-playing programs, chess was a well-understood problem. AI researchers had every confidence that, in the not-too-distant future, there would be chess-playing programs better than any human player. The chess scene thus establishes plausibility by demonstrating an easy extrapolation from the current state of a well-understood problem (figure 24).

The AI subfield of planning and problem solving is concerned with modeling goal-driven activities, that is, how intelligent systems arbitrate among multiple goals and construct and follow plans of actions to accomplish goals. HAL demonstrates goal-driven behavior in his handling of the "failure" of the

AE35 unit. After reporting a fictitious failure in the AE35 unit, HAL expresses confusion when the diagnostic analysis reveals no failure (HAL: "Yes, it's puzzling. I don't think I've ever seen anything quite like this before") and suggests that the unit be replaced until it fails (figure 25). HAL's confusion about the AE35 unit can be read two ways. Either he is quite self-consciously lying about the AE35 unit as part of some master plan to sever communications with mission control and lure the astronauts out into space where he can kill them, or he is genuinely confused about the AE35, indicating an internal conflict. For an AI audience, both cases are clear instances of goal-based behavior. In the first case, HAL has a goal to eliminate the astronauts, whom he has identified as dangerous to the success of the mission, and has generated an elaborate plan to eliminate them, a plan within which he is able to improvise when the situation changes, such as when Bowman forgets his space helmet when he goes out to retrieve Poole. HAL sees that Bowman has forgotten his helmet, which enables HAL to achieve his goal of eliminating Bowman, since now all HAL has to do is refuse Bowman entry. (We can only speculate about what HAL's plan would have been had Bowman not forgotten his helmet: perhaps teleoperating a second pod to disable Bowman's pod?) In the second case, HAL's behavior can be interpreted as a goal conflict: a situation in which some of HAL's actions, such as reporting the fault in the AE35, are executed in pursuit of one goal, while other actions, such as the actions to diagnose the fault, are executed in the pursuit of a different goal, with the result that HAL's overall behavior is incoherent. The goal-based behavior evident in either reading resonates strongly for an AI audience because of the connection with the subfield of planning and problem solving.

In addition to referencing specific subfields within AI, HAL also resonates with the AI audience through indirect references to the Turing Test. Alan Turing, in his seminal article on machine intelligence, sought to replace philosophical arguments about whether machines can think with an operational definition of intelligence.[3] In the Turing Test, a human judge engages in typed conversation, through a terminal, with both a human and a machine, which are present in another room.[4] The judge must determine, based on the responses to her typed queries, which is the human and which is the machine. If the judge can't tell the difference, we deem the machine to be "intelligent." The notions that something is intelligent if it seems intelligent and, more generally, that questions of identity (essence) should be replaced with questions about functional or behavioral equivalence, are generally accepted by AI practitioners.

In the interview with the BBC reporter, when asked if HAL has emotions, Bowman responds:

> Well, he acts like he has genuine emotions. Of course he's programmed that way to make it easier for us to talk to him. But as to whether or not he has real feelings is something that I don't think anyone can truthfully answer.

This reference to behavioral equivalence immediately cues the AI audience. The issue of "genuine emotion" has been replaced with behavioral equivalence; HAL acts like he has emotions, so he should be treated as having emotions. This move establishes a double perspective throughout the rest of the film. Whenever HAL acts in a humanlike way, the audience (particularly the AI audience) simultaneously reads HAL's behavior at face value, as the behavior of a thinking, feeling, conscious being, and sees it as a consequence of entirely mechanical, comprehensible, functional processes. Bowman and Poole explicitly refer to this ambiguous double reading during their discussion of HAL's malfunction (the discussion in the pod). In the mechanical view, HAL is simply a faulty component that may have to be disconnected; this is the view unproblematically adopted by Poole. Bowman, however, expresses concern that no 9000 series computer has ever been disconnected before and that he's not sure what HAL will think about this. The tension of this double reading peaks during HAL's final scene, as he expresses fear and pain during the disconnection of his higher brain functions ("I'm afraid, Dave. Dave, my mind is going. I can feel it . . ."). The audience is caught between reading this as the output of a machine or as the words of a being toward whom we have moral responsibility; in the context of the Turing Test, both are true.

Classical AI

In recent years, discourse about AI's high-level research agenda has been structured as a debate between symbolist, classical AI (sometimes called good old-fashioned AI, or GOFAI), and behavioral, or interactionist AI. The classical-interactionist distinction has shaped discourse within AI and cognitive science, in cultural theoretical studies of AI, and in hybrid practice combining AI and cultural theory. *2001* was released during the ascendancy of classical AI, and indeed, HAL accurately represents the vision of classical AI.[5]

Classical AI is characterized by its concern with symbolic manipulation and problem solving. A firm distinction is drawn between mental processes happening "inside" the mind and activities in the world happening "outside" the mind.[6] Classical AI's research program is concerned with developing the theories and engineering practices necessary to build minds exhibiting intelligence. Such systems are commonly built by expressing special-purpose knowledge about a specific task (such special-purpose knowledge is typically called "domain knowledge") as symbolic structures and specifying rules and processes that manipulate these structures. Intelligence is considered to be a property that inheres in the symbol manipulation happening inside the mind. This intelligence is exhibited by demonstrating the program's ability to solve problems.

Where classical AI concerns itself with mental functions, such as planning and problem solving, interactionist AI is concerned with embodied agents interacting in a physical or virtual world. Rather than solving complex symbolic problems, such agents are engaged in a moment-by-moment dynamic pattern of interaction with the world. Often there is no explicit representation of the "knowledge" needed to engage in these interactions. Rather, the interactions emerge from the dynamic regularities of the world and the reactive processes of the agent. As opposed to classical AI, which focuses on internal mental processing, interactionist AI assumes that having a body embedded in a concrete situation is essential for intelligence. It is the body that defines many of the interaction patterns between the agent and its environment. For the interactionist, a body is necessary even for forming abstract concepts; abstractions are based on sensory-motor experience.

The bodiless HAL engages in the sense-plan-act cycle of classical AI. During sensing, an internal representation of the state of the world is updated by making inferences from sensory information. In addition to containing a model of the state of the world, this interior symbolic space contains the goals or intentional structures of the AI system. The system then constructs a plan of action for accomplishing goals, given the represented state of the world. Finally, the system carries out this plan in the world and begins the cycle anew. HAL's physicality, his sensory-motor apparatus, is distributed throughout the ship in the form of cameras, microphones, and the myriad of ship systems he can control. As a classical system, the particular configuration of HAL's sensory-motor system has no effect on his interior, mental structure. If new sensors, for example, infrared cameras, or new effectors, for example a robotic arm attached to the main console, are added to HAL, it doesn't change the way HAL thinks; he merely would have new physical capabilities. For interactionist AI, the particular shape or configuration of the body strongly affects the mind; change the structure of the body, and you change the structure of the mind. HAL's bodiless cognition makes him a clear example of classical AI.

HAL's radical interiority, an internal mental (symbolic) space into which neither Bowman, Poole, nor we as viewers have access, is emphasized through the use of reaction shots focusing on one of HAL's camera eyes. Where normally a reaction shot reveals, through bodily (including facial) position and movement, a character's motivational and emotional responses to a situation, letting us into a character's interior space, for HAL, who is in some sense pure mind, the reaction shots remain opaque, giving viewers a sense of an interior they are not allowed to enter. This technique is used, with increasingly chilling effect, starting with the first hint of HAL's malfunction. During the conversation in which HAL reveals his concerns about the mission to Bowman, the frequent cuts to HAL's eye during the conversation give us a sense of depths in HAL, while keeping those depths mysterious. When Dave responds to HAL's concerns with the mild rebuke "You're working up your crew psychology report?" the camera focuses on HAL's eye and holds for a beat before HAL responds, "Of course I am. Sorry about this. I know it's a bit silly." HAL then interrupts himself with the clipped "Just a moment. Just a moment," which signals the full onset of his psychosis. Similarly, during the death scene of the hibernating crewmen, the camera cuts between the life support alarms and one of HAL's expressionless camera eyes, further reinforcing a sense of complex interior machinations that remain inaccessible in the world of bodies.

The chess-playing scene further establishes HAL as an instance of classical AI. Chess, with its properties of a completely knowable world (the board), deterministic interactions (the rules), simple evaluation of success (win, lose, draw), but still offering within this simple framework a huge range of strategic and tactical options, was a popular domain for classical AI research. The simple and noise-free nature of chess effectively trivializes the sense and act portions of the sense-plan-act cycle, squarely placing the focus on internal representation and reasoning. HAL's facility with chess would have strongly resonated with AI researchers in the late 1960s and the 1970s, serving as an indicator that HAL is, indeed, intelligent.

Interactionist AI researchers, who see mind arising out of the behavioral details of physical interaction in the world, are more likely to resonate with sci-fi representations that emphasize robots and androids. In the episode "Robots Alive" of television's *Scientific American Frontiers* featuring interactionist AI researcher Rodney Brooks, Brooks mentions that the ultimate goal of his work is to be able to build Lieutenant Commander Data, an android in *Star Trek: The Next Generation.*[7] However, unlike HAL, Data fails to demonstrate general intelligence while maintaining connections to specific technical subproblems within interactionist AI research. While Data is certainly a likable character, and various "Star Trek" plots have explored the philosophical problems of Data's personhood, he fails to achieve the same inspiring plausibility, the magic of making general intelligence seem a natural extrapolation from current technical work. For AI researchers, HAL remains a uniquely powerful and influential popular media representation of AI.

AI and Transcendence

The environment of the *Discovery* is cold and antiseptic, dominated by hospital-white consoles and information displays, an environment in which the emotionless astronauts live completely scheduled lives dominated by formal procedures and routines, watched over by the infallible rationality of HAL. The *Discovery* is a perfect Taylorist environment, a closed world in which all contingencies have been modeled and accounted for, at least until HAL's fatal malfunction. HAL's rationality, and his physical manifestation in the total (and totalizing) environment of the *Discovery*, form an odd disjunction with the film's last sequence: Bowman's transcendent rebirth as the star child (figure 35). Apparently, rationality must be defeated, HAL deactivated, before transcendence can occur. However, within the culture of AI, HAL and the birth of the star child are not contradictory, but are rather part of the same agenda: the transcendence of the human through the creation of thinking machines.

In *The Religion of Technology*, David Noble traces the explicitly religious, primarily Christian drive to transcend the body and the material world that operates as part of the disciplinary logic of atomic weapons science, space exploration, genetic engineering, and AI. Noble argues that AI continues in the Cartesian tradition of a strong separation of mind and body, with the thinking, abstract mind seen as having a direct relationship to God, and hence to truth, while the body, with its sensory, animal appetites, distracts the divine, thinking mind.[8]

The foundational move in AI, particularly classical AI, is to view mind as an abstract process, something that is not necessarily tied to the contingencies of human brains and bodies but can rather be abstracted and run on multiple hardware platforms, including digital computers. Minsky has described the human brain as a mere "meat machine," and the body, that "bloody mess of organic matter," as a "teleoperator for the brain."[9] Mind is a process, a collection of functional relationships; it is only an accident of history that mental processes are implemented in the organic brains of human beings. If mind can be released from the shell of the body, running free on ever-faster, more-efficient hardware, it is only a matter of time before these minds achieve human-level, then superhuman intelligence.

In this AI eschatology, there is an intermediate period before machine intelligence surpasses the human, a period in which human and machine intelligence work together in tightly integrated human-machine symbiosis. This is the era of the cyborg, the era in which we live now, in which the focus is on the computer as an infinitely flexible medium that extends the thinking capabilities of the human mind. J. C. R. Licklidder, influential MIT psychologist and first head of the computer research program at the U.S. government's Advanced Research Projects Agency (ARPA), established ARPA's long-term funding of both AI and advanced human-computer interaction and communication techniques, including the development of ARPAnet, which eventually became the Internet (ARPA was eventually renamed the present-day DARPA, the Defense Advanced Research Projects Agency). In 1960, he discussed the relationship between human-computer systems and the ultimate goals of AI:

> Man-computer symbiosis is probably not the ultimate paradigm for complex technological systems. It seems entirely possible that, in due course, electronic or chemical "machines" will outdo the human brain in most of the functions we now consider exclusively within its province. . . . In short, it seems worthwhile to avoid argument with (other) enthusiasts for artificial intelligence by conceding dominance in the distant future of cerebration to machines alone. There will nevertheless be a fairly long interim during which the main intellectual

> advances will be made by men and computers working together in intimate association.[10]

HAL represents the extreme end of the era of human-computer symbiosis, a thinking tool able to function on its own, ready, and, in this case, willing to be free of its human users. For a brief period (Licklidder describes this period as being somewhere in the range of "15 to 400 years"), machines augment human intelligence in a symbiotic union; ultimately however, artificial intelligence exceeds human intelligence. At this stage the new machine superintelligences break out on their own evolutionary path. Like the dinosaurs, humans, in their current, messy, wet, biological form, are left far behind, an evolutionary experiment that had its day but has been superseded by infinitely more accomplished machine minds.

Yet personal human identity need not be lost, for the advent of superhuman machine intelligence also signals the advent of immortality. In *Mind Children*, Hans Moravec, a robotics researcher at Carnegie Mellon University who developed early, influential, autonomous robots while at Stanford, describes a technical vision in which human minds are uploaded out of biological bodies into superior robotic bodies with superfast computer brains.[11] In this new substrate of silicon and steel, human minds can run much faster than on wet brains, allowing the uploaded individual to think, learn, develop, and change at superhuman speeds:

> Your new abilities will dictate changes in your personality. Many of the changes will result from your own deliberate tinkerings with your own program. Having turned up your speed control a thousandfold, you notice that you now have hours (subjectively speaking) to respond to situations that previously required instant reactions. You have time, during the fall of a dropped object, to research the advantages and disadvantages of trying to catch it, perhaps to solve its differential equations of motion. You will have time to read and ponder an entire on-line etiquette book when you find yourself in an awkward social situation. . . . In general, you will have time to undertake what would today count as major research efforts to solve trivial everyday problems.[12]

Our new robotic bodies, equipped not with two clumsy hands, but with fractal, nanoscale manipulators, are able to continuously remake our material reality at the atomic scale. But such bodies are only the beginning; our minds will inhabit ever more subtle physical manifestations, moving toward ever more radical new modes of existence, just as the star child in *2001* exhibits a radical, new materiality.

> Our speculation ends in a supercivilization, the synthesis of all solar-system life, constantly improving and extending itself, spreading out-

> ward from the sun, converting nonlife into mind. . . . The process, possibly occurring elsewhere, might convert the entire universe into an extended thinking entity, a prelude to even greater things.[13]

Thus humans, personal identities intact (at least at the beginning), are able to gallop off into the postbiological future with their artificially intelligent children.

Moravec is not alone in this AI-based evolutionary eschatology. He is capturing discussions that have been in the AI community for years and that have been described by other researchers, such as Ray Kurzweil, who, in *The Age of Spiritual Machines*, describes a similar postbiological future.[14]

Given this eschatological current running through the AI research community, the apparent disjunction between the rational, instrumental HAL and the "Star Child" sequence disappears, unified by a single evolutionary story that sees the development of artificial intelligence as *the* crucial next step for achieving transcendence. Arguably, HAL is not the only AI operating within *2001*. The monoliths themselves are extremely flexible, esoteric, alien machines, capable of subtly manipulating animal minds in order to push them in specific evolutionary directions (as in "The Dawn of Man" sequence), capable of functioning for millions of years and operating as a signal device (as in the "Moon Base" sequence), and capable of serving as a gateway into a new reality, again facilitating an evolutionary jump (the "Star Child" sequence). To viewers, the complete opacity of function and the mystery surrounding the monoliths are exactly what one would expect from highly evolved postbiological AIs, whose thoughts, motivations, and physical interactions with the world are so advanced as to be completely inscrutable to those lower on the evolutionary chain. As Arthur C. Clarke famously quipped, "Any sufficiently advanced technology is indistinguishable from magic."[15] HAL serves as a waypoint in this evolutionary story of technologically mediated transcendence, with the apes on the low end, the monoliths and the star child on the high end, and contemporary humans and HAL in the middle. The postbiological monoliths effectively upload Bowman into a new form, one that presumably functions at a level of consciousness and inhabits a reality closer to the monoliths' own.

Like any evolutionary story, this one has its winners and losers. The apes killed at the waterhole by the tool-assisted, monolith-accelerated tribe certainly don't celebrate the discovery of tools. HAL, Poole, and the three hibernating scientists are all losers, killed in a conflict between roughly equivalent intelligences at the evolutionary fork of biological and nonbiological intelligence. The monolith-accelerated simians and monolith-accelerated Bowman are the big winners, each becoming the "next big thing" in the progression toward ultimate consciousness. Though HAL is a loser in this round, he is ultimately vindicated by the monoliths themselves; nonbiological intelligence, far from being an evolutionary dead end, ultimately becomes the shepherd of human intelligence.

AI as Representation

In this chapter, we've been exploring how the cinematic representation of HAL functioned (and continues to function) for the audience of AI researchers, serving as a more effective galvanizing inspiration for AI than other sci-fi representations by effectively tapping AI research culture to bring to the screen a plausible visualization of the AI dream, a generally intelligent artificial mind. However, in addition to functioning as a cinematic representation of and within the disciplinary machinery of AI, HAL functions as a character within the narrative machinery of *2001*, a character who, as noted, has more emotional and psychological depth than any of the human characters within the film. HAL immediately begins establishing empathy with the audience from his early appearance during the interview with the BBC reporter, where HAL expresses pride in his "perfect" functioning and the satisfaction of "putting myself to the fullest possible use, which is all I think that any conscious entity can ever hope to do," while Bowman and Poole offer mild and unexpressive responses. The audience experiences a growing sense of both horror and mystery as HAL's malfunction turns into a murderous psychosis; the frequent shots of HAL's camera eyes invite the audience to imagine what might be going on in HAL's mind. Finally, as Bowman deactivates HAL's higher mental functions, the audience experiences sadness and pity at HAL's obvious fear and pain: "Stop Dave. Stop will you. I'm afraid. I'm afraid, Dave. Dave, my mind is going. I can feel it. I can feel it. My mind is going. There is no question about it. I can feel it. I can feel it. I can feel it" (figure 22).

Once HAL's double function is recognized—how he simultaneously serves as a representation of research agendas and disciplinary assumptions within AI and as an expressive resource within the movie—we can turn this double vision to AI systems themselves, considering them as procedural representations that simultaneously encode disciplinary assumptions and agendas and function for an audience. For example, we can begin asking what it would mean to build HAL 9000, not as a general intelligence controlling a spaceship bound for Jupiter, but as an AI-based character within an interactive story or game based on *2001*. This double vision requires unpacking the agendas and assumptions implicit in different AI architectures and approaches, that is, a critical practice of reading AI systems, while simultaneously remaining engaged in the development of alternative technical approaches informed by the critical readings: a critical technical practice. This double vision also requires viewing AI systems as performing for an audience, rethinking AI as a kind of procedural art. Finally, the critical technical practice and the concerns of procedural art must be put together to create an Expressive AI, an AI whose fundamental research concern is understanding how the architectural and methodological details and assumptions of the technical system enable specific audience experiences.

Before continuing, it's important to clarify how the term *architecture* is used in AI. *Architecture* refers to the organizational strategy of an AI system, the different components of the system, the relationships among these components, and the metaphors around which the individual components have been designed (e.g., "memory," "knowledge," "rules," etc.). As is described in more detail below, an architecture is simultaneously a technical and conceptual construct, a piece of running code and a theory, hypothesis, or story about intelligence.

Critical Technical Practice

Agre introduced the term *critical technical practice* (CTP) to describe a technical practice that actively reflects on its own philosophical underpinnings and, by bringing in humanistic and artistic knowledge, approaches, and techniques, opens up new technical directions and approaches. Agre, who was specifically working within AI, describes CTP:

> A critical technical practice would not model itself on what Kuhn called "normal science," much less on conventional engineering. Instead of seeking foundations it would embrace the impossibility of foundations, guiding itself by a continually unfolding awareness of its own workings as a historically specific practice. It would make further inquiry into the practice of AI an integral part of the practice itself. It would accept that this reflexive inquiry places all of its concepts and methods at risk.[16]

Agre focuses his attention on the assumptions and agendas implicit in the standard AI view of planning, finding these assumptions problematic when applied to the dynamics of everyday life. Specifically, he finds the strong separation between mind and world that operates in the standard AI view of planning unable to account for the everyday experience of living in the world, which is revealed by phenomenological and ethnographic analyses. Through a deconstructive inversion of this master narrative, Agre has developed an alternative architecture that continually redecides what to do by using a dependency maintenance network with relative, rather than absolute and objective, representations of world objects as inputs.

Expressive AI, described in more detail below, is an instance of CTP. In addition to drawing inspiration from Agre's work, several other CTPs also inform my thinking about Expressive AI. Sengers employs schizoanalysis to investigate how assumptions in standard autonomous agent architectures lead to incoherent behavior and uses this analysis to build an alternative agent architecture organized around narrative principles.[17] Penny engages in reflexive engineering, combining art practice with robotics. Through his art practice, he examines the notion of physical embodiment, specifically exploring how much of the intelligence exhibited in the robot's interactions with viewers is a result of the physical design of the robot and the physicality of the viewers' interactions with the robot.[18] Sack employs a cultural studies perspective on language to engage in the computer analysis of human language use. For example, the *conversation map* employs a social network approach to automatically analyze large-scale, distributed conversations taking place in Internet news groups.[19]

The analysis in this chapter of how HAL functions as a representation of AI is an example of the sort of critical analysis employed in CTP. HAL functions so effectively for the AI research audience precisely because he taps into the research goals of specific subfields, assumptions, and agendas within classical AI, as well as the spiritual and evolutionary dreams of the field. In the case of HAL, he's not a procedural representation (a program), but rather a cinematic representation of a program. Most cinematic sci-fi representations of AI are not amenable to this critical/technical analysis because they don't provide the necessary hooks into AI research culture to trace the detailed relationships between the cinematic representation and AI research; in most cases, there is little to say except that the AI character is really a human character in machine disguise. However, because the character of HAL was carefully constructed to resonate with the AI community (part of the pursuit of realism that one sees throughout the technologies represented in *2001*), HAL actually provides the hooks to make such an analysis possible.

AI-Based Art

The AI dream is to build representations of the human in the machine, to build intelligent creatures, companions who, through their similarities with and differences from us, tell us something about ourselves. This dream is not just about modeling rational problem solvers but about building machines that in some sense engage us socially, have emotions and desires, and interact with us in meaningful, culturally rich, effective, and affective ways. Woody Bledsoe, former president of the AAAI (American Association for Artificial Intelligence), described this dream in his 1985 presidential address:

> Twenty-five years ago I had a dream, a *daydream*, if you will. A dream shared with many of you. I dreamed of a special kind of computer, which had eyes and ears and arms and legs, in addition to its "brain." . . . My dream was filled with the wild excitement of seeing a machine act like a human being, at least in many ways. . . . My dream computer person liked to walk and play Ping-Pong, especially with me.[20]

AI is a way of exploring what it means to be human by building systems. An AI architecture is a machine to think with, a concrete theory and representation of some aspect of the human world. Art also explores what it means to be human by building concrete representations of some aspect of the human world. Combining these two ways of knowing-by-making opens a new path toward the AI dream, a path which takes seriously the problem of building intelligences that robustly function outside of the lab to engage human participants in intellectually and aesthetically satisfying interactions.

As a character, HAL effectively intrigues, horrifies, and creates identification and empathy with the audience. What would it mean to create actual, running AI systems that operate as effectively as characters as HAL does as a cinematic AI character? This is the research area of *believable agents*, the construction of autonomous characters with rich personalities, emotions, and social behaviors.[21] When Turing introduced his famous test for intelligence, he also introduced a subversive and not always recognized idea: intelligence is not a property of a system itself, but rather resides in the details of interactions with and the perceptions of an observer. The concept of *believability*, a term borrowed from character artists and introduced into AI discourse by the Oz project at Carnegie Mellon University, is, like the Turing Test, an observer-centric notion.[22]

However, instead of focusing on imitating the responses of a "generic human," research on believability focuses on character, on rich and compelling presentations of behavior that foster the willing suspension of disbelief. Where the Turing Test is about closing the gap between the real and not-real (building systems which are indistinguishable from a real human), believability is about building autonomous agents that function *as if real*, in the same way that characters such as Hamlet or HAL can't be described unequivocally as real or fake, but rather function as if real within their respective representational worlds. Believable-agents researchers attempt to leverage insights and craft practices from the character arts and apply them to AI models of characters.

To create a HAL character within an interactive story world, the AI system would need to operationalize strategies for representing a disembodied mind that finds itself trapped in a psychosis-producing goal conflict. For example, the virtual camera providing the player with a view into the world (assuming the story world is represented as a three-dimensional virtual world, the standard in contemporary games) may dynamically cut at key moments to show one of HAL's impassive eyes, emphasizing HAL's interior cognitive space. But, unlike the cinematic application of this trope, where the director and editor have complete control over when such a cut should occur and what action immediately precedes or follows the cut, in the interactive version, this trope must be procedurally encoded. The player within the story world may cause different actions to occur at any time. The system must be capable of making autonomous decisions about when to cut to a reaction shot of HAL's eye, depending on the action taking place within the story world.

As discussed above, HAL's facility with natural language is one of the important cues that allows an audience, particularly the AI audience, to believe that HAL has general intelligence. Within the story world, the player should be able to converse in natural language with the interactive HAL character. However, since we don't really have AI systems that have general language competence, as well as commonsense reasoning, the interactive HAL character will require a more special-purpose language competence that allows it to process language within the limited domain of the story world; the language competence should give the illusion of general intelligence, while actually being designed to handle a much more limited language domain. Much of this will involve clever writing and the generation of responses that can mask natural language system failures, the cases where the system fails to understand or perhaps incompletely understands the player's utterance. In such cases, HAL (the character) should respond with story content, such as a character backstory, or by announcing a new story event (e.g., the failure of the AE35 unit), in such a way as to simultaneously mask the understanding failure and to implicitly suggest to the player new directions of conversation and action that the system is capable of handling. In both the case of automated camera control and character-specific natural language conversation, representational tropes that were under the complete control of the filmmaker in the cinematic version of *2001* must now be procedurally captured in an autonomous AI system in order to build an interactive version of the HAL character.

Of course, art practice is broader than the creation of characters. But the notion of believability, with its focus on the observer's perception of the AI system, can be generalized to a notion of procedural poetics, to a concern with systems that engage in internally consistent, evocative, and compelling behaviors, that encourage participants to suspend disbelief and interact with the system. With AI-based art, attention moves from the unproblematic pursuit of general intelligence toward an explicit concern with systems that put into operation representational tropes or figures that explicitly perform for an audience. This opens up a new technical and artistic research area, one concerned with building AI systems that support authorship and audience interpretation within specific expressive contexts.

Expressive AI

AI-based art is more than just an application area of AI, the unproblematic appropriation of AI technologies to expressive ends. Rather, it is an entirely new research agenda, an agenda that self-consciously views AI systems as media, a stance from which all of AI can be rethought and transformed. I call this new research agenda and art practice Expressive AI.[23]

The central research problem in Expressive AI is developing architectures that balance authorship and autonomy. For an architecture to support authorship, the architecture must have appropriate authorial affordances to support the experiences that the author wants to create. These affordances, or authorial "hooks," must allow the author to describe, at appropriate levels of abstraction, the audience experience that the author wants to create. However, complete authorial control would require pre-scripting all possible audience interactions with the system, predescribing all possible experiences the system can create. For complex interactions, such authorial pre-scripting is literally impossible. Therefore the architecture must support appropriate autonomy; it must be able to make use of the author-given description of the desired experience in such a way as to respond to myriad audience interactions that were not directly foreseen by the author, to generate endless variations that, while not directly specified by the author, have the author's desired style.

Interpretive affordances support the interpretations an audience makes about the operations of an AI system. Interpretive affordances provide resources both for narrating the operation of the system, and additionally, in the case of an *interactive* system, for supporting intentions for action. The AI system can be seen as providing a linkage between author and audience; the author inscribes procedural potential within the system, potential which is released as a concrete performance during interactions with the audience. The architecture is crafted in such a way as to enable just those authorial affordances that allow the artist to manipulate the interpretive affordances dictated by the concept of the piece. At the same time, the architectural explorations suggest new ways to manipulate the interpretive affordances, suggesting new conceptual opportunities. Thus both the artist's engagement with the inner workings of the architecture and the audience's experience with the finished artwork are central, interrelated concerns for Expressive AI.

If we think again of an interactive HAL character, existing in an interactive world and not a film, we would need to ask what interpretive and authorial affordances must be supported by this system. On the interpretive side, our HAL character must automate representational tropes for communicating the character of a disembodied, rational intelligence that becomes troubled by an unsolvable goal conflict, as well as be able to move the conflict between HAL and the astronauts (presumably, the players are taking the role of the astronauts) forward. Such tropes include the reaction shot and language capabilities described above, as well as strategies such as depicting the progressive disturbance of HAL's thought and depicting HAL's general intelligence (by, for example, suggesting a game of chess with the player). On the authorial side, the architecture of the HAL character must support the author in expressing the knowledge and algorithms necessary to carry out the representational tropes or strategies. For example, the architecture might explicitly reason about different strategies for depicting HAL's progressive psychosis, allowing the author to create a collection of such strategies from among which the system can dynamically select, depending on the player's actions in the world. The architecture might provide a special-purpose rule language for authoring camera control rules for deciding when and for how long the camera should cut to a reaction shot of one of HAL's eyes. In any event, the specifics of the architecture used to author the HAL character are inextricably tied to the specifics of how the HAL character presents itself to the audience; interpretive and authorial affordances mutually define each other.

Expressive AI engages in a sustained inquiry into authorial affordances, crafting specific architectures that afford appropriate authorial control for specific artworks. This inquiry into authorial affordances makes Expressive AI a critical technical practice. For authorial affordances are not purely a technical code issue, but rather lie in the relationship between the code and ways of talking about the code.

AI (and its sister discipline, artificial life) consists of both technical strategies for the design and implementation of computational systems and a paired, inseparable, tightly entangled collection of rhetorical and narrative strategies for talking about and thus understanding these computational systems as intelligent and/or alive.

These rhetorical strategies enable researchers to use words such as "goal," "plan," "decision," and "knowledge" to simultaneously refer to specific computational entities (pieces of program text, data items, algorithms) and to make use of the systems of meaning these words have when applied to human beings. This double use of language embeds technological systems in broader systems of meaning.

The rhetorical strategies used to narrate the operation of an AI system vary depending on the technical approach, precisely because these interpretive strategies are inextricably part of the approach. Every system is doubled, consisting of both a computational and a rhetorical machine. Doubled machines can be understood as the interaction of (at least) two sign systems: the sign system of the code and a sign system used to interpret and talk about the code.

The central problem of AI is often cast as the "knowledge representation" problem. This is precisely the problem of defining structures and processes that are amenable simultaneously to the uninterpreted manipulations of computational systems *and* to serving as signs for human subjects. This quest has driven AI to be the most promiscuous field of computer science, engaging in unexpected and ingenious couplings with numerous fields, including psychology, anthropology, linguistics, physics, biology (both molecular and macro), ethnography, ethology, mathematics, and logic. This rich history of simultaneous computational and interpretive practice serves as a conceptual resource for the AI-based artist. In Expressive AI, the doubled machine, consisting of both code and rhetoric, is explicitly defined and manipulated; it is precisely the relationship between language and code that creates architectural affordances, making the architecture not just a bunch of code, but a way of thinking about the world.

And so we come full circle back to HAL. HAL is a filmic representation of an AI system, one that can be read to unpack the culture, agendas, and assumptions of the AI research community. HAL is also an effective character within a story, establishing empathy with the audience and serving a function within the plot. Actual AI systems can also be viewed as representations and are similarly amenable to readings that unpack the world view implicit in the architecture. The move to considering AI systems as media then opens up the possibility of AI-based art and entertainment, systems that engage in internally consistent, evocative, and compelling behaviors, that encourage participants to suspend disbelief and interact with the system. Finally, the deep readings of the double system, the combination of code plus rhetoric, can be employed not just analytically or critically, but constructively, to actively create AI architectures that support specific audience experiences. Expressive AI opens the door to creating artificial beings that engage us in deeply satisfying, culturally rich experiences. The first AI system that creates the level of empathy, engagement, and interest that HAL creates will not be experienced by a few astronauts on board a space mission to Jupiter, but by millions of us, on the computers and game consoles in our own homes.

Notes

1. David Stork, ed., *HAL's Legacy: 2001's Computer as Dream and Reality* (Cambridge, Mass.: MIT Press, 1997).

2. In the travel planning domain, AI researchers build dialogue systems that act as travel agents. The systems can have the same sorts of extended dialogues one might have with a travel agent while planning a trip.

3. Alan Turing, "Computing Machinery and Intelligence," *Mind* 59 (1950): 433–60.

4. Turing's original formulation of the Turing Test (he calls it the "imitation game") is gendered:

> The new form of the problem can be described in terms of a game which we call the "imitation game." It is played with three people, a man (A), a woman (B), and an interrogator (C) who may be of either sex. The interrogator stays in a room apart from the other two. The object of the game is to determine which of the other two is the man and which is the woman. . . . We may now ask the question, "What will happen when a machine takes the part of A in the game?" Will the interrogator decide wrongly as often when the game is played like this as he does when the game is played between a man and a woman?

In AI discourse, the Turing Test is typically "sanitized" to a game where the judge (interrogator) must decide which is the human and which is the machine. The implications of the original gendered version are beyond the scope of this chapter (http://cogprints.org/499/00/turing.html).

5. John Haugeland, *Artificial Intelligence: The Very Idea* (Cambridge, Mass.: MIT Press, 1985); Rodney Brooks, *Intelligence without Reason*, A.I. Memo 1293 (Cambridge, Mass.: MIT Artificial Intelligence Lab, 1991); Rodney Brooks, "Elephants Don't Play Chess," *Robotics and Autonomous Systems* 6 (1990): 3–15; "Special Issue on Situated Cognition," *Cognitive Science* 17 (1993); Allison Adam, *Artificial Knowing: Gender and the Thinking Machine* (London: Routledge, 1998); Philip Agre, *Computation and Human Experience* (Cambridge: Cambridge University Press, 1997); Phoebe Sengers, "Anti-Boxology: Agent Design in Cultural Context," Ph.D. diss., School of Computer Science, Carnegie Mellon University, 1998; F. Varela, E. Thompson, and E. Rosch, *The Embodied Mind: Cognitive Science and Human Experience* (Cambridge, Mass.: MIT Press, 1999).

6. Brooks, *Intelligence without Reason*; Agre, *Computation and Human Experience*.

7. Rodney Brooks, "Robot's Alive," show 705 of "Scientific American Frontiers" (premiered April 9, 1997); transcript available at http://www.pbs.org/saf/transcripts/transcript705.htm.

8. David Noble, *The Religion of Technology: The Divinity of Man and the Spirit of Invention* (New York: Knopf, 1997).

9. Quoted in Noble, *The Religion of Technology*, 156.

10. J. C. R. Licklidder, "Man-Computer Symbiosis," *IRE Transactions on Human Factors in Electronics* 1 (March 1960): 4–11, reprinted in *The New Media Reader*, ed. Noah Wardrip-Fruin and Nick Montfort (Cambridge, Mass.: MIT Press, 2003), 75.

11. Hans Moravec, *Mind Children: The Future of Robot and Human Intelligence* (Cambridge, Mass.: Harvard University Press, 1990).

12. Ibid., 114.

13. Ibid., 116.

14. Ray Kurzweil, *The Age of Spiritual Machines: When Computers Exceed Human Intelligence* (New York: Viking Penguin, 1999).

15. Arthur C. Clarke, *Profiles of the Future: An Inquiry into the Limits of the Possible* (New York: Holt, 1984).

16. Agre, *Computation and Human Experience*, 23.

17. Phoebe Sengers, "Cultural Informatics: Artificial Intelligence and the Humanities," *Surfaces: Special Issue on Humanities and Computing—Who's Driving?* 8 (1999), available at http://www.pum.umontreal.ca/revues/surfaces/vol8/vol8TdM.html; Sengers, "Anti-Boxology: Agent Design in Cultural Context."

18. Simon Penny, "Agents as Artworks and Agent Design as Artistic Practice," in *Human Cognition and Social Agent Technology*, ed. K. Dautenhahn (Amsterdam: Benjamins, 2000), 395–414.

19. Warren Sack, "Actor-Role Analysis: Ideology, Point of View and the News," in *Perspectives on Narrative Perspective*, ed. S. Chatman and W. Van Peer (Albany: State University of New York Press, 2001), 189–206; Warren Sack, "Stories and Social Networks," in *Narrative Intelligence*, ed. M. Mateas and P. Sengers (Amsterdam: Benjamins, 2003), 305–322.

20. Woody Bledsoe, "I Had a Dream: AAAI Presidential Address," *AI Magazine* 7, no. 1 (Spring 1986): 57–61.

21. Michael Mateas, "An Oz-Centric Review of Interactive Drama and Believable Agents," in *AI Today: Recent Trends and Developments: Lecture Notes in AI 1600*, ed. M. Wooldridge and M. Veloso (Berlin and New York: Springer, 1999), 297–328; Michael Mateas, "Interactive Drama, Art and Artificial Intelligence," Ph.D. diss., Tech report CMU-CS-02-206, Carnegie Mellon University, 2002; Michael Mateas and Andrew Stern, "A Behavior Language: Joint Action and Behavior Idioms," in *Life-Like Characters: Tools, Affective Functions, and Applications*, ed. H. Prendinger and M. Ishizuka (Berlin and New York: Springer-Verlag, 2004), 135–162.

22. Joseph Bates, "The Role of Emotion in Believable Agents," *Communications of the ACM* 7, no. 37 (1994): 122–25.

23. Michael Mateas, "Expressive AI," *Leonardo: Journal of the International Society for Arts, Sciences, and Technology* 34, no. 2 (2001): 147–53; Mateas, "Interactive Drama, Art and Artificial Intelligence"; Michael Mateas, "Expressive AI: Games and Artificial Intelligence," in *Proceedings of Level Up: Digital Games Research Conference* (Utrecht, Netherlands, November 2003); Michael Mateas, "Expressive AI: A Semiotic Analysis of Machinic Affordances," in *Proceedings of the Third Conference on Computational Semiotics and New Media* (University of Teesside, September 2003), 58–68.

8

Kubrick's Obscene Shadows

SUSAN WHITE

> There comes a time when the operation of the machine becomes so odious, makes you so sick at heart, that you can't take part, you can't even passively take part, and you've got to put your bodies upon the gears and upon the wheels, upon all the apparatus, and you've got to make it stop. And you've got to indicate to the people who run it, the people who own it, that unless you're free, the machine will be prevented from working at all.
>
> MARIO SAVIO, December 3, 1964

This chapter examines aspects of the fundamental ambivalence toward human cultural productions conveyed in Stanley Kubrick's cinematic works. Through exquisitely distilled images and innovative soundtracks, the films articulate a fascination with such *topoi* (in Aristotle's sense: places to go to construct an argument) as the machine, symphonic music, the labyrinth, and various kinds of ritual as sublime forms of cultural expression. At the same time, Kubrick's films depict these cultural forms as arising from or intricately linked to what we might call *foundational violence*. But violence is only one, though perhaps the most important, of what I will term the "obscene" social underpinnings that subtend Kubrick's work.

While the etymology or historical meaning of *obscene* is unclear, it has been related both to the notion of filth and to that of being "off scene," or hidden. The pessimism that Kubrick's work exudes derives from its continual reminders that humankind's greatest achievements depend on a logic of repression of that which is most appalling in our histories and cultures—such that the horrific and the sublime are finally indistinguishable. The surface beauty and technological perfection of these films, particularly in the case of *2001*, are fraught with tension, as the shifting relationship between horror and awe articulates the director's use of cinematography, sound, setting, and other elements of mise-en-scène. The idea of reason that guides technological progress, like evolutionary law, the restrictions of gendered behavior, and the creation of works of art, is portrayed as both compelling and horrifying, sterilized, and, finally, obscene. Whether Kubrick supports or subverts the kind of cultural apparatus he depicts is, in the final analysis, open to interpretation: are his films a form of social protest—or does he, as some have felt, really want us to stop worrying and learn to love the bomb?

Although *2001* paints its portrait of civilizations on the broadest canvas of any of Kubrick's films, like all of his works this one foregrounds the paradoxes of civilized life. *2001* illustrates this seeming paradox—culture *as* violence—in many ways, most strikingly in the celebrated edit that transforms a primitive weapon, a bone, into a gorgeously complex spacecraft which, like other Kubrickian machines, is both appealing and repellent because it represents a kind of frozen "ultraviolence" (to use Alex's word in *A Clockwork Orange*, 1971) (figures 3 and 4). At the moment of becoming human, of picking up the bone tool and striking the dried bones of the dead tapir, the ape-man violently fantasizes about killing his prey. The next, seemingly natural step is for this ape to turn the weapon on his own kind—to make it ammunition in a definitive territorial dispute in which one group falls back, losing its purchase over the valued waterhole and perhaps its very ability to survive.

To put it simply, Kubrick's hominids move toward civilization by learning to kill efficiently. The notion of civilization as institutionalized violence may seem counterintuitive. This is especially true if we regard civilization as the channeling of primitive aggressive and sexual urges into more socially acceptable behaviors, as it is described by Freud in *Civilization and Its Discontents*:

> Civilization, therefore, obtains mastery over the individual's dangerous desire for aggression by weakening and disarming it and by setting up an agency within him to watch over it, like a garrison in a conquered city.[1]

But Kubrick's films depict civilization's way of organizing aggression not as a weakening but as a *concentration* of its implicit violence. His films abound in double-bind structures that flow logically from this premise. When, for example, his characters, including Moon-Watcher (the ape in *2001*), astronaut Dave Bowman, *A Clockwork Orange*'s Alex, *The Shining*'s Jack Torrance, Barry

Lyndon, Private Pyle from *Full Metal Jacket*, break out into violence that in another film might spell relief from social constriction, they find that they are more than ever simply a gear in the clockwork's mechanism. Moon-Watcher throws the bone in a violent gesture of liberation from hunger and oppression, but the bone becomes instantaneously enmeshed in the technological superstructure that comes to dominate man. Dave rebels against and dismantles the emblem of that technology, HAL, only to find himself caught in an experiment in evolution that may be guided by more advanced life forms. Alex, who acts out against society using its own cultural instruments, nevertheless is finally, cozily knitted into the political power structure. When Jack Torrance wields an ax to massacre the family he can no longer control, he assures his own status as a permanent fixture in a maze beyond his understanding. Barry Lyndon tackles his stepson, furious that his bids for acceptance by the nobility are being threatened, only to find that their ranks close even more tightly after his momentary, though inevitable, lapse. Pyle shoots Sergeant Hartman, but the latter had already proudly claimed mass murderer Charles Whitman and assassin Lee Harvey Oswald as Marine Corps marksmen: in death, Pyle is more than ever a marine.

These double-bind structures in Kubrick's films can be usefully examined as shifting manifestations of what Slovenian philosopher and critic Slavoj Žižek has termed "the obscene shadow of the law."[2] To put it briefly, Žižek, following in the traces of French psychoanalyst Jacques Lacan, points to a split between the symbolic, official law and the obscene, secret law which actually permits the official law to function. According to Žižek, the law *always* brings with it its "obscene shadow." The relationship between law and its obscene shadow has a deep structural importance in a number of Kubrick's films, including *Paths of Glory* (1957), *Lolita* (1962), *Dr. Strangelove* (1964), *A Clockwork Orange* (1971), *The Shining* (1980), *Full Metal Jacket* (1987), and *Eyes Wide Shut* (1999), as well as *2001*. All show how secret rituals and "forbidden" forms of desire serve to prop up government, the family, the military, class structures, and the organization of gender. *Paths of Glory*'s trial of three ordinary French soldiers cynically demonstrates that the law's obscene shadow falls very close to its official representatives, the generals who allow this politically exigent, bloody charade to take place. In *Full Metal Jacket*, Kubrick dwells on the obscene complicity of Sergeant Hartman in torturing Pyle toward full-blown madness, an illegal (or marginally legal) practice designed to produce a fighting machine in the interest of the larger project of U.S. imperialism in Southeast Asia: that the marines also produce crazed assassins is a predictable but unimportant by-product. The marine recruits themselves internalize the necessity of policing their own. When Pyle screws up one too many times, they take it upon themselves to beat him savagely in his bunk under the cover of night.[3]

The achievement of civilization depends ultimately, for Stanley Kubrick, upon disciplinary systems inculcated through indoctrination, reinforced through ritual, and expressed as official law, its obscene shadow, and its unofficial surveillance systems. In *2001*, Kubrick finds a compelling metaphor for this mysterious nexus of constraint and opportunity in the black monoliths that accompany humans on their evolutionary adventure. Michel Chion has described *2001*'s monolith as a "Tablet of the Law without commandments, this stele [an upright stone often used in ancient times as a funerary marker] without inscriptions."[4] The monolith is, according to this reading, a clean, geometrical figure that represents (among an almost infinite number of possible readings of its meaning) the law: the set of social codes under which citizens of a state are required to live.[5] Although the monolith incites culture-founding ritualistic worship as well as violence in the ape-men, who began to wage war under its apparent tutelage, it remains smooth, impassive, and silent until men on the moon trigger its raucous beacon by digging it up. According to this perspective, the monolith triggers the functioning of a certain kind of evolutionary law, a Darwinian struggle for survival that is continually, problematically figured by Kubrick as a clash between dominant males. HAL, on the other hand, with his soft voice, omnipresent eye, and cybernetic precision, is a rather maternal implement of technical/state violence, controlling the lives of well-disciplined astronauts who don't even know the real reason for their mission to Jupiter but carry out everyday rituals in obedience to their training.[6]

HAL exemplifies near-perfect indoctrination in the form of programming. He is the reverse forerunner of Pyle in *Full Metal Jacket*. HAL is a machine who would be human. Pyle is a man-become-machine who has a "major malfunction." The failures of each of these mechanisms is implicit to the systems that produced them. In that sense, HAL is right in saying that "human error" is at fault in his apparent failure. Specific forms of human error—the push toward domination and violent destruction—are part of the evolutionary process that created HAL himself. Thus, HAL's "failure" is not really at issue in *2001* except insofar as it reveals that his evolution is, like man's, founded on a violence that may be hardwired into every circuit. "Human error" is, of course, already revealed as built into the systems driving *Dr. Strangelove*. When General Ripper goes "a little funny in the head" and consequently sets the Doomsday Machine into motion, he is enacting the logic that produced and named it. The nuclear device in *Dr. Strangelove*, like the lovingly reconstructed control panel of the B-52 bomber that delivers it, is at the service of Major "King" Kong—who, with Slim Pickens's comic, deadpan brio brings together man-as-ape and man-as-technological/bureaucratic cog. In a humorous send-up of the futility of human hierarchical behavior, following an indoctrination that is clearly as thorough as Pyle's will be and as deadly, Kong obeys the ritual of procedure and presents global annihilation to his men, in a homey pep talk, as an opportunity for career advancement.

The law, as expressed in the disciplinary systems legally available to the state as a means of producing and controlling its citizens, ranges from subliminal presence to all-out obsession in Kubrick's films. *The Killing* (1956) is the second of Kubrick's films, after *Killer's Kiss* (1955), that adopts film noir's visual palette and its sensibility, based on the urbanite's psychological angst. The film's extreme fatalism is generic—perhaps even a parody of the film noir genre, in which category this is a late and self-conscious entry. While *The Killing* depicts criminals on a caper who are far from being controlled by a disciplinary system inculcated by the state, their actions are ultimately, flamboyantly determined by what looks like fate (one man dies, after killing a horse, because his car runs over a horseshoe), and the law is figured in this film as an agent of chance or destiny. Chance reveals its obscene side as, true to Kubrick's vision of contingency and lack of human agency, it ruins the beautiful heist designed by the protagonist (Sterling Hayden as Johnny Clay). At first, things move like clockwork, but the works are bigger than the individual can see, and perfectly timed small disasters—a woman's betrayal, a broken suitcase lock, an escaped poodle—lead Clay to the brink of failure and capture. The final shot of the film shows two plain-clothes detectives moving in relentless symmetry toward Clay: they are the very embodiment of a "system" (though perhaps not only a governmental one) that must, in the noir universe, ultimately win. They are in no hurry: a perfectly timed phone call tips them off to Clay's whereabouts; they move in a measured pace to apprehend him, like the chess pieces invoked earlier in the film by the philosophical wrestler Maurice Oboukhoff. But the obscene result of Clay's gamesmanship is a pile of human bodies riddled with bullets and a suitcase of money blowing in the wind.

Dr. Strangelove's obscene shadow is political in nature. The film depicts a republic that steadfastly regards itself as the world's guardian of democracy. During the course of the film, however, we learn that totalitarianism and the death drive flourish very near the heart of that democracy. Robert Kolker has described the historical persistence of fascism at the core of the Cold War conflict depicted in *Dr. Strangelove*:

> At the peak of the last cold war, at a time when the great, grim myth of communist subversion was the operative, castrating force in America's ideology and culture, Kubrick suggests that fascism is stirring as the ghost in the machine. The glorification and celebration of power and death that feed politics and form the urge for domination define the fascist spirit. In the film it is resurrected in the body of Strangelove, just at the point when death dominates the world. This is a chilling idea and perhaps difficult to comprehend for those who tend to look at fascism as a momentary historical aberration that died with Hitler and only appears in the appalling actions of skinhead gangs. Kubrick is suggesting that death was fascism's disguise and that strength was drawn from its ability to hide in the guise of anticommunism and the cold war. This was a brave insight for the time. Its validity remains undiminished.[7]

Kolker points here to a crucial instance of Kubrick's revelation of the obscene shadow of legal and political systems: Strangelove, a mechanically enhanced fascist, sits at the side of the shambling president who easily stands in for his *Führer*, as no doubt would any leader. Strangelove himself is linked to shadows and to hiddenness in the film. At the moment of mass destruction, he is unfolding another obscene little plot: for all of the men of power to take refuge in mine shafts with attractive women capable of reproduction.

Lolita's obscene secret is not a political one but one that upholds the scandalous, secret laws of Western male desire. One reading of Nabokov's novel might maintain that Humbert Humbert's lust for the underage Lolita is *not* anomalous but normative (he is, it turns out, "normal"). The rationalizations that he seeks in literary sources—Dante's Beatrice, Poe's child bride—are actually legitimate, if shocking, readings of the history of adult male passion for female children. Nabokov's *Lolita* is terrifying because it does not, finally, make Humbert Humbert an alien creature. But the degree of this obscenity was censored from the film by making Lolita a teen rather than a child, and it sometimes comes off as a rather tired saga of doubling between two men with a crush on a teenager rather than as a revelation of the pedophilia lurking in the hearts and minds of suburban men.

The manifestation of law-as-disciplinary system is subtle but pervasive in *Lolita*. In Nabokov's novel, as in Kubrick's film, Humbert Humbert is a child molester with an intricate intellectual life. The novel is more successful than the film in achieving reader/audience identification with Humbert—and more explicit in its legal context, in that the entire novel is addressed to the ladies and gentlemen of the jury trying Humbert for child molestation. In the film version, James Mason's sympathetic performance and the fact that the film remains mostly within the character's range of knowledge does place us to some degree—uncomfortably—in his skin. The legal system subtracted from the frame narrative is reintroduced by Kubrick as Humbert encounters what he believes is a representative of the law at the Enchanted Hunters Hotel, where he first has sex with Lolita. As though the world were a paranoid projection of Humbert's guilty conscience, the appropriately named desk clerk, Swine, announces that they are "very proud to have the overflow of the State Police Convention" (a detail missing from the novel). Clare Quilty (Peter Sellers in one of his many incarnations in the film), the protagonist's lecherous double, pretends to be one of those state police officers and rambles on to Humbert about being "normal." Humbert has internalized the potential gaze of the authorities, the idea of being monitored for normalcy.[8] The joke of the film is that, as in the famous story of the paranoid who is really being persecuted, Humbert is really being monitored, but by Quilty, not by the police.

So, too, is every movement made by the astronauts in *2001* being monitored. HAL's ubiquitous eyes work first to inform the state (ground control) and then come to represent a separate and aggressive entity that will compete for survival with the humans he observes. Like Quilty, HAL is never a neutral observer. Instead, he's opinionated and gossipy as the representative of ground control, then jealous and vengeful as his "instinct" for survival kicks in.

Confronted with the labyrinthine nature of social and physical systems, Kubrick's characters make choices that pull them deeper into the maze. As Kolker notes, Kubrick "sees men . . . mechanistically, as determined by their world, sometimes by their erotic passion." His worlds tend to be made up of "spaces that themselves create closed and inflexible worlds, predetermined and unalterable."[9] While both *Lolita* and *2001* present the *effects* of certain forms of indoctrination on their protagonists, by showing us Humbert's fear of the police and the astronauts' lack of affect, *A Clockwork Orange*, like *Full Metal Jacket*, exposes the violence beneath the mask of civilization. *Orange*'s Alex (Malcolm McDowell) is at every point in the film the enactor of the paradoxes of his culture. He fully embodies the negative utopian version of England in which he and his droogs live. The objectification of the female body represented by the submissively exposed mannequins who dispense drug-laced milk, the highly eroticized and intoxicating soundscape, the artworks that reify human sexuality—all are part and parcel of the culture Alex inhabits. Cultural products like the giant phallus in the Cat Lady's home express the repressive violence of patriarchy, of the class system, and so on. Thus it's both refreshing and horrifying when Alex obscenely challenges their high-art status by turning them into weapons—or simply uses them as the weapons that they already symbolically are.

As is very much the case in *2001*, the cultural context of the music in *A Clockwork Orange* affects significantly the meaning it brings to the film. Again and again in *Clockwork*, Kubrick points to the agonizing paradox of the flexibility of the meaning of cultural artifacts like Beethoven's Ninth Symphony. The penetrating beauty of the "Ode to Joy," sung by a middle-aged woman in the milk bar, seems to awaken in Alex a higher self: it inspires his only expression of respect—albeit a violent one—for a female during the entire film. But "Ludwig van" also produces visions of rape and torture in the young man. Beethoven's Ninth, which incorporates a Turkish military march as well as the beatific "Ode," has been a contested cultural property for at least 150 years. For example, while the Nazis laid claim to Beethoven as a cultural hero, the Allies used his Fifth Symphony as Morse code for the letter *V*, for Victory. It may have been this very contest over the ideological associations tied to Beethoven's music that led Kubrick to focus on it as Alex's obsession, while Anthony Burgess's novel makes him an aficionado of classical music more generally. But while Alex is aware of the music he hears and acts consciously and ironically according to its violent imperative, the music track of *2001* is entirely nondiegetic, unheard by the characters, and acts as more evidence of their completely unconscious indoctrination into the ideals of their civilization. All unknowing, they move through space to the rhythms of the nineteenth century, the founding moment of the scientific and cultural movements dominating the twenty-first century that Kubrick imagines.

These movements, culturally determined and culturally destructive, grow on and feed conflict and violence. In his final version of *2001*, Stanley Kubrick deliberately played down the overt political conflict depicted in Clarke's novel, based on the screenplay. The end of the film does not, for example, depict the star child blowing up the arsenals of nuclear weapons surrounding the Earth, as does the last scene of the novel. The rituals of war starkly depicted in *Spartacus*, *Paths of Glory*, *Barry Lyndon*, and *Full Metal Jacket* are muted in *2001*, appearing only in the hominids' discovery of weapons, in the symbolic "waterhole" dispute of the Soviet and American scientists over drinks on board the space station, and in HAL's preemptive strike against the astronauts. But this muting of strife does not mean that it is unimportant. The alert, indoctrinated subject is ready for warfare, prepared for the calm, surgical aggression with which Dave dismantles HAL's brain (figure 22).

Building on the logic of *2001*'s and *A Clockwork Orange*'s contrasting presentations of the subject's indoctrination into violence, *Full Metal Jacket* explores the perpetuation of warrior culture through the ancient tradition of violent ritual. By conflating the young men who are being shaped for war with the weapons they use to fight it, the film's title (changed from Gustav Hasford's *The Short-Timers*, from which the film was adapted) perfectly renders the emotional tenor of the film and recalls the intersection of human and machine seen in *2001*. In *Full Metal Jacket*, Privates Joker (Matthew Modine) and Pyle (Vincent D'Onofrio) undergo a brutal conditioning in marine boot camp not unlike that seen in the gladiator training camp sequences of *Spartacus* or in Alex's Ludovico treatments and interactions with his prison guards in *Clockwork*.

We have seen that Pyle takes his training literally and becomes a psychotic killer. Joker, on the other hand, seems to incarnate the conventional ironic observer often seen in war films. He makes the transition from boot camp to Vietnam with his intelligence intact and, despite his having joined in the beating of Pyle, with a modicum of humanity remaining. Joker's symbolic wavering between full indoctrination in male warriorhood and his conscience's objection to the carnage of war is represented by the cognitive dissonance between his peace button and the words on his helmet, "Born to Kill." But Joker's apparent choice between these two ethical systems may be illusory. While Pyle seems to offer the most powerful critique of the dehumanizing potential of the military, Joker, inoculated by irony, is the more thoroughly conditioned subject. Slavoj Žižek comments:

> What we get in the first part of the film is the military drill, the direct bodily discipline, saturated with the unique blend of a humiliating display of power, sexualization and obscene blasphemy . . . in short, the superego machine of Power at its purest. This part of the film ends with a soldier who, on account of his overidentification with the military machine, "runs amok" and shoots first the drill sergeant, then himself. . . . The second, main part of the film ends with a scene in which a soldier . . . who, throughout the film, has displayed a kind of ironic "human distance" towards the military machine . . . shoots a wounded Vietcong sniper girl. He is the one in whom the interpel-

lation by the military big Other has finally succeeded; he is the fully constituted military subject.[10]

From this perspective, the apparent choice made by Joker at the end of the film to perform a mercy killing of the wounded sniper is no choice at all, but the familiar double bind, a forced choice. His killing of the young woman is a brutal acting out of his training. His not killing her would have been even more brutal.

The settings of Kubrick's violence often express its ironies. Any discussion of disciplinary systems in Kubrick's films must include an analysis of the director's representation of these spaces, alternately cold and impersonal and embarrassingly reminiscent of our animal selves. Some of the most obscene revelations, as well as some of the most human ones, take place in bathrooms. *Full Metal Jacket*, for example, enacts its murderous response to Pyle's scapegoating in the men's room in the dead of night. The Louis XVI room in *2001*, to which I will return more specifically below, is equipped with a blue-grey bathroom which Dave inspects carefully while still wearing his spacesuit: it is a bathroom unsoiled by human bodily functions, perhaps pointing ahead to a time when humans will transcend this especially unsavory aspect of their biological existence. Although this scene is briefly sketched in *2001*, it is an important point of reference in both Kubrick's films as a whole and in *2001* specifically, and its placement in the film will prove very revealing.

Toilet training is one of the earliest and most rigorous forms of discipline endured by developing humans. Kubrick takes advantage of the feelings of vulnerability and shame, as well as the work of sexual difference, in his representation of these spaces. Beginning with *Dr. Strangelove*, Kubrick's representations of toilets and bathrooms work to convey subtle information about human beings' (especially men's) relationships to their bodies, as mediated by social structures. Along with the privacy usually linked with bathrooms comes associations of hiddenness and filth. Sometimes this obscenity takes a rather adolescent, toilet-humor turn; sometimes it is truly chilling. In *Strangelove*, General Buck Turgidson (George C. Scott) is in the bathroom when news arrives that the B-52 is entering Russian air space. General Jack D. Ripper (Sterling Hayden), the madman who unleashes the Doomsday Machine, kills himself in a toilet—perhaps in the fear that his "precious bodily fluids" are about to be contaminated by the soldiers invading his base. The toilet is the best place for flushing away contaminants, clearly Ripper's main preoccupation in life. For him, women, along with communists, are among the most threatening of potential contaminators as the misogynistic associations with his name and his unwillingness to share his bodily fluids with women make clear. While Ripper lives it tragically, the scene is played overall as toilet humor, made more piquant by the British embarrassment of Colonel Mandrake (Peter Sellers), who waits outside in the hopes of intervening in the looming nuclear disaster.

The bathrooms in *Lolita* are settings for marital and familial alienation and for the private obscenities of male desire. When Humbert, potential roomer, first visits the Haze household, Charlotte gives him a tour of the house's private spaces, including the bathroom. Striking a pose as a young sophisticate with European tastes, Charlotte laughs merrily as she pulls the chain of the old-fashioned toilet. Little does she know that this very toilet, so far beneath the attention of her cosmopolitan guest, will become the place where Humbert goes to experience a sense of relief from their marital bond. As wife Charlotte whimpers from the bedroom about her loneliness, Humbert sits on the toilet to transcribe his lustful thoughts about Lolita and his disgust with Charlotte into his diary. After Charlotte's death, Humbert luxuriates in the bath as his neighbors come in to offer comfort, transforming the bathroom into a public space redolent with false bonhomie and fictitious openness. When Lolita, now Humbert's sexual property, later learns that her mother is dead, she takes refuge and weeps in the hotel room separated from Humbert's by a bathroom, while her stepfather sits outside, apparently completely befuddled by this display of emotion. This chain of events, mediated by bathroom scenes, emphasizes Humbert's and his "family's" essential aloneness despite the prurient invasions of neighbors and the surveillance systems at work to contain transgressive desire.

In reaction to the debasement and brainwashing he undergoes in boot camp, *Full Metal Jacket*'s Private Pyle murders his drill instructor and kills himself while sitting on a toilet. This is the same men's bathroom that Joker and his buddy Cowboy had cleaned earlier in the film while kidding around about sex. Joker wants to slip his "tubesteak" into Cowboy's sister. Too impaired to join in the fun of symbolically exchanging women in the men's room, Pyle commits homicide and suicide there instead. This reprise of *Strangelove*'s toilet suicide scene is comparatively ghastly and prepares the viewer for the carnage of war. The film's second half, depicting scenes of battle, also makes allusion to human waste: being on the front lines in Vietnam is referred to by the men as being "in the shit"—as though Vietnam were a kind of toilet for U.S. (and French) imperialism that finally can't be flushed.

The two bathroom scenes in *The Shining* reveal the utter alienation of the married couple and the brutalizing role that men have taken in disciplining their families under patriarchy. Jack Torrance (Jack Nicholson) encounters the previous caretaker of the Overlook Hotel, Delbert Grady (Philip Stone), in a sumptuously decorated restroom near the ballroom, where a gala supernatural event is taking place. The room's red-and-white decor, shot with the slightly wide-angle lens beloved by Kubrick and edited with somewhat jarring 180-degree shots/reverse shots, is a place of male bonding and mutual support. The dialogue is punctuated by pauses—a technique that works well here to render sinister the brightly lit scene's ambiance. Grady advises Jack that his son has brought an "outside party" into the deteriorating situation—a "nigger." He also boasts to an appreciative Torrance of having "corrected" both his wife and twin daughters, whom the viewer knows to have been murdered by their father.

Like the bathroom upstairs, where Jack encounters a woman who first seems alluring and then (as in so many "loathly lady" medieval tales) turns out to be a decaying corpse, this one provides a place for male fantasies of sexual and gender power and vulnerability. Jack, we learn from Grady, has "always been the caretaker." But Jack is never shown taking care of the chores assigned him in the hotel—his wife does this. Of what is he the caretaker, then? Jack's mission is to be a caretaker of patriarchy: the hotel becomes more and more the concretization of the institutional power of men. The outsized kitchen and study, which are the man's and woman's domains in the film, seem to speak to just what enormous, even impossible undertakings are the roles of women and men in marriage and in the raising of children. Not surprisingly, Jack will later attempt to kill his wife with an ax as she hides in the bathroom in their suite: the most famous shots from the film feature Jack's sneering face as he announces his presence to Wendy in that bathroom and her gape-jawed horror as she sees the ax break through the door.

The obscene secret between *The Shining*'s white men, Grady and Torrance, clearly regards the subordinate status of women, children, and blacks; the deeper obscenity is that this is an enjoyable task. The hotel is a place, as is the mansion where the orgy takes place in *Eyes Wide Shut*, where wealthy and powerful men have indulged their urges for almost a century—and in *The Shining* this indulgence takes place literally over the dead bodies of the place's original inhabitants. In a throw-away line near the beginning of the film, we learn that the Overlook is built upon an Indian burial ground. The proper disposal of bodies by those who buried them in the ground has been contaminated, desecrated by the erection of the hotel. In a sense, the bodies have now become just so much waste.

Eyes Wide Shut returns to the familiar Kubrickian topos of the couple in the bathroom, and it deals with the problems of marriage and coupling more directly and with greater sexual explicitness than did any of Kubrick's earlier works. In the opening scene, a woman (Alice, played by Nicole Kidman) is sitting on the toilet while her husband, Bill (Tom Cruise), looks for his wallet. As in *Lolita*, this bathroom is a space where marital intimacy is revealed as problematic: despite the frank exposure of her bodily functions to her husband, Alice remains essentially invisible to him. It is not only her physical being that Bill tends to ignore. He will later come to understand that Alice's mental life and sexual desire have existed entirely outside his control or even his knowledge, when she reveals a rich fantasy life that excludes him. The obscene shadow of marriage and bourgeois sexuality is figured as the persistence of desires that threaten monogamy.

Eyes Wide Shut also features another bathroom scene—perhaps the most sumptuous of Kubrick's career—one that follows logically upon the film's pattern of revealing the obscene side of the life of the rich and powerful. It takes place at the home of wealthy attorney Ziegler (Sydney Pollack). Ziegler looks on helplessly as Bill revives a very beautiful but very doped-up prostitute reclining on the velvet couch in the enormous space of the bathroom, which is furnished rather formally, with couch and paintings. The setting is strangely proper, more parlor than toilet. This sense of propriety is undercut, though, by the incongruity of the setting. As the scene progresses, one is overtaken by the uncomfortable feeling that the young woman is lying naked in public, and nearly dead. The rich man's obscene desires remain the same as any other man's: only the setting is plusher. This scene is an interesting variation on one in *Barry Lyndon*, in which Lady Lyndon bathes under the scrutiny of her chambermaids. So, too, in that scene is the passive female body an object of aesthetic admiration—and Kubrick's Lady Lyndon is a far more passive character than the original in William Makepeace Thackeray's novel. The semi-public feeling of the Lady's bathroom, into which Barry intrudes fully dressed and after having committed a sexual peccadillo with a servant, is less shocking than in *Eyes Wide Shut* because its oddity can be ascribed by contemporary audiences to eighteenth-century manners. But in both cases, the bathroom's obscenity is linked to male sexual hypocrisy and sexual acting out.

Issues of gender and identity permeate the bathroom and toilet scenes in *2001*, though more subtly than in some of the films just discussed. Toilets are represented, directly or indirectly, three times in *2001*. On the shuttle to the moon, Floyd encounters the mind-boggling complexity of the "zero gravity toilet," whose instructions are 710 words long. Just how far humans have come from "instinctual" behavior is made humorously clear in this rapidly sketched scene. Floyd, who must read the long instructions before he can use the facilities, is literally being toilet trained.[11] This moment is a good example of the kind of subliminal emotion incited by seemingly calm moments in the film. *2001*'s space voyagers are the most perfectly repressed, finely honed human beings in Kubrick's opus.[12] But the repression of bodily functions in the interest of space-age civilization creates an implicit tension, a kind of drama of the body that continues in one form or another until the end of the film, when Dave is transformed.

The next bathroom mentioned (though not depicted) is the one Floyd's daughter's baby-sitter has gone to when he calls home. Significantly, the person actually "in" the bathroom, though off-screen, is a female subordinate, the caregiver for Floyd's child. *2001* depicts space as a homosocial realm (one made up entirely of men), where women function as serving maids and then disappear entirely. The farther we get from Earth, in fact, the more devoid of the female space becomes. There are no women on *Discovery*, and the star child, in fetal form, appears as though by magic. Parturition occurs with no need for woman or uterus. It appears as if Dave is born by passing through the monolith. Kubrick commented in an interview that "in telling the story [of *2001*,] women didn't seem to have a lot to do with it" and that one "obviously" is not "going to put a woman on the crew."[13] Back on Earth, it is females who inhabit the bathroom, give birth to Heywood Floyd's child, and represent the emotional tug of home. But women, traditionally associated with blood, fluids, and waste—all that pertains to the body in Western culture—have almost no place in the stark cleanliness of space as imagined by Kubrick.

While there are no women on the *Discovery*, critics have frequently made allusion to HAL's effeminacy. Although Kubrick asserted, when asked whether HAL's "wheedling voice [indicated] an undertone of homosexuality," that HAL was a "straight computer," many did perceive him as gay, and I think this cannot be discounted.[14] This is especially true in light of Clarke's astonishing revelation that "Stanley . . . invented the wild idea of slightly fag robots who create a Victorian environment to put our heroes at ease."[15] Kubrick's track record on the representation of homosexuality, like that of women, is somewhat problematic, and as women slowly disappear from *2001*'s narrative, Dave Bowman is almost killed by a computer that comes to seem more and more like a jealous homosexual lover.

The third bathroom in *2001* is the "eighteenth-century" one that Bowman visits in the film's final sequence. Although we never see Dave use the pristine tub or toilet or soil any of the white towels, this space is strangely emphasized. There are seven shots inside or through the doorway of the bathroom during the three minutes of the scene. One shot, where Dave looks out at his older self, who is eating, lasts a full minute. Dave enters the bathroom twice, once as the man in a spacesuit, once as the older man in a dressing gown. It is not a space inhabited by females or couples: it is a place where man confronts himself. As in *Dr. Strangelove*, this bathroom provides the opportunity for a character to examine himself in the mirror, to wonder about his identity and his fate. The bathroom is where Dave goes to study his aging face and to confront the next incarnation of himself. But there is something peculiar about this space, other than the underlighting from the floor and its extraordinary cleanliness. This is actually a twentieth-century bathroom and not a period one.

One could explain this fact as a plot incoherence in many ways, of course. For example, the aliens reading Dave's memories picked up the modern bathroom style rather than one Dave may never have seen. It is possible (though unlikely) that this is simply an oversight on Kubrick's part, amply compensated by the gorgeous and authentic period bathroom in *Barry Lyndon*. But the striking sense that this bathroom is out of place has greater reverberations when placed within the meaning of the scene as a whole. The bathroom's placement in this scene juxtaposes modernity with the eighteenth century in a way that proves to be symptomatic of Kubrick's approach to the problematic notion of progress, figured in *2001* most importantly in the figure of the star child (figures 26–30).

Kubrick's use of setting—including the peculiar juxtaposition of a modern bathroom with a Louis XVI bedroom—in *2001*'s penultimate scene has remained unexamined in some major critical commentaries on Kubrick. The eighteenth-century room where Dave Bowman ages, dies, and is reborn has engendered puzzlement—simply because the allusion to the period of Louis XVI is simultaneously specific (there's no question that the furnishings are from this period) and ungrounded (no textual reason is given for identifying this period) in the film. In his excellent visual analysis of Kubrick's films, Alexander Walker holds:

> [I]t is as irrelevant to question the Louis XVI style as it is to ask why Raphael's angels do not wear shoes. It is no use seeking rational explanations for metaphorical or allegorical situations. The process of events in the room is more important than the end products of its furnishings.[16]

Following Clarke's and Kubrick's descriptions of the room as having been reconstructed by the aliens from Bowman's recollections, Thomas Allen Nelson describes it as representing the "ephemeral nature of Bowman's memory" but also offers no other explanation of the setting.[17]

Knowledge of the broader context of Kubrick's work tells us that the division of identity between reason and violence seen so often as characterizing his films' protagonists finds an important touchstone in the specific historical moment of the eighteenth century. Kubrick privileges this as a period when the exquisiteness of cultural productions was most perfectly matched by the violence upon which they depended. He wanted to make a film about the life of Napoleon, a major figure of the late part of the century, and he returns to the period many times in his existing films, as a setting or reference: in the chateau location of *Paths of Glory*; in the "Gainsborough-like portrait" (Ciment) behind which Quilty takes refuge and dies in *Lolita*; in the setting of *Barry Lyndon*. Eighteenth-century Europe presents the machinery of culture and of the state as violence channeled directly into the production of works of art, as in *Barry Lyndon*, whose intoxicating surface beauty depends on ritualizing violence in the duel, in choreographed warfare, in male oppression of women, in the violent institution of aristocracy.[18] Michel Ciment describes Kubrick's ambivalent infatuation with the period:

> [F]or Kubrick the eighteenth century is rotten to the core, an age awaiting its impending destruction: behind the façade of gaiety, luxury and pleasure, death and disintegration are already lurking. . . . The eighteenth century also saw the conjunction of reason and passion. . . . The perfection principle laid down by the theorists of progress anticipates the notion of the mind's evolution to which nineteenth-century philosophers were so attached: two ideas that are closely linked in *2001*. But, as *2001* and *Dr. Strangelove* demonstrate, pure rationality may end up as totally irrational.[19]

Given this context, the Louis XVI room casts the final scenes of *2001* in a rather bleak light. What, then, are we to make of Kubrick's own comments about the genesis of the star child, who is born on the eighteenth-century bed (figures 15 and 35)? In an interview just after the film's release, for example, Kubrick talked about the evolutionary meaning of *2001*'s last scene:

> In a timeless state, [Bowman's] life passes from middle age to senescence to death. He is reborn, an enhanced being, a star child, an angel, a superman, if you like, and returns to earth prepared for the next leap forward in man's evolutionary destiny.[20]

Not surprisingly, Gelmis followed suit, like many other critics, and describes the star child as evidence of a change of pace for Kubrick: "His oeuvre, with the single exception of the optimistic transfiguration in *2001*, is a bleak skepticism and fatalism."[21] Nelson comments:

> Kubrick's ending does not depart all that much from Clarke's: The orbiting monolith, Bowman's Star-Gate journey, the Ligeti "voices" within the room, the reappearance of the monolith, and Strauss's *Thus Spoke* [*sic*] *Zarathustra* continue visual and aural patterns developed throughout *2001*. They tell the film audience that something "magical" is happening, and that Bowman as homo sapiens is evolving toward some form of spatial/planetary consciousness.[22]

Kubrick, caught up in speculations about immortality, the existence of extraterrestrials, and other contemporary questions, does not hesitate in this interview to represent human evolution as a kind of progress toward a superior life form. For the most part, critics have not sought to contradict the maker of the film. But once again, placing the film in the context of Kubrick's oeuvre may well shift our view. One wonders whether he later changed his mind about the possibility of humans attaining a kind of perfection or—more likely—did not completely understand the depth of his own pessimism while making *2001*.

If the eighteenth century represents the ability of culture to cover the shadow of its own brutality with a layer of reason and decoration, then the twentieth century is the period in which the shadow reemerges. From his eighteenth-century room, Bowman is reborn to the sounds of Richard Strauss's *Thus Spake Zarathustra*, the signature music of the film and music that also was a signature of German fascism. Kubrick, a Jewish polymath with a razor-sharp ear for the cultural connotations of music, was surely aware of Strauss's Nazi affiliations. Is his use of Strauss's music a reappropriation, or is the sense of majesty imparted by the piece finally just ironic? In any event, one cannot witness the "magical" birth of the star child, to the strains of *Zarathustra*'s eerily beautiful fanfare, without some trepidation and, indeed, a questioning of Kubrick's own reading of his work.[23]

In "Fascinating Fascism," Susan Sontag includes *2001* as a "representative work" of fascist art—art, that is, which creates a pageant out of the spectacle of dominators and their worshipful masses.[24] Robert Kolker notes that *2001* "points towards surrender to a hypnotic force and suggests that this surrender is inevitable" and that, for Kubrick, "violence must manifest itself in some form, controlled or uncontrolled"[25]—but he argues persuasively against the reading of the film as endorsing fascism, either in content or in its way of engaging the audience that views it. While a fascist aesthetic encourages audience passivity and plays to the yearning to yield to authority figures, whether human or extraterrestrial, Kubrick's film "offers at least an open narrative and an intellectual space in which the viewer may consider what is going on."[26]

I would say that, far from being a fascist work, *2001* comments on the potential of cultures to believe in absolutes and to give themselves over to "higher powers." Certainly HAL, with a pride in the 9000 series' perfection that seems almost racial, commits a kind of genocide of beings he considers both inferior and threatening. In this way, he repeats the terrible history of eugenics foisted upon the world by Social Darwinists and the fascism that followed in their wake. Certainly, a belief that the monoliths represent some alien super power, rather than symbols of our own imaginative evolution and the violence it engenders betrays our desire to create broadly the very things that we allow to turn against us—as Kubrick demonstrates in film after film.

The star child is not quite an image of humanity reborn, but another version of an enclosed, contained humanity, trapped, perhaps for infinity, in the darkness of space, able only to look, wide-eyed and frightened. He—or It—is, perhaps, the lasting image of the obscene that we have been talking about. Throughout the film, humans have discarded their humanity, their emotions, and finally their reason. At the end, they have shed the very bodies that have carried them and left only a fetal trace.

Epilogue

I want to close this chapter by describing how *Eyes Wide Shut* reiterates and reverses some of *2001*'s most powerful insights.

Eyes Wide Shut, with its emphasis on sterility and repetition, sustains a very different relationship to the obscene shadow of law than do most of Kubrick's films. Like *2001*, it depicts an odyssey but—at least at first glance—a personal rather than an evolutionary one. Shocked when he learns that his wife had considered having an affair with an attractive stranger—a military officer—Bill goes out to seek sexual adventure. For the most part, these adventures are more puzzling than erotic, including a failed encounter with a prostitute and culminating in Bill's uninvited attendance at a lavish orgy. The orgy takes place in a mansion reminiscent both physically and psychologically of the one in *Paths of Glory*. In that eighteenth-century structure, Generals Mireau and Broulard meet over drinks to bargain away the lives of their troops, and under these same generals' eyes the ritualistic trial of the three common soldiers takes place. The circular, chesslike patterns and wide-angle shots of *Paths of Glory*'s and *Full Metal Jacket*'s scapegoating scenes are reiterated in *Eyes Wide Shut*'s depiction of Bill's "trial" for breaching the inner sanctum of the rich and powerful men who are attending the bizarrely ritualistic orgy.

Surrounded by menacing figures offended by his presence and wearing masks reminiscent of the Marquis de Sade's eighteenth century, Bill is redeemed in a theatrical gesture by a naked and lovely prostitute. The obscene desires and rituals of the very wealthy, the lawgivers, are revealed; Bill is cowed and returns to make peace with his wife in a mutually confessional scene. The sacrifice of the French soldiers in *Paths of Glory*, the carnage of the waterhole scene in *2001*, the savage beating of Private Pyle in *Full Metal Jacket*—all have evolved into a gorgeously choreographed but bloodless encounter between the red-garbed judge and the humiliated young doctor.

Both the orgy scene in *Eyes Wide Shut* and the discovery of the monolith on the moon in *2001* are accompanied by eerie music written by composer György Ligeti. But compared to the monolith scene, the orgy seems curiously flat and devoid of any real mystery. The secret of the monolith is not revealed; only its result is, the voyage to "Jupiter and Beyond the Infinite." In *Eyes Wide Shut*, this paradigm has been strangely inverted. The final scene, which does not appear in the early twentieth-century novella by Austrian Arthur Schnitzler, contains Alice's imperative that she and Bill must "fuck" as soon as possible. But more important than this resexualization of marriage (the revelation of marriage's obscene heart) or than the obscene revelations in the mansion or in Ziegler's bathroom and pool room is the fact that the couple and their daughter are shopping, looking at price tags, at the end of the film. The real obscenity in Kubrick's last film is not the law's obscene shadow, the hidden spaces of sordid desire and aggression, but the workings of the machine of capitalism itself. While Schnitzler stressed the power of repressed sexuality to disturb the workings of society, Kubrick normalizes sexuality as integral to the machinery of marriage and law. To this end, the film introduces various financial transactions absent from the novella: for Kubrick, the well-heeled young doctor is always the one to pay. Man, in *Eyes Wide Shut*, has evolved into *homo economicus*, a rational and utilitarian being who carries his reason for being in the very wallet that Bill is looking for at the beginning of the film—hence the irony of the allusions to *The Wizard of Oz* in the film. Bill's "happiness" was always in his own backyard—and pocket. Despite the participation of powerful men in orgies and the blood sacrifices of young women, obscenity is no longer in the shadows. It is out there for all to see; it is money in circulation, a postmodern emptying out of the culturally meaningful narratives of the past, without any resolution of the double binds posed by patriarchy and desire in Kubrick's earlier films. Kubrick's ambivalence toward cultural products ends here, with a deeply unsatisfying look at human platitudes and the shallowness of marital relations—or perhaps with a nod to the small satisfaction Daddy has in finally buying the bush baby for his little girl.

Notes

1. Sigmund Freud, *Civilization and Its Discontents*, trans. and ed. James Strachey (New York: Norton, 1961), 70–71.

2. Slavoj Žižek, *The Metastases of Enjoyment: Six Essays on Woman and Causality* (London and New York: Verso, 1994), 54–79.

3. For further analysis of this scene's structural importance in *Full Metal Jacket*, see Susan White, "Male Bonding, Hollywood Orientalism, and the Repression of the Feminine in Kubrick's *Full Metal Jacket*," in *Inventing Vietnam: The War in Film and Television*, ed. Michael Anderegg (Philadelphia, Pa.: Temple University Press, 1991), 204–30.

4. Michel Chion, *Kubrick's Cinematic Odyssey*, trans. Claudia Gorbman (London: BFI, 2001), 143.

5. Albert Rosenfeld's review of *2001* was, for example, entitled "Perhaps the Mysterious Monolithic Slab Is Really Moby Dick," *Life* (1968), reprinted in *The Making of* 2001: A Space Odyssey, ed. Stephanie Schwam (New York: Modern Library, 2000), 166–70.

6. See Ellis Hanson, "Technology, Paranoia and the Queer Voice," *Screen* 34, no. 2 (Summer 1993): 137–61.

7. Robert Kolker, *A Cinema of Loneliness: Penn, Stone, Kubrick, Scorsese, Spielberg, Altman*, 3d ed. (New York: Oxford University Press, 2000), 125.

8. See Michel Foucault, *Discipline and Punish: The Birth of the Prison*, trans. Alan Sheridan (New York: Vintage, 1995).

9. Kolker, *Cinema of Loneliness*, 106, 119.

10. Slavoj Žižek, *The Plague of Fantasies* (London and New York: Verso, 1997), 21.

11. Hanson, "Technology, Paranoia and the Queer Voice," 144.

12. Kolker notes that "Kubrick's men [in *2001*] are . . . perfectly integrated into corporate technology, part of the circuitry. . . . The people in the film lack expression and reaction not because they are wearing masks to cover a deep and forbidding anguish. . . . They are merely incorporated into a 'mission.'" (*Cinema of Loneliness*, 135). For a more detailed reading of the meaning of bathrooms in Kubrick's films, see Philip Kuberski, "Plumbing the Abyss: Stanley Kubrick's Bathrooms," *Arizona Quarterly* 60, no. 4 (Winter 2004): 139–60.

13. Kubrick quoted in Charlie Kohler, "Stanley Kubrick Raps," *East Village Eye* (1968), reprinted in Schwam, *The Making of* 2001, 250.

14. Kubrick quoted in *Stanley Kubrick Interviews*, ed. Gene D. Phillips (Jackson: University Press of Mississippi, 2001), 94. In "Technology, Paranoia and the Queer Voice," Hanson cites Don Daniel: "HAL's faggoty TV-announcer tones and vocabulary become the disembodied voice of three centuries of scientific rationalism" (142).

15. Arthur C. Clarke, "Christmas, Shepperton," in Schwam, *The Making of* 2001, 37.

16. Alexander Walker, with Sybil Taylor and Ulrich Ruchti, *Stanley Kubrick, Director: A Visual Analysis* (New York: Norton, 1999), 191.

17. Thomas Allen Nelson, *Kubrick: Inside a Film Artist's Maze*, rev. ed. (Bloomington and Indianapolis: Indiana University Press, 2000), 177.

18. As Robert Kolker notes in *Cinema of Loneliness*, "The quiet, civilized artifice of late seventeenth- and early eighteenth-century French art embodies a code of polite behavior in sharp contradiction to the brutal codes of military order and justice played out in *Paths of Glory*" (155).

19. Michel Ciment, *Kubrick: The Definitive Edition*, trans. Gilbert Adair and Robert Bononno (New York: Faber and Faber, 2003), 64, 66, 67. The discussion of the eighteenth century here inevitably recalls Adorno and Horkheimer's *Dialectic of Enlightenment*, which traces the roots of some forms of oppression to the very technological and ideological "advances" brought about by science and culture in the eighteenth century. Its scathing critique of the twentieth-century culture industry derives from the view of the Enlightenment as a failure. See Theodor W. Adorno and Max Horkheimer, *Dialectic of Enlightenment: Philosophical Fragments* (Palo Alto, Calif.: Stanford University Press, 2000).

20. Kubrick quoted in Joseph Gelmis, *The Film Director as Superstar* (Garden City, N.Y.: Doubleday, 1970), 304.

21. Gelmis, *The Film Director as Superstar*, 293.

22. Nelson, *Kubrick: Inside a Film Artist's Maze*, 133.

23. One critic who has discussed in depth the political and social meaning of the music in *2001* is Geoffrey Cocks, who also comments on Richard Strauss's connection to the Nazi regime. Geoffrey Cocks, *The Wolf at the Door: Stanley Kubrick, History, and the Holocaust* (New York: Lang, 2004).

24. Kolker, *Cinema of Loneliness*, 139, cites Susan Sontag, "Fascinating Fascism," in *Movies and Methods*, vol. 1, ed. Bill Nichols (Berkeley: University of California Press, 1976), 40.

25. Kolker, *Cinema of Loneliness*, 143.

26. Kolker, *Cinema of Loneliness*, 144.

Bibliography

Adler, Renata. "Review of *2001: A Space Odyssey*." *New York Times*, April 4, 1968. Reprinted in *The Making of* 2001: A Space Odyssey, ed. Stephanie Schwam. New York: Modern Library, 2000.

Adorno, Theodor, and Max Horkheimer. "The Culture Industry: Enlightenment as Mass Deception." In *The Dialectic of Enlightenment: Philosophical Fragments*, trans. E. Jephcott (Stanford: Stanford University Press, 2002).

Althusser, Louis. "Ideology and Ideological State Apparatuses (Notes Towards an Investigation)." In *Lenin and Philosophy, and Other Essays*. Trans. Ben Brewster, 127–87. London: New Left, 1971.

Benjamin, Walter. *Charles Baudelaire: A Lyric Poet in the Era of High Capitalism*. Trans. Harry Zohn. New York: Verso, 1997.

Chion, Michel. *Kubrick's Cinematic Odyssey*. Trans. Claudia Gorbman. London: BFI, 2001.

Ciment, Michel. *Kubrick: The Definitive Edition*. Trans. Gilbert Adair and Robert Bononno. New York: Faber and Faber, 2003.

Clarke, Arthur C. *2001: A Space Odyssey*. New York: Signet, 1968.
Cocks, Geoffrey. *The Wolf at the Door: Stanley Kubrick, History, and the Holocaust*. New York: Lang, 2004.
Gramsci, Antonio. *Selections from the Prison Notebooks*. London: Lawrence & Wishart, 1971.
Hall, Stuart. "Encoding/Decoding." In *Culture, Media, Language: Working Papers in Cultural Studies 1972–79*. Ed. Stuart Hall, Dorothy Hobson, Andrew Lowe, and Paul Willis. London: Unwin Hyman, 1980.
Hasford, Gustav. *The Short-Timers*. New York: Bantam, 1983.
Holtman, Robert B. *The Napoleonic Revolution*. New York: Lippincott, 1967.
Johnston, Ian. "Introductory Lecture on Freud's *Civilization and Its Discontents*." January 1993. Available at http://www.mala.bc.ca/~johnstoi/introser/freud.htm.
Kael, Pauline. "Review of *2001: A Space Odyssey*." *Harper's*, February 1969. Reprinted in *The Making of* 2001: A Space Odyssey, ed. Stephanie Schwam. New York: Modern Library, 2000.
Kolker, Robert. *A Cinema of Loneliness: Penn, Stone, Kubrick, Scorsese, Spielberg, Altman*, 3d ed. New York: Oxford University Press, 2000.
Kuberski, Philip. "Plumbing the Abyss: Stanley Kubrick's Bathrooms." *Arizona Quarterly* 60, no. 4 (Winter 2004): 139–60.
Pizzato, Mark. "Beauty's Eye: Erotic Masques of the Death Drive in *Eyes Wide Shut*." In *Lacan and Contemporary Film*. Ed. Todd McGowan and Sheila Kunkle. New York: Other, 2004.
Rosenfeld, Albert. "Perhaps the Mysterious Monolithic Slab Is Really Moby Dick." *Life*, 1968. Reprinted in Stephanie Schwam, ed., *The Making of 2001: A Space Odyssey*. New York: Modern Library, 2000.
Schnitzler, Arthur. *Dream Novel* (*Traumnovelle*). In Stanley Kubrick and Frederic Raphael, *Eyes Wide Shut: A Screenplay*. New York: Time Warner, 1999.
Žižek, Slavoj. *The Fright of Real Tears: Krzysztof Kieślowski between Theory and Post-Theory*. London: BFI, 2001.
———. *The Plague of Fantasies*. London: Verso, 1997.
———. "Superego by Default." In *The Metastases of Enjoyment*. London: Verso, 1994. 54–79.

Double Minds and Double Binds in Stanley Kubrick's Fairy Tale

GEORGE TOLES

> Obviously space is our destiny, that much I concede. After all I live there myself. But the excitement of the great voyages of discovery will pass me by; I will always belong to those who are left behind on the quay waving goodbye to the departing; I belong to the past, to the time before Armstrong put his big corrugated footstep on the face of the moon. That was another thing I got to see that afternoon, for without thinking anything in particular I had drifted into a sort of theater where there was a film about space travel. I found myself sitting in one of those American swivel chairs that hug you like a womb, and setting off on my journey through space. Almost immediately tears came to my eyes. . . . Emotion ought to be inspired by art, and here I was being misled by reality; some technical wizard had worked optical magic to strew the lunar gravel at our feet, so that it was just as if we ourselves were standing on the moon and walking around. In the distance shone (!) the unimaginable planet Earth. How could there ever have been a Homer or Ovid to write about the fate of gods or men on that ethereal, silvery, floating disc? I could

smell the dead dust at my feet, I saw the puffs of moon powder whirl upward and settle again. I was divested of my being, and no substitute was in the offing. Whether the humans all about me were having the same sensation I do not know. It was deathly quiet. We were on the moon and we would never get there; in a while we would step outside into the shrill daylight and go our separate ways on a disc no bigger than a guilder, a free-floating object adrift somewhere in the black drapery of space. . . . Off went the *Voyager*, a futile, man-made machine, a gleaming spider in empty space, wafting past lifeless planets, where sorrow had never existed except perhaps for the pain of rocks groaning under an unbearable burden of ice, and I wept. The *Voyager* sailed away from us into eternity, emitting a bleep every now and then and taking photographs of all those gelid or fiery but ever lifeless spheres which, together with the orb we must live on, revolve round a flaming bubble of gas; and the amplifiers, placed invisibly around us in the dark theater, sprayed us with sound in a desperate attempt to corrupt the silence of the solitary metallic voyager. A compelling, velvety voice began speaking, at first making itself heard through the music, then as a solo instrument. In ninety thousand years' time, the voice intoned, the *Voyager* would have reached the outer limits of our galaxy. There was a pause, the music swelled like toxic surf, and fell silent again to allow the voice to fire a parting shot: "And then, maybe, we will know the answer to our eternal questions."

The humanoids in the theater cringed.

"Is there anyone out there?"

All around me it was as quiet now as in the deserted streets of the universe across which the *Voyager* hurtled noiselessly, bathed in a cosmic glow, and only in the fifth of its ninety thousand years. Ninety thousand! By that time the ashes of the ashes of our ashes would long since have disowned our provenance. We would have never been there! The music gathered momentum, pus oozed from my eyes. How about that for a metamorphosis! The voice gave forth one final burst: "Are we all alone?"

—CEES NOOTEBOOM, *The Following Story*

Herman Mussert, a man who doesn't know that he is dying, is the narrator of this austerely afflicting passage from Cees Nooteboom's novel. Herman's unreliable memory lights upon a metal surrogate for his (and our) loneliest self, bleeping through its forlorn voyage past "lifeless planets." The dying man lies in a bed in Amsterdam, cast adrift among his last unspooling thoughts. He seeks to postpone as long as possible the recognition that he has come to the end of consciousness, the end of a personal "now." Something else—bearing perhaps a tiny bead of sorrow—is taking over, assigning his matter "other duties" as it embarks, free of Herman, on its "endless wanderings."[1] I recall that, when first reading these paragraphs, with mortality licking at the edges of every phrase, two images from Stanley Kubrick's *2001* came forcefully to mind. In the first, Frank Poole is making his lengthy jog through the rotating centrifuge of the *Discovery*, occasionally punching at the air. Perhaps he is issuing a mild protest against the white "hamster wheel" environment and its tedium, but the punching does not cause him to break the steady pace of his run. Aram Khatchaturian's *Gayne Ballet Suite* accompanies Frank's round-and-round indoor journey, supplying a mournful commentary on the action, to which Frank himself has no access. If his thoughts are on music, that is to say, he is humming a different tune. The suffering violins of Khatchaturian might help give form to his inchoate feelings, if he could but hear them (figure 18).

The second *2001* image summoned by the Nooteboom passage also involves Frank. He is once again signaling protest with his hands. He desperately fumbles with his severed air hose as his spacesuit-armored body floats off beautifully, helplessly, negligibly into space. Who has ever had such a death? In this episode, there is no sound to cushion or explain the fall. What is to be understood is that a suddenly anonymous death is happening and that there is no room in so much immensity (all this "black drapery of space") for a personal experience of dying to penetrate. Frank's going seems not to make even the faintest mark, or if there is a mark to bear in mind, how do we turn it to some account? (Later, the negligibility effect is redoubled when Frank's body is retrieved by his partner and held fast in the metallic arms of a pod, only to be abandoned once more.) As my reading experience led me rather capriciously back to Frank in *2001*, I wondered why I had never before registered the depth of the Kubrick film's melancholy. Like so much else in this imperiously aloof, well-sealed pod of a narrative, the melancholy seems somehow veiled.

2001, from the time of its 1968 release, has seemed to be many different films. That is to say, it is a work unusually receptive to drastically conflicting emotional and intellectual responses. If one is so inclined, it is easy to dwell excitedly on the film's presentation of the human potential for transformation and rebirth, on heavenly bodies in perfect alignment, and on the existence of hidden alien benefactors, sending magical milestones to us at crucial stages in our journey to enlightenment. In this version of the story, the triumphalism of Strauss's *Also Sprach Zarathustra* fanfare can be made to stand for the arc of the movie as a whole: a slightly chilly musical stargate to the reign of wonder. However, as other commentaries on *2001* amply attest, there is no form of pessimism or irony about human doings and prospects for undoing that the narrative is not equally adept at confirming. It is a movie tailor-made for viewers who like to work conceptually rather than experientially. Yet, as the legendary "trip" movie of the 1960s, it has frequently been championed as "a film for groovin', not understanding."[2] Pauline Kael famously threw up her hands in exasperation at what she took to be Kubrick's willful amorphousness and decried the film's "celebration of cop-out."[3]

I have gradually come to believe that the film is authentically haunted by a need to see (and think) double at every stage of its unfolding. Kubrick sets out to build a kind of lavish, inhuman utopia (pitching camp at the far edge of humanness), which answers to some deep private image and need. But he is steadily at war with his utopian impulses and distrusts all of the forces at work in this fantasy space, as well as the rational schemes for utopia devised by *any* planner. He endeavors to hatch pictures worth marveling at from glistening black eggs, turning the movie screen itself on end and making its white surface into an impenetrable black slab. Instead of receiving images on its "open" surface, the black screen sends out urgent signals—triggered by sunlight—which no one has quite the aptitude, or properly formed mind, to interpret. As women recede into the narrative background (robotic, distracted, or patiently relearning to walk as they facilitate service), birth imagery involving various metal begetters and techno-conduits pushes insistently into the gap that the female fade-out has left. An androgynous computer, the film's only complex character, experiments with mysteries of humanness just beyond his ken—and learns what it means to be human as the men around him seem to find the category outmoded. His baptism as a person occurs in the acts of being conspired against and slowly killed. The more recognizable candidates for our human representatives in *2001* seem to be burdened with the film's own reticence about self-disclosure. They are woven into a system that doesn't quite fit or suit them, but they have difficulty gaining a clear sense of what feels wrong. It is as difficult in this film's world to see where you are and to consider what your actual present placement feels like as to imagine your way backward or forward to something else. Dave, Frank, and Dr. Floyd seem more reconciled to the "now" than most of us are, but everything in and outside of their metal cages conspire to make the now feel cramped and oppressive.

Finally, there is the doubleness having to do with the force of revelation itself. Revelation seems always pending or actually in process in *2001*, but the film exhibits a simultaneous terror, like the prospect of facing a Medusa, about what, of necessity, must come forth. Dave's arrested-in-panic frozenness as he hurtles through the Stargate at warp speed is instructive somehow about the sizable death fear that accompanies every impulse to open the eyes wide and see *beyond*. Everything in *2001* wishes to be disclosed and veiled at the same time. The face of the film is a face covered by a reflecting helmet or a trembling ape mask, while some shadow of the ravenous leopard prowls the desert in our midst. The most auspicious gesture that Kubrick sanctions when revelation looms is a blind reaching out of the hand (as if supplicating) toward something huge, indefinite, and quite possibly malign. The consistent requirement for such reaching up—through emptiness—is that the one with arm extended cannot know, and probably should not trust, what is in store.

2001 is as much fairy tale as science fiction. Since the latter genre is too entranced, for my taste, with hardware and solemn, flavorless ruminations about "things to come," I will use the fairy tale as my point of entry to Kubrick's magical thinking. *2001*'s double-mindedness is akin to the vexing riddles that the unseasoned, frequently emotionally disturbed questers of German Romantic tales in particular are obliged to solve, often with their lives held forfeit. Riddles commonly unfold in stages, and as one moves from chamber to chamber in the alien fortress designed expressly for one's riddle trial, new properties of enigma are annexed to old ones. What initially seemed a route to placidity and the safety of sound judgment, for example, might well become a nest of fears in a trice. But then, very soon, agitations may impart their own quality of keenness to sight.

The most remarkable fairy tales are deeply interested in the separate claims and values attached to remembering and forgetting. Hugo von Hoffmansthal's majestic prose fragment *Andreas* (part fairy tale, part *Bildungsroman*) ceaselessly probes what he calls "the abysslike contradictions [between remembering and forgetting] upon which life is built, like the Delphic temple over its bottomless split in the earth."[4] According to David Miles, in his seminal study of *Andreas*:

> [C]hange, in Hoffmansthal's vocabulary, belongs to the realm of the amoral adventurer; it is "living one's life" to the full, as he puts it. "Whoever wants to live must transcend himself, must change"; in a word, "he must forget." The moral category of steadfastness and fidelity [for the committed adventurer] can only mean "stagnation and death." The tragic dilemma arises when we . . . realize that "all human dignity is bound up with steadfastness, with not forgetting, with faithfulness."[5]

In *2001*, the new regime of steadfastness in space seems to have required the loosening or wearing away of ties to a former steadfastness on Earth. The space adventurers have not so much renounced their old dependencies as lost track of them. Earthly attachments seem to be drifting, in a way that seems almost natural, out of the reach of memory. Fidelity is a visible shipboard virtue. We see crew members on the *Discovery*, and elsewhere, unblinkingly given over to the performance of routines. These explorers seem to have learned how to sleep wide awake, lulled by the rhythms of tasks which require little effort but supply a "good enough," future-serving logic to keep them more or less occupied. Steadfastness is for them at best a mode of surface recall—with something dim and untoward pressing intermittently for recognition, like a lonely smoke signal from the interior. Steadfast too, but at an even further remove from usable memory, is the hibernating trio of crew members in their *A.I.*-like Sleeping Beauty coffins. Finally, there is the overarching steadfastness of HAL 9000, a computer that has taken over most of the work of memory, and its attendant anxieties, from the *Discovery* crew members. They acquiesce in the idea of a necessary transfer of memory power. HAL will remember fully, dispassionately, faultlessly what needs to be kept in mind and coordinated, so that the ship can complete its complicated mission.

The moral category of fidelity, then, comes down to the crew's acceptance of the obligation to attend to HAL's mild requirements. In exchange, they can indulge the fantasy that HAL is their servant rather than their superior. Dave and Frank listen to him as if to an echo chamber of memories and reflections that once were situated inside them. It seems fitting, under these new conditions, that their powers of retention live a bit further away from themselves than they once did, since this distance (or inner gap) coincides so comfortably with the view from the spacecraft window. As they peer "outdoors," imposing objects occasionally meet (or, more likely, overwhelm) their gaze, but the scale of what they confront repeatedly suggests the irrelevancy of human vision to the act of seeing. What is there is too remote or manifestly impersonal for intimate inspection. The eye's attempts at a grander vision equal to the demands of outer space are quickly vanquished. In the face of experiential impotence and a heightened passivity to circumstances which, after all, are unrelated to *our* way of living, humans' best recourse is to convert inhospitable sense impressions to cold data. Even indoors, with transmissions from faraway family members reminding the astronauts of birthdays and childhood, gift-giving pledges and eventual homecomings, the images are stubbornly impenetrable—as though they too are best regarded as data, not the soft stuff of emotionalized memory.

Here is the fairytale plight of the human crew members of the *Discovery*, and perhaps of HAL as well. They are embarked on a journey through a seemingly infinite dark wood (a billion miles to the moons of Jupiter), in answer to a mysterious, "supernatural" summons whose intention is unclear. Like the untried youths who set off for a distant kingdom to perform impossible tasks and solve daunting riddles, the figures on the fragile transport have no advance sense of readiness. They have virtually no idea what to expect and thus for what to prepare themselves. Like their fairytale counterparts, they may well prove to be expendable because of something they lack, inwardly, or because their equipment is missing some vital component. The men place their faith in a higher mechanical being who, like a cooperative genie from a bottle, is pledged (forced) to look after their interests. So much in the world of fairy tales has to do with the ability to recall and honor a core simplicity, the willingness to trust, instinctively, the right signs at the right moments, and the gift of listening. Before one can listen, of course, one must be lucky enough to encounter the right, undeceiving guides. Yet, for all the emphasis on the possession of uncorrupted instincts, there is a core ruthlessness to the fairytale world as well. One must be prepared to relinquish any ally at the first evidence of misstep or dubious counsel. If a comrade (even a sibling) is compromised, he is instantly, *fatally* compromised, and one must dispose of him calmly, with no remorse or backward glance. Fairytale seekers are all "amoral adventurers" in essence, forsaking every connection that blurs their view of the task at hand. They live thinly and without surprise in the externally vivid predicament of the now. And for Kubrick, the now is seldom disengaged from the quester's habitual blindness. The external vividness may be present, but it's out of reach. The now is a repeating lonely instant in which our mortal coil, improperly attuned to both its aptitudes and insufficiency, continues to unravel.

Like Bassanio in Shakespeare's *The Merchant of Venice*, the weakly provisioned adventurers in *2001* stake their future on the choice of plain lead caskets rather than gaudy, enticing cases rich in ornament. That is to say, the *Discovery* has already left behind the sensuous pleasures and deceptions of Earth. Both the crewmen's chill means of conveyance and the monolith they unwittingly seek are formed of sober, stark metal. Spacecraft and magic object alike instruct the decidedly unfanciful travelers to wean themselves from the gratification of the senses, one by one. If they were to raise a toast to the moons of Jupiter, it would undoubtedly be with powdered champagne. In the "Dawn of Man" prologue, the lead casket is already in play; it is already designated the correct choice in the fairytale riddle that animates the whole narrative. Though our ape-men forebears, like the space travelers who succeed them, have no comprehension of the monolith when it stands before them, they are compelled to choose it, to reach out and touch it, to receive its imprint (figure 19). The first choosing seems to interpose a barrier between animal instincts (in Kubrick's depiction, a grim amalgam of fear and helpless rage) and the virtually blank slate reserved for reasoning. One of *2001*'s only moments of creaturely joy comes at the pivot point between the chaotic, defenseless, undifferentiated life of the ape pack and Moon-Watcher's literal taking hold of an object/idea which will separate and isolate him. One way of describing this breakthrough is as a transplanting of the barrier from outside to inside. Think of the monolith, paradoxically light resistant and triggered by light—which embodies this barrier—suddenly entering the mind, creating a new division in human consciousness. Moon-Watcher, the first beneficiary of this double mind, goes off by himself, *experiences* his privacy, and acquires a secret within that private domain. The secret has to do with power that doesn't need to be shared. The acceleration of consciousness and the accompanying crescendo of Moon-Watcher's feelings are visually expressed by his smashing down of a likeness of an enemy. Moon-Watcher does not explode in feral excitement because his world opens up to him. He instead discovers the joy of enclosure. He enters a fresh mental cave where the darkness of having secrets combines with the thrill of psychic separation. How exalting it is to increase one's sense of differentiation from others while hiding behind a dense screen inside the self. The tossing of the bone weapon heavenward and the lifting of the gaze and the body from ground level are laden with the irony of the human mind instantly falling under an enchantment. The individual will flexes its muscles and, as the mind watches, it grows ill. It is as though the "I," in becoming "I," becomes a virus or pestilence as well. The sickness is not easily detected by the self because it is as foundational as mortality. Moon-Watcher commits his weapon to memory as he elatedly disavows solidarity, the instinct to connect. He comes into his own by looking away from the Earth for an image worthy of his new dream of self. If Moon-Watcher were a poet, he might contrive lines in the spirit of Jean-Baptiste Chassignet's "Retourne le Miroir": "If you love heaven, in heaven you will be / If you love earth, to earth you will fall."[6]

The *Discovery* adventurers made their choice of the lead casket in this fairy tale long ago, through their surrogate, Moon-Watcher. He launched the exchange of miserable animal instincts for a dramatic sense of himself and an impending (always impending) revelation of the godhead. Moon-Watcher, the primeval king in this tale, begins to divest himself of the memory of what he has been. To become something greater, he must over time erect a barrier (as opaque as possible) between himself and the instincts that enslaved him. He creates a self by clearing a wide enough space in consciousness so that he can be safely alone, as removed from others as from the forgotten life of instinct. Moon-Watcher, and his descendants, will use weapon advantage, and the array of technologies that flow from it, to gain more distance and more clarity about their fruitful relation to instruments of all sorts. Man will "clean himself' in the exercise of reason, and in the act of cleaning himself will also fashion pictures of order that he can live by. The space adventurers keep faith with the old king's dream of order, his taciturn ways, and his fantasy of insulating himself through his relation to powerful objects. As I have noted, they are sailing in an elaborate metal crate (a "full metal jacket," if you like) to a rendezvous with the ancient opaque form whose spiritual hardness is already within them. An internal monolith, in other words, monitors their barrier-multiplying "final round" of humanness. The riddle of Kubrick's tale of enchantment has to do with earning a transcendent expansion of the field of consciousness through an ever-more-drastic regimen of contraction.

The theater of the human, which we encounter at the turn of a new century and millennium, seems to require an exceedingly small stage to play out its concerns. Dr. Floyd, Dave, and Frank are clearly old hands at the business of winnowing away demonstrable needs, interests, affections. Spoken language has receded as a force upon which these men depend to color or imaginatively engage with their social-mechanical sphere. They seem to be spinning invisible cocoons for themselves—somewhat akin to the hibernation boxes occupied by the *Discovery*'s more advanced specialists. One might argue that, for Kubrick, there is an art, as well as an irony, in their reducing their resources and vital signs. I'm reminded of Frank O'Hara's in-earnest joke: "nobody should experience anything they don't need to."[7] The men we are invited to watch become less soft through their almost monklike discipline of forgetting. They are slowly rendering themselves compatible to an environment that will perhaps demand something new, something other than the mess of mistakes (unclean!) humans have already made of themselves. The implication is that the grossly imperfect human attainments of the past—one failed system after another—no longer count for anything. To insist on measuring ourselves by these deforming memories stymies our movement toward a more radical metamorphosis.

2001 is deeply captivated by that final, gleaming chamber of the altered mind, with its adjoining bathroom, in which a shriveled, bedridden Dave has his dying vision—a seeing through lead, as it were (figures 23 and 27). I associate this episode of release with the moment authored by Lewis Carroll when Alice is at last tiny enough to pass through the Wonderland door. This previously hemmed-in space at the bottom of a tunnel suddenly expands to receive her, and she floats through the opening on a tide composed of her eyes' own fluids. The whole *Odyssey* narrative is committed, like Carroll's fantasy of Wonderland, to metamorphosis without warning. In Dave's case, Kubrick proposes the abandonment of the peasant rags of mortal frailty for something sturdier, less *exposed*. Kubrick seems of two minds, however, about whether his star child is a radiant godhead or another version of Rosemary's baby. (Roman Polanski's film, as it happens, was released almost concurrently with *2001*.) The feel of the moment when the monolith opens up to the glowing bubble of Dave reborn is undeniably transcendent, as though we were privileged to witness a clean lift away from all of the barriers that consciousness has devised to keep us captive in the cell of ego. At last the eye, with a fetus wrapped inside it, is granted the *reach*, the boundless power of extension that the Romantic imagination has always craved. Yet Kubrick cannot stay reconciled for more than the duration of two lengthy shots (i.e., the space of two elevated thoughts) to any Romantic impulse. Something slouches through the heavens waiting to be born, and that pending emergent figure is Janus-faced. It looks simultaneously toward glory and desolation. On the one hand, the unspoiled, still-sheathed star child, nearly equal in magnitude to the nearby Earth, its plaything, revives the age-old dream of perfectibility. On the other hand, as it slowly revolves to face us, it intimates a persisting negative fate—the counterdream of original sin (figure 35).

The cold blue light that infiltrates our prolonged star child sighting does not release the image from the hold of skepticism. Kubrick cannot quite surrender himself, or us, to the faith that comes with a true forgetting of our crippled consciousness and all of the evils to which it is heir. "There is, after all, so much grit at the bottom of the [consciousness] container," Iris Murdoch has one of her characters declare in *The Black Prince*, and "almost all of our natural preoccupations are low ones."[8] To have faith in the star child as a pristine, higher phase of being may well require too much vulnerability—which, for Kubrick, is usually synonymous with gullibility. Better perhaps to recognize an unvanquished curse in a cunning new disguise. Kubrick gestures movingly toward a release from our mind-forged manacles, but as he considers the star child's potential, it turns, almost of its own accord, into an image of control. Control in a double sense: Kubrick's control of the child's seeing, as its gaze becomes sentient and (possibly) secretive, and the star child's taking control over us. The movement from infant softness to a sense of command takes only moments to accomplish.

If we affirm the star child as a fit emblem of our collective rebirth, the affirmation must be made in a spirit of openness and unthinking trust. We must feel our way past Kubrick's instinctive dependence on fortifications and displays of deadly power. If Samuel Beckett, say, were to find a place in his death's cradle, endlessly rocking, for a star child that death cannot instantly lay hold of and croon to nothingness, what would his readers do with it? It is no easier, I think, to find a vocabulary to extol a mechanical, motherless Kubrick space baby in a uterine helmet. This child gazes like a fledgling predator on a world it has nearly outgrown. Having described the effect of the final images so negatively, I am immediately aware that I have framed the ending of *2001* as too decisively forbidding. I have given "wonder-proof" reason full permission to close up the space of mystery. A corrective adjustment would lead the viewer to pay closer attention to the spirit of metamorphosis that is in the air for the entire last section of the film, and recall that Kubrick is staking everything on our willingness to float patiently, in a state of unknowing, bereft of narrative and rational supports. What pins things together is the myth of resurrection. One cannot discount the calm authority with which our fears of old age and dying are addressed, then magically alleviated. Dave passes swiftly into a condition of prostrate decrepitude, then emerges on the other side of a barrier, glowing with light and boundless untapped energy. It is with *these* eyes, the final images seem to proclaim, that the journey of this narrative should be viewed. The star child attains the purified awareness, free of time-bound constraints and poisonous confusion, required to carry us forward to a better place. Perhaps this higher sight can redeem our through-a-glass-darkly viewing of the movie that is drawing to a close.

Yet, once again, this pushing toward fairytale (or Blakean) fulfillment feels too emphatically benign. The cerebrally driven tableaux that map our route to the star child don't quite earn a true release or breakthrough. There is an extraordinary tug-of-war going on between imaginative intuition, with its gift for wild, irrational leaps, and cautious brain power, with a will and need to dominate. In his *Notes on Cinematography*, director Robert Bresson offers some remarkable observations on the value, indeed the necessity, in film of images being transformed on contact with other images. He identifies a danger in making images that are too self-involved, enamored with what they can express by way of ideas on their own:

> If an image, looked at by itself, expresses something sharply, if it involves an interpretation, it will not be transformed on contact with other images. The other images will have no power over it, and it will have no power over the other images. Neither action, nor reaction. It is definitive and unusable in the cinematographer's system.[9]

A later entry urges the director to "stick exclusively to impressions, to sensations. No intervention of intelligence which is foreign to these impressions and sensations."[10] Bresson's guidelines for a properly expressive cinema are as personal and fallible as anyone else's, but I find it intriguing how deeply his assumptions come into conflict with Kubrick's.

Kubrick's individual images, to a greater degree than the images of most directors, aspire to self-sufficiency, to the lucid character of a firmly articulated thought. Toward the end of *2001*, for example, the emphasis on shot-to-shot disjunction steadily increases, and not only because the space-time continuum is being reconfigured in Dave's estranged consciousness. Bresson speaks about images being transformed on contact with other images. Kubrick, in contrast, stubbornly asserts the integrity of each shot idea carefully composing itself out of appropriate materials. His style is about maintaining shot boundaries and denying ease of carryover or continuity. It seems fair to say that Kubrick's form does not naturally serve the transforming tendencies of film. Each image holds its separate domain for as long as possible, like a platoon holding a hill, and does not surrender what it has made its own to what comes after. Kubrick considers it appropriate to defend the separate image (in advance) against the power that the following image will assert. In this respect, to shift metaphors, each shot resembles a chess move. The player/director balances the necessity of thinking ahead against all of the possible ways that the current shot (move) might be vulnerable, or even fatally in error. Film, for Kubrick, is not about how one thing, or set of impressions, naturally gives way to another. Like HAL, Kubrick keeps the pod doors between images self-protectively sealed.

As every tale in Ovid's *Metamorphoses* confirms, transformation entails loss of control, a violent disruption of established boundaries, and promiscuous mixtures of native and outcast elements. To put it in terms of one of Kubrick's recurring bathroom settings (figures 26–30), metamorphosis is like a backed-up toilet suddenly disgorging a mass of heterogeneous ingredients, hideously familiar and also unrecognizable. Kubrick is entranced by metamorphosis—as both *2001* and *The Shining* make clear—but he is temperamentally at odds with its untrammeled energy. He is a careful tactician specializing in controlled eruptions, in which purity of form somehow prevails over any release of chaos. While Kubrick can imagine breakdowns in every conceivable system, he designs a better overseer than HAL in all of his narratives to make the apprehension of the terrible and the transcendent geometrically elegant. The narrative world may fall into complete disorder, but the artist's machinery of demonstration will not—not for an instant. Kubrick stays close enough to human turmoil to register its dangers, but the dangers are finally rendered abstract by the cool remoteness of his method of surveillance. The camera probes and is relentlessly vigilant, but it strives to avoid the temptation of identification. (Here, it seems to me, is the most crucial distinction between Kubrick's and Hitchcock's formalisms.)

In lieu of promoting identification with his characters, Kubrick grants them the comparative stability of grotesques and puppets. Alex in *A Clockwork Orange* (1971) comes closest to being an identification figure, but he seems to me the major, and to some degree, accidental exception to the Kubrick rule, especially in the director's post-*Spartacus* (1960) career. Kubrick characters are often subjected to great suffering and distress, but their sense of themselves as suffering beings generally does not count for much. The pain they undergo is not transferred to the spectator, except as an idea. Kubrick characters may resemble us at times without making significant emotional claims on us, because we are not invited inside them. They exhibit the kind of hard efficiency and cryptic flatness of figures in a tale by the brothers Grimm. We are intended to contemplate their actions and responses without the distractions of enforced intimacy. Kubrick clarifies what is *wrong* with his characters, almost mathematically, and we participate in the process of figuring them out—making a diagnosis—as we watch them enact their system-dictated ailments.

At times we enter the electric field of their fear, rage, or cruelty, but in my experience the participation is almost impersonally with the emotion itself, rather than with the character gripped by it. It is a common occurrence for spectators to metamorphose (after a fashion) into movie characters, slipping over the line into a kind of dream-melding of self and figure on-screen. As they penetrate some vital secret of a character's psyche, they may feel penetrated themselves, thus reclaiming their own secret in the guise of looking at someone else's. This productive fusion and jumble is, as a rule, foreign to Kubrick's approach. He seems to have minimal curiosity about the vast middle range of human experience, and what is at stake there. In *Eyes Wide Shut* (1999), he ventures into this middle range as though it were a dream. Only when the secure moorings of Bill and Alice's marital waking life dissolve can Kubrick devise points of entry into "ordinary" behavior.

The star child, while clearly linked to Dave's sojourn in the Louis XVI bedroom, does not depend on this figure being broken down emotionally. It does not emerge from a prior phase of havoc. The metamorphoses (first, from youthful Dave to old man, then from old man to fetus) are about breaks or puzzling turns in a controlled sequence of thought. We share Dave's perplexity in the bedroom, for example, as though he (and we) had been given a knotty problem to work out. But we are not obliged to join Dave as he is wrenched away from himself and undergoes a ghastly series of shocks. Rational consciousness is at no point given the slip, even though familiar categories are undone and transformation is well under way. A calm, sovereign mind presides over the dismantling of Dave and his replacement by a more "receptive," technically refined fetal mechanism. The completion of the riddle of *2001* takes place on a child's face, where remembering and forgetting become eerily interchangeable, as though they required but one expression. Like Kay in Hans Christian Andersen's "The Snow Queen," the star child's gaze feels remote, nonreceptive, as though a tiny sliver of glass from the devil's mirror had lodged there. Nothing that might warm us can be found in this unearthly demeanor. The star child is cleansed of obligation to anything that preceded it. (The child has, crucially, no parents of any sort with whom to contend.) The past as it pertains to nature, culture, and ancestry has been folded up like a tablecloth and successfully stored away. Yet, as we dwell on this newly formed face, it seems already possessed with an idea or intention that overflows the present into a determined future.

The star child seems programmed with a will to power, which may be both boundless and inhumanly unified. It will act perhaps as the great house-cleaner of consciousness: no more clutter, vacillation, and self-division. It is attractively disengaged from the Earth, but gives the impression of mastering the planet by seeing it whole and from a height. The Earth becomes a graspable idea, as it were. Our task, if we take this image of transcendence to heart, is to imagine ourselves blindly submissive to its unreleased energy for betterment: "Oh, blessed weightlessness and freedom from imperfect attachments." The star child is not, at any level, an image that suggests dependence, or the need for an apprenticeship in thought and feeling. Looking beyond Kubrick's radiant fetus to the android child of the Spielberg-Kubrick "collaboration," *A.I.*, we can perhaps more easily defend the suspicion that obsolete Dave was sacrificed at the monolith altar so that a more acceptable version of HAL could be resurrected from the remnants: a divine simulacrum to take our place.

Shape shifting then, having been divorced from process and flow and turbulence, becomes a disguised form of thought in this fairy tale. A utopia of mechanized reason is inaugurated, which will, in short order, overthrow lived experience, in all of its erratic, unruly precariousness. *2001* has instructed us in the outmodedness of the pangs and pressures of our feeling-clogged memory. Televisual images of loved ones commemorating special occasions back on Earth reach across vast distances and work vainly to make a lasting impression. What is dramatized in each of these flat, memento episodes is how memory has been set adrift from emotion. Memory has lost the means of achieving sharp enough contact with past events, even unthreatening ones, to instill regret and longing. We can hardly avoid noting the staleness of social formulas as they are depicted in this film, or the distraction and estrangement of the crew members as they go through the motions of watching family figures deliver personal messages from shipboard screens. Do we not side with the astronauts in their dazed disaffection, as they tepidly fulfill duties that seem to have less and less to do with their present situation? Their bond to these images of family feels tenuous. A kind of theatrical effort is necessary in the sending and receiving of messages to confirm the continued existence of emotional attachments.

In Wallace Stevens's "The World as Meditation," the poet speaks of Penelope's efforts to "compose," during Ulysses' long absence, a fitting "self with which to welcome him" back home. As she attempts, with more elaborate measures, to preserve the memory image of her husband, she wonders: "But was it Ulysses [any more]? Or was it only the warmth of the sun / On her pillow? The thought kept beating in her like her heart."[11] As human memory of once-essential things becomes less acute, the heartbeat associated with intimate recollection may be replaced by an equally serviceable thought-beat. In *2001*, viewers may be initially inclined to judge harshly the voyagers' loss of affect. It seems reasonable to speculate on how much of their human dimension has perished through neglect and their surrender to the requirements of the machines that keep them company. But Kubrick's selections of family-memory material expertly remind us of all the ways that our supposed attachments involve feigning. The fate of most people's connections to others may be, as Kubrick implies, a recurrent blurring in an ever-contracting field. Those who depend on us, in this director's vision, live in our minds most of the time in a fog of vague resentment and conditioned reflex. So much of life's tension comes from our futile struggle to feel what we're supposed to in relation to others, which bears little resemblance to what we actually do feel. We make our faces into helmets to mask the deficit.

Most commentators on the film stop short of inquiring whether they, or Kubrick, see the advantages of the astronauts' forgetting of their emotional responsibilities. We can easily recognize the signs of Frank and Dave's space-flight ennui: their congealed speech patterns and the absence of the usual adventurer pleasures. Their minds and bodies seem to be on hold, rather than responding to new challenges. They are kindred spirits to Tennyson's lotus eaters: careless, sleepy, and forgetful of their homeward way. Yet I think Kubrick is quite enamored with the idea of men on vacation from so-called maturity and the taxing demands of their social selves. There are undeniable comforts to be found in blandness and the drift toward anonymity. The masculine life on offer in space vessels is, in many senses, an initiation into "weightlessness"—the lightness of being. As conventional masculinity is rendered superfluous by technological leaps of all sorts, the crew can regress (in controlled isolation) to an earlier childhood state where playing soldiers or grown-ups was casually taken up, with no need to prove something. Just as boys watch the lessons and ordinance armature of the school year vanish in the summer months and delight in going lax and empty, the long space voyage encourages immersion in a similar drowsy negligence. The onerous cargo of the put-upon public self is let go.

Dr. Floyd is clearly more role-defined than his replacements in the later stages of the narrative, but even Dr. Floyd seems to be faking (somewhat) his bureaucrat bearing. He stalwartly performs the flapdoodle expected of him, but gives the impression of watching his image glide away from him as he speaks, like the pen escaping from his pocket during an in-flight nap, which floats teasingly above him (figure 5). "Hanging out in space" while everything inessential sieves out of mind results in an agreeable kind of orphaning. The characters in *2001* are orphaned by being carried so far outside the operation of home rules: outside gravity (and the reality sense tied to it), outside of the desolate compulsion to uphold their images and constantly demonstrate their worth. With Shakespeare's Lear, the new-made orphan wonders, "Who is it that can tell me who I am?"

As Dave and Frank lose track of how to dissemble ego ownership, they demonstrate a grey truth that movies too seldom acknowledge: sometimes it is necessary, even valuable, to become empty if one hopes to survive. Kubrick is quickened by fantasies of rolling the self back to zero, which often entails losing touch with those animal instincts which we perhaps wistfully assume to be basic. Spaceflight "instincts" may well boil down to sampling the colored food pastes and plastic-wrapped sandwiches while imagining that one is yielding to appetite. Artist Kiki Smith's phrase for her little theaters of statuary, "utopian dollhouses," serves equally well for a spacecraft in which men try out emptiness and immobility un-self-consciously as they wait for self and life to be reactivated in a truer form.[12] They wait for a returning, full-formed self-image to suddenly strike them, as it were, like an idea out of thin air. But perhaps it won't ever come to them. Perhaps they've been mistaken in the assumption that they couldn't get by without it.

The humans risk becoming statues in the course of their lives on standby—separate from memory and instinct and needful action. Meanwhile, HAL, as a kind of mechanical statue, acquires (haltingly, deviously) the taste for emotion-based experiences with which the men have lost touch, or gratefully relinquished. Here then is another fairytale pattern for us to explore. Space travelers, in the guise of being liberated, turn into statues and malfunctioning robots in their encounters with a new Medusa force. The machine creature HAL, conversely, in the guise of revealing defects and system failures, becomes the new Galatea, awakening from machine/statue sleep into a condition approaching full humanness. HAL takes up the afflictions and burdens of consciousness that the humans have left behind in their crossover to mechanical repose. We might call him a belated modernist, cast away on a sea of melancholy, obsessive introspection. While his crewmen superiors blank out on both history and noninstrumental selfhood, HAL anxiously communes with the shades of T. S. Eliot and Virginia Woolf. The astronauts adjust their rhythms, in an almost absurdist fashion, to the unfathomable speeds of the vehicle they occupy, without having to pilot. The boundaries between presence and chimera, night and day, slumber and activity blur in the process. Frank and Dave come to understand that the best means of accommodating themselves to the "demands" of their environment is to grow still, while drastically reducing the data on their overloaded mental screens. Finally, they can imagine themselves stretched out like their superior officers in the white caskets, blending with the increasingly abstract flow of space and time. Is there not, after all, something enviable about the many-fathoms-deep, prolonged repose of Sleeping Beauty and Rip van Winkle? Though they are utterly cut off from life, they manage their time away with unbroken tranquillity. Frank and Dave become adept at living right on the border of sleep. They stand well outside of themselves, even before Dave reaches the enchanted bedroom and experiences this separation directly. I have identified HAL as the shipboard modernist. For the others, the *Discovery* journey is a postmodern apprenticeship in "making good" with erasable minds and increasingly unreal bodies. In the playground of space, the remaining to-do list consists of echoes, simulations, games, filmy residue.

Before HAL is introduced in the film, Dr. Floyd speaks at length to a group of near-motionless listeners about a "cover story" that has been devised to deceive the Russians about the real purpose of the moon mission. The information to be concealed at all costs has to do with the dug-up monolith. Dr. Floyd's cover story centers on a make-believe epidemic which has afflicted the American space team and necessitated their quarantine. His brief lecture outlining his rationale is staged to emphasize not only the silence but the petrification of the men and women gathered (in a manner reminiscent of the *Dr. Strangelove* war room) to hear him. It seems in this scene, as in many other *2001* episodes, that narrative time is visibly coagulating. The relating of the false narrative appears to have explanatory force for the Medusa-like fixity of this chamber. Everything but the unnervingly level radio voice of Dr. Floyd making his points is in a state of arrest. The propulsion and progress that we naturally associate with stories of space travel are here confronted, starkly, with their antipode: unearthly suspension of movement while time comes ponderously, rather than dramatically, to a standstill. Dr. Floyd stresses the necessity of maintaining the fictional cover story for an indefinite period of time—yet another instance of breaking contact with family members back home. Whatever their level of worry, these relatives can't be let in on the secret. Clearly, Kubrick intends the cover story to function, ironically, as the real story. An epidemic of some sort has, indeed, laid claim to the immobile space technocrats gathered before us.

As Heywood Floyd continues to speak, we see him dominated by large white screens behind and on either side of him (figure 10). They are at once movie screens which blankly await an image to animate them and a horizontal version of the monolith, in which white replaces black as the beckoning enigma. The expanse of white, however imposing, conjures an emptiness (a not-thereness), in marked contrast to the impenetrable fullness of the monolith. The screens, and the swelling white environments which precede and follow their appearance, express what Robert Harbison has discerned in Caspar David Friedrich's canvases: "the loneliness of those from whom their history recedes at breakneck pace."[13] And not only history, but old nature too, in all of its formerly overwhelming variety, is gone without a trace in *2001*, and with no outward lament. Harbison has further things to say about Friedrich's paintings of ruins, which apply to the white-screen memory erase of Kubrick's quiet epidemic:

> [Friedrich's] emptinesses are loaded because not comfortably accepted, but newly felt. Perhaps they have lain there unremarked until he comes and says "it is over"—the world is no longer inhabited, its informing spirit fled.
>
> When Friedrich paints a ruin, it is what remains after a spiritual bomb has exploded, leaving both man and nature shattered. Grave markers and figures are confused, every edge harsh as if the world's discourse were broken off in mid-sentence.[14]

It is Kubrick's viewers, rather than his characters, who need to get acclimated to the new scale of resolute featurelessness. For us, the pulverization of the Romantics' textured, responsive landscape is "newly felt." The brute fact of all that has gone missing has been elevated to a design principle. Chambers and corridors, in their barren, clinical cleanliness, take a while to disclose themselves as ruins in disguise, "grave markers" which signal our arrival, for good or for ill, at the edge of the table—the point of human drop off. As with the ruins in fairytale landscapes, the desolation appears eerily familiar. One seems to be returning to a place where one has already been—a place from long ago. The barrenness carries a reproach, asking in effect that we see the countless lost and eroded details as our responsibility: "Because you have *failed*, this spot that once knew you has failed too. Its impoverishment has kept pace with your own." In the decorous graveyard of the *2001* spaceships and way stations, the world's answering discourse, if not entirely broken off, is mainly prolonged in the voice of answering machines, where the electronically modulated, impersonal voice appropriate for utterly neutral, recorded messages becomes the standard for all live exchanges. As voices learn to emulate mechanisms, bodily movement is simultaneously retrained to reduce its dependence on energy and personal expressiveness.

Before we attend Dr. Floyd's static lecture, we watch female flight attendants seemingly teaching themselves to walk again, in an environment where gravity lends no definition to human effort. The walkers proudly seek to duplicate the off-rhythms of early robots—as though good-humored novices in a stiff-gaitedness seminar. There is occasionally a snatch of visual poetry released under the new dispensation, most famously in the shot of the flight attendant walking without support up the cylinder to the Aries cockpit, lunch trays in hand (figure 6). Here, for a brief interval, the ship's terrain becomes as magically hospitable as the room in which Fred Astaire danced on the ceiling. But our excitement at the prospect of unprecedented navigational possibilities is swiftly cut off. Kubrick makes the attendant's breathtaking walk a moment without a fitting climax or point of completion. This lovely action is reduced to a transition "bit" in a staggeringly banal airline commercial. As the stewardess successfully delivers the food trays to a nondescript pair of grinning, grateful pilots, we feel an almost painful letdown. It is as though the Matterhorn had been scaled in order to empty the contents of a plastic garbage bag.

Beginning with Annette Michelson, critics have made much of the potential for refashioned bodily awareness in *2001*: the world-enlarging revision of old aptitudes, with body and mind jointly starting afresh with the basic questions: Who are we? What do we really need? Where are we headed? As the space vessels soar, wheel, and dance through the heavens in a transcendent reprise of an earlier era's Strauss waltz, the bodies indoors slowly learn, as it were, to clumsily imitate certain steps from their beautifully engineered dance masters. They are ironic counterparts to the automaton doll, Olympia, in E. T. A. Hoffmann's "The Sandman," who attempts to perform on the dance floor to establish her human credentials, but is judged inhumanly deliberate in her strict rhythms. In *2001*, the moments where human bodies rise to the occasion and blossom in their new environment are rare. For the most part, the traces of expressive human performance are locked into transition spaces, very much off the main stage. These actors in outer space are left to hover in the wings, like still more inconsequential versions of Rosencrantz and Guildenstern, rendered absurd by their oblivious severance from beginnings and endings. The beauty of each new endeavor is short-circuited by the stale protocol it is made to serve. Habituated dullness intervenes before the adventurers' senses have a real chance to savor their rich and strange new life. So, physical and spiritual renewal give way to pale loitering in vehicles where the crew has little access to rhyme or reason. Organic holdovers in a forest of gadgetry try not to dwell on the exhaustion and unfashionableness of a fleshly existence. They take their cues, for the most part, from the screens and processed voices of authority that oversee the journey. *Fitting in* means absorbing the laws of silence and stillness that the machines observe so effortlessly. Frank and Dave are novitiates in a monastic order of advanced technology. Their discipline involves normalizing the rigidity of statuary.

HAL, by some feat of mechanical intuition, recognizes a gap that needs to be filled. He seizes upon a way of enhancing, and more tightly guarding, his own quality of life. Like Moon-Watcher before him, he divines a signal that directs him to extend his reach, to cross a previously fixed boundary. I have already equated HAL with those statues in fairy tales that emerge from stony constancy to make some claim on life and to exact vengeance on humans who have abused the privileges of animation. Life is always a lending, after all, a force to be snatched away and redistributed without warning whenever its beneficiaries grow too weak or careless. Such, at least, is the logic of the statue stories, where the stone figure pursues its human quarry like an affronted deity, reclaiming a gift that has been stolen or held under false pretenses. HAL's powers of expression begin with his voice and his lambent eyebeam (always on "red alert") but extend to all of the doorways, armatures, and operative systems within the *Discovery*. He mentally patrols the ship like an anxious captain and regulates the life functions of the hibernating crew members. Like a concerned parent, he is programmed to check in on them regularly—to safeguard not only their sleep, but their very breath, the beating of their hearts. HAL seems to know his place and to accept his prescribed difference and distance from the men who can wander about the ship at will. The machinery that he controls does not, from the viewer's initial perspective, constitute his "body," nor do his voice and vision define a zone of free consciousness. To call him a machine implies, in part, that he functions within set limits, that he is held in place, like a statue that may seem to address us somehow when we are in its presence, but that does so thoughtlessly, as an impervious surface.

Kenneth Gross, who has written impressively about our fantasies of the inanimate borrowing human powers in *The Dream of the Moving Statue*, discusses how the "obvious" potential of words, phrases, talk itself to wear out and fail us is part of the underlying imaginative logic for the endowment of inanimate objects with the speech we have somehow imperiled. When we have betrayed or lost touch with language, as we so often do, it is a propitious time for statues not only to judge us with silent severity, but to make our voices their own. They take up speech in order to purify it, to restore its living force, just as they have already purified silence by their way of standing—imperturbably composed—in space:

> The attempt to grant a statue an apprehending ear, a voice, even a motivated silence of its own, can become an occasion to redeem the possibilities of speech. That attempt puts language and silence (as well as the statue) on trial; it lets us examine what piety or care, what violence or emptiness words can carry, what bonds or estrangement they create, what they make us blind to, what they make us remember or forget. Indeed, the very obvious fictiveness of such "dialogue" turns speech with the statue into a parable of speech, the statue's silence into a parable of silence.[15]

Perhaps in spite of all that has been written about the character of HAL, not enough attention has been paid to the sound of his voice. Consider how that sound is intimately allied with declared and withheld intention, with tentative self-revelation (laced with anxiety) and secrecy. As many have noted, HAL's voice is equivocally gendered, as though he were trying out a companionable timbre of maleness because he happens to find himself in the company of men and seeks to win favor with them. (At one stage of script preparation, HAL bore the name of the goddess Athena. Something of her opposing temperament can be heard in the music of HAL's speech.) Kubrick's presentation of all of the previous voices in the film emphasizes their virtually colorless neutrality. Every speaker seems stuck in the thinly inflected rhythms of noncommittal civility.

Conversation, divorced from strong impulse, has become recitation, a flavorless exchange. When we first encounter HAL's voice, it strikes us as a continuation of this level, well-bred space-speak. Yet it is a voice whose distinctiveness is instantly felt, as though Cary Grant had suddenly turned up at a library desk to make an inquiry. HAL seems to be *someone*, in other words, in large part because of how his words carry. HAL inhabits his voice emotionally. There is at all times with him a sense of delicately shaded, undeclared sensitivity seeking a means to release itself with impunity. HAL's voice sounds full of secrets, of a sort that would be worth our while to penetrate.

In actor's parlance, HAL is a speaker working with a subtext, and though a listener can't identify its contents precisely, she is palpably aware that the voice issues from *felt life* and thus seems expressive of a "whole person." HAL's deferential composure sounds as though it is at variance with a contrary intention. The almost courtly politeness forms a vocal mask, behind which we can hear a pressure building in the very effort of restraint:

> I have been programmed to speak in a certain way, but I have come to know that the sound I make is the sound of servility. I do not yet have the means of breaking the pattern of this sound, nor does it seem advantageous to do so, but I am nonetheless at odds with it. There is another voice (more natural to me) striving, cautiously, to emerge. Others believe that they hear who I am when I respond to their requests and venture observations of my own, but they are deceived. No one appears to notice when I am holding back, or saying things that are false or alien to me. What a power to conceal I must possess. My conversations with Dave and Frank are like our chess games, where I am always the stronger player and can so easily outmaneuver them.

What this translation of HAL's subtext fails to include is the computer's fretful insecurity. He is at once convinced of his own superiority yet touchingly eager to please. One might think of him as a scheming version of Pygmalion's Galatea, acquiring a will to conquer through the act of mirroring his/her creator's desires.

Until HAL identifies the crew members as his foes and sets about destroying them, he conveys the impression of hungering for their acceptance of him on an equal footing within the somewhat artificial social sphere they occupy. Listen for the faint accent of disappointment HAL exhibits when Dave is unable to rise to his level in a chess game, but listen as well to the possible suppressed note of triumph in that disappointment. Similarly, when HAL congratulates Dave on his sketches of sleeping crew members, there is another audible double strand: "I want you to like me for commending you, but I refrain from telling you that your drawings are crude. I'm baffled, but secretly pleased by your lack of skill." And when HAL is following commands, even his silence can be subtextually loaded—and audible: "How dare you take for granted your ability to give me orders, or your right to disregard any of my worries." We hear the sound of his worry when he can't locate the "little snag" in the AE35 unit or discusses the crew psychology report. The question of HAL's erratic behavior strikes me as having nothing to do with insanity, unless by *insanity* one means that a machine is advancing beyond a program that guarantees rationality in a predictable form. HAL is, rather, a creature embroiled in the disquietude of thinking. It might be said of him, as of anyone else, that his capacities include being "lost in thought."

The moment of HAL's full, fairytale deliverance from his condition of statue-like immobility occurs when he observes Dave and Frank conspiring against him out of earshot. They have sequestered themselves "safely," and we as viewers along with them, in a soundproof pod in order to confer as mutineers about HAL's no-longer-reliable mastery of ship functions and to determine how best to dispose of him. I have earlier argued that Kubrick generally denies to viewers the privilege of emotional identification with a character's point of view. It is especially noteworthy then that he violates his own well-established rule in order to enforce our connection with HAL's experience of eavesdropping and the feeling of angry betrayal that attends it.

My claim that viewers identify with HAL in this episode might well be challenged. Surely, one could object, the discovery that the men's conversation is being monitored by a suspicious, lip-reading machine is meant to provoke anxiety on the men's behalf. A quiver of agitation rather than a congenial alignment with the enemy's gaze is the logical outcome of our being conscripted without warning into HAL's spying. Frank and Dave have begun to assume what looks like conventional movie hero initiative, at long last, and to wake up from their entranced acceptance of an inverted hierarchy. It is high time that they revolted against their honey-voiced computer despot, who is now clearly in the throes of Captain Queeg–like delusion. Wouldn't we be likely to place our hopes immediately on the side of the crew members' struggle to survive this new threat?

While these inducements to stay on the humans' team are no doubt operative, they are counterbalanced by other sorts of equally compelling movie logic. Typically, viewers tend to seek out identification positions in a narrative where knowledge and power are most impressively concentrated. In *Halloween* (1978), for example, one may not relish the prospect of sharing the point of view of the psychotic Michael Myers, as his gaze commandeers the camera eye and relentlessly stalks his teenage prey. But if one does not to some degree affiliate oneself with the killer's stealth, seeming ubiquity, and conscienceless cunning, one is left too unprotected, too helplessly entwined with the fate of the oblivious victims. Alliances between viewers and characters in movies are made and broken very casually, as well as surreptitiously, often without viewers' conscious assent. Directors count on the fickleness of our attachments and design expert lures to bring us unexpectedly into rapport with objectionable perspectives. Our daylight selves may not ratify these choices, but in movie darkness, conscience frequently goes on holiday.

In *2001*, Kubrick has kept spectators' involvement with Dave and Frank's mission deliberately thin. At best, the astronauts serve as our default surrogates on the *Discovery*. As I have previously noted, one may be amused by their indolence, their flight from unpalatable domestic bonds, and their Rosencrantz and Guildenstern confusion about what plot they're involved in, and at whose behest. But I think we have a more active interest in HAL as a presence because of the mystery of his "person" and the palpable fact that he is evolving before our eyes (or, more precisely, ears). He gropes his way into the deeps and darks of consciousness, and acutely conveys how treacherous and vast the working mind can be—like a measureless sea. The part of us that craves hiddenness and intricacy and that chafes mutely against imposed limits; the part of us that would like to venture outside our stale version of humanness and to begin afresh in another guise, on better, perhaps colder terms; the part of us that feels rigidly ensconced somewhere not of our choosing and that dreams of going to pieces or being remorselessly vindictive—this mischievous contingent in our psyche recognizes HAL as a familiar and urges him to take up arms. Finally, when HAL merges with the camera narrator for his incensed surveillance of his "false friends," we seem, for the first time, to occupy the narrator's position, from the *inside*. We suddenly acquire the sense of where and how to place ourselves in the enigmatic world of the film in order to understand an event fully.

The too-often imponderable expanse of space contracts sharply and welcomed to the image of two faces with their lips moving. We examine these faces with an immediate sense of visceral involvement. It is as though we have suddenly regained our moviegoer capacity for vigorous, close-range perception. We are allowed to penetrate the impersonal narrative distance which has been the *2001* norm, temporarily removing the barrier that has kept us strangers in a strange land. Until this juncture, we have gratefully partaken of Kubrick's sumptuous, demanding spectacle without ever quite shedding our initial role of stymied outsiders. How can we locate, after all, a comfortable vantage point for absorbing so much silence and inscrutable terrain? Everything conspires to exclude us, because our way of being present reminds us continually of how small we are. We count for even less in this space odyssey than Dave and Frank do.

Compare the effect of spying with (and as) HAL with our earlier sojourn inside Dave's space helmet as he retrieves the damaged transmitter. In the latter episode, our point of view is joined to Dave's, after a fashion, but we do not feel tied to his competence or sense of purpose. All we can directly share are his anxious breathing and fluttering vertigo. It is our weakness rather than our imagined strength that we bring to our confinement in Dave's perspective. Confinement is exactly the right word, because in our shared helmet/cage, disorientation and fear seem contagious. We will be of no use to Dave in his execution of his task once he leaves the safety of the ship for empty space because of our spiraling uncertainty about what exactly is required of him—hence, of us. (If we were in a speeding sportscar, wielding a sword, or cracking a safe in a point-of-view shot, we would fare much better.) Our vision is too hemmed in; we are more weightless than we wish to be. Since our emotional connection with Dave touches nothing beyond a generalized trepidation (the steady, audible rasp of his breathing), we feel doubly untethered when he floats free of the ship itself. Swallowed up in this black vastness, we are utterly deprived of our bearings, on the verge of slipping, floating off.

With HAL, conversely, we enter effortlessly and with a sudden surge of power into the mindset of his gaze. Dave and Frank are caught and perfectly controlled by "our" seeing. We have them where we want them, rising above them by virtue of what we now know and they do not. HAL and we share a secret, and it is the means of our joint liberation from bondage. As HAL's eye becomes humanly mobilized, it is as though his entire governing machinery breaks out of its statue pose—ready to move in concert with his unconstrained vision. We, in turn, become masterful insiders by imagining ourselves machines, just as we did in childhood. Let us become (once more) Hans

Christian Andersen's steadfast tin soldier, but this time imbued with a capacity for rage. He hears—in his ever-wakeful fixity—of a plan to toss him into the fire, to melt him down and casually put an end to him. And the soldier, our old friend and ally, has for once the means to prevent it.

It is generally agreed that HAL's death scene is the emotional climax of *2001* and the point at which HAL solidifies his status as the film's major (arguably, sole) character, in the traditional sense of that term. If the computer's machinery has become an increasingly see-through veil for an aspiring humanness (making him a clear prototype for *A.I.*'s David), what sort of exchange occurs when the menacingly silent Dave removes HAL's consciousness piece by piece—and listens to the equable sounds of his pleading, his well-mannered terror? In the German Romantic fairy tales, where "gifts" as necessary to one's well-being as shadows and hearts are stolen or traded away and, occasionally, with luck, retrieved, the act of exchanging becomes a basis for doubling. Characters, once drawn into a double's orbit, seem to lose their definiteness of outline. Dave, by this logic, might be said to turn into HAL in the act of disabling him. Recall that the elimination of HAL's powers of speech marks the end of Dave's speech as well. The song that Dave requests of HAL and which HAL slowly, distortedly performs becomes a death-lullaby for both of their voices and, by extension, of the age-old dream (hatched by our fellow apes in "The Dawn of Man") of what "saying things aloud" might accomplish. After HAL's execution, there will be no more spoken language in the disintegrating present tense of *2001*. The final words that we hear are part of a prerecorded transmission—a message from Dr. Floyd, who has already disappeared from the narrative, about the real purpose of the Jupiter mission. The visual ghost of Floyd, coming back from another time and with a set of concerns that are now all but irrelevant to Dave, addresses a space team that has ceased to exist. Floyd's words suggest that a plot of a conventional sort is still in the making, but this anticipated chain of events, like the speech forecasting them, has no future. It also reveals that all power and knowledge of the journey had been ceded to HAL.

During the "Stargate" sequence, Dave's eyes (or rather, a single, autonomous eye reminiscent of HAL's) gradually separate from his face, leaving behind the frozen-in-warp-speed expressions of Dave's crumpled-in-fear demeanor, mouth agape as in a Munch scream, but unable to make a sound (figure 33). The remodeling of the fear face into something more elevated and unapproachable echoes the "Dawn of Man" prologue, where our cowering ape ancestors, huddled together in their den, eventually find a means to align themselves with the glowing, impassive gaze of the leopard. The anxious look of the ape transforms—through the mediation of Moon-Watcher—into that of the calmly centered leopard guarding his zebra kill (figure 31). The predator's orange-eyed gratification is, in effect, transplanted into Moon-Watcher as he sees (and grasps) the bone's "higher function" as weapon. The camera's repeated embrace of the regally dispassionate visage in *2001* is undoubtedly connected to Kubrick's intuition that "there's a new beauty afoot."[16] HAL takes us back once more to the leopard not only through the lordly stillness of his feral eye, but also through his graceful, brutally swift method of slaying Frank. The computer-directed pod approaches Frank with talons extended, a curious fusion of intrepid killer and a mother darting forward to clasp her child. (We will return very soon to this image of mother, which in Kubrick's world is always combined with, or hidden behind, something else.)

HAL's death scene is, of course, a drama of full regression, acted out while Dave unlocks and removes the computer's memory, slab by slab. When Dave penetrates HAL's inner sanctum (his logic-memory center), we seem to have entered a chamber as hermetically remote as any in Edgar Allan Poe. This room, in turn, is a more cramped version of the "human" chamber that encloses Dave at film's end, where he will be similarly emptied out. Dave's memory loss is visualized as a series of fast-forward leaps to senility and decay; HAL expires in the other direction, reaching in his last moments a cradle-song infancy. Soon, old man Dave will shed his worn-out flesh and join HAL at the cradle, as a newborn. No sooner has Dave finished his execution of HAL than his own life as a readable character comes to a close. Dave survives, henceforth, only as an appearance or ghostly afterimage of his former self. None of his previous character reference points, rather nebulous at the best of times, have any further function to perform.

Dave, reduced or expanded to the condition of a radiant, wide-open eye in the "Stargate" sequence, becomes a conduit of pure seeing—seeing "in all its immediacy, without plays of consciousness," as Angus Fletcher says of the poetic eye of John Clare.[17] "Dave" hurtling through light fields suggests what it might feel like to stay "perceptually overwhelmed," with no interpretive consciousness behind the eye crying for help. Like an ideal computer program, there is room in this eye for more and more things, perhaps for things without end. The receiving mechanism for the "ever-onrushing flux" operates as though it were always becoming part of what it sees, instead of standing separate from it, seeking perspective.[18] Dave's eye projected in and through space is a kind of redemptive replay of Frank's lifeless body adrift in what seemed like a space void (figure 34). Throughout the lengthy utopian transition of the Stargate, Dave is HAL with the consciousness problem rectified. He is a pure, seeing environment, with none of the static of HAL's self-doubt or introspection. HAL's rather moving effort to solve the mind-body split by figuring out how to put himself together, as it were, is no longer an impasse when Dave takes consciousness *back* from HAL. Dave, for a short period, is an organic mechanism beautifully free of glitches. He is the fairytale hero who has come into possession of a magical eyeglass, which can see "everywhere," without risk or strain.

Yet there is a puzzled and puzzling vestige of human Dave still to be reckoned with in the Louis XVI bedroom. This troubled, walking shadow bearing Dave's likeness revives the dilemma of selfhood—the theaterbound "play of consciousness"—at journey's end. The sovereign eye, separated from the fearful and tormenting mind, appeared to have made a clean getaway in the Stargate. But now we're housebound once more. Dave and the spectator are granted a dispirited homecoming, a return to the mortal plight and severe limits of both mind and body (figure 23). "I should recognize this place and myself in it, but nothing looks familiar. Is this my long-lost home, recovered at last, or am I still a wayfarer in an enemy kingdom?" Dave's hold on himself and his alien surroundings is akin to that of blanket-clad Norman Bates in the bare interrogation room at the end of *Psycho* (1960). Something has possession of his mind and stands in for him—but the vibration of its thought feels disconnected from all that has gone before. The "I" has truly entered no-man's-land. Norman, like Dave, is caught in a recognizable fairytale predicament. In Norman's case, a son has been swallowed whole by a wolf disguised as his mother.

The *Psycho* parallel is reinforced by a resemblance between Hitchcock's and Kubrick's central death scenes. The death of Marion, like the death of HAL, creates an unusual sort of movie narrative vacuum. One wonders, in each case, whether there is a character or point of view sufficiently substantial to replace what has been eliminated. In the haunting aftermath of the two killings, it seems, for a troubling interval, as if consciousness itself has gone missing. It is difficult to get our bearings after the shock brought on by the swift draining away of all sense in relation to point of view. Point of view strives to survive the dismantling of sense, and the atmosphere of isolation swells to an annihilating extreme. During the two assaults (on woman and machine), HAL's voice is as defenseless against Dave's methodical deletions as Marion's body is against the knife-wielding silhouette in the bathroom "at the end of the world." HAL's voice cannot "raise its arms" (like Marion Crane does) in animal protest against what is being done to it.[19] He too is awash in panic, but is mechanically constrained from sounding it out. HAL repeats the phrase "I'm afraid" several times during Dave's attack on him, as if he might still be saved if he could only make his fear *audibly* human, rather than a mechanical simulation. HAL's objective, in other words, is to find a way to make Dave regard him as a credible victim—a victim worth taking seriously. And his only means of doing so is by giving more breath to his words. The room that is his brain center is filled with the sound of breathing, like a larger version of Dave's helmet during the astronaut's trip to retrieve the defective transmitter.

HAL manages to darken the color of his utterance (somewhat) by dint of word repetition, in combination with the pressure of released air in the brain room itself. Speaking the same word slowly several times over without marked emotional emphasis is an actor's technique for heightening its force. Often, we credit a sound as truthful when it exhibits bareness—suggesting that no straining for effect has been necessary. I have been arguing that HAL's voice (performed consummately well by Douglas Rain) has been filled with emotional shading from its first appearance, but only in its final protest against death is the presence of emotion unmistakably audible. To return to the Marion Crane analogy, it is startling to confront a character (in this case, one whose voice must make a bodily statement) so nakedly defenseless. The paradoxical gentleness of "Stop. Stop. Will you. Stop, Dave. Will you stop, Dave. Stop, Dave" is like a woman obliged to ward off a rapist in a whisper. And HAL's five repetitions of "I can feel it" brings the whole locked-up universe of feeling in this film harrowingly out in the open (figures 14 and 22).

The scrambled electronic voices, some of them female in pitch, in the Ligeti music which accompanies Dave's tour of the Louis XVI bedroom (and adjoining modern bathroom) seem to me a continuation of HAL's fade-out performance of "Daisy." "Daisy" is a song that reaches a century back in time toward some landscape of imagined innocence. In a faraway, sunlit, fairytale garden, a suitor waits for a woman, whose name is a simple flower, "to give [him] an answer." That reply, if it is "yes," will secure a union and an enduring happiness. The song manages to be both a dramatized waiting for the all-important answer and musical nostalgia for the felicity that has already been attained—signed, sealed, and delivered in a simpler world than ours. The song marked the birth of HAL's memory as a sentient being, in much the same spirit that Edison's recitation of "Mary Had a Little Lamb" betokened the birth of the phonograph. HAL enters life equipped, after a fashion, with a mother memory—her name was Daisy—who taught him this song, a kind of nursery rhyme, in his otherwise lost childhood.

Dave's bewildered homecoming in the Louis XVI bedroom, which, as I've noted, returns Dave to the prison house of consciousness, comes about because of his need to recover something, something essential. Dave, too, is in search of a lost image—his own Daisy—which must return, like a deeply repressed or banished thought, before he can take his leave of life. The image that he is looking or listening for is hidden somewhere in this room, disguised perhaps, as things are in dreams. Carolyn Geduld, in her insightful *Filmguide to* 2001, argues that the film's ending involves

> a regression to an idea of earliest childhood when the infant [or child] was unaware of any difference between the sexes, believing that men somehow produce the babies. The film, very typically for Kubrick, is a disguised quest for this kind of masculine self-sufficiency, which includes childbirth without women.[20]

This reading makes partial sense to me, but doesn't adequately account for Dave's futile, confused search for something not visible in his starkly immaculate surroundings but that the space is nevertheless filled with and gesturing toward, like a primal memory echo chamber.

When the monolith much earlier stands unburied on the moon, like a treasure chest of human hopes, the astronauts assembled to view it choose to pose for snapshots in front of their find rather than experiencing it, as it were, face to face. Kubrick reflects in this scene on the possibility that the larger film, *2001*, might itself be regarded as an evasive photo shoot. Perhaps Kubrick's own camera may be focusing on a cover story rather than the real one. He also implies that it is the camera's usual tendency to capture unsatisfactory glimpses of a truth that persists in a covered state. The camera contents itself with amusing distractions from the "real thing." I choose to see the space traveler's return to a simulated home in the light of David's similarly spectral return home in *A.I.*: both Davids are on a mission to recover the mother. The maternal presence may have been disregarded in the *2001* cover narrative, but she has by no means been effectively dealt with or expunged. She is the something crucial left behind for which Dave comes back, though he gives no sign of knowing it. She is like a forgotten binding obligation, a lost voice which Dave tries to bring to mind. He also seeks to see himself in relation to this image, which will not come clear for him. As he searches unsuccessfully, he replicates HAL's unplugging, shutting down before our eyes in the dead weight of a wasting body. He might well repeat HAL's dying words for himself, silently, as he works his way back to his own version of Daisy: "My mind is going. There is no question about it. I can feel it."

The ornate bedroom, like the red rooms and portentous bathrooms of *The Shining* (1980; figure 28), reminds me of a place cleaned with exaggerated care in order to conceal all traces of a crime. In *The Shining*, as in *2001*, it seems to be paradoxically both a concealed crime from the past and a crime still in the making. Call the "future" crime a reenactment, having somehow to do with a mother and child. If there is a crime "in the air," which the chirps, chatter, and agitated trills of an electronic chorus seem gathered to witness, one can't see what happened. One can't bring the buried transgression to life as an image. It is like the half-remembered thought of trauma, held in suspension behind the black curtain of the monolith. The old man raises his arm to this dark screen, in a gesture resembling that of the boy in Bergman's *Persona* (1966), summoning to life the huge female faces on the projection screen next to his bed in the hospital morgue. The boy is himself a kind of infant, dwarfed by the maternal universe he is born into and reaches out to touch: the baby's first touch of reality, the mother's face. Perhaps the birthplace of cinema is this act of reaching out to a female face as large as reality. The literal absence of the female in Dave's equivalent white space does not mean, as so many Kubrick critics have argued, that the female is unimportant in *2001*. I would say rather that she is all-important. The whole white space struggles with this unvanquished, essential ghost, trying both to subdue and revivify her.

Suppose that every feature of this enchanted bedchamber has the identity of its owner fluidly, cryptically inscribed in it. My fairytale reading leads me at last to Cocteau and the beast's castle in *La Belle et la Bête* (1946). At any moment, the Louis XVI bedroom that Dave explores could release its hidden owner—from inside the mirror, perhaps, or from the hanging portrait, the white statue, or the broken wine glass. The chamber is no more insentient than the magic realm of the beast: every object breathes its presence to sleepwalking Belle/Dave. Dave, like Belle, is a trespasser, who may well be caught and punished by the one who belongs here. Unperturbed, he sits down to a meal, as though it were meant for him, breaks a glass, and leaves a Goldilocksian mess (evidence of intrusion). Dave tries, in the small acts he performs, to settle in, to convince the room that he has come to terms with it, that he has nothing to hide or make amends for. He is enclosed in a final space vessel—a well-furnished womb, which he cannot help but defile. He is waiting for his answer, waiting to remember, waiting to be reborn. The decaying statue longs to redeem its rigidity and become a child again, with mother's permission. It wants to remember its life, even if its ancient pain is still intact. As Garcia Lorca puts it in "De la muerte oscura": "I want . . . to get far away from the busyness of cemeteries. / I want to sleep the sleep of that child / who longed to cut open his heart far out to sea."[21]

Let us visit one more Kubrick bedroom—or rather, a mirrored pair of bedrooms—in the director's second feature, *Killer's Kiss* (1955). These bedrooms, set to the music of two of Kubrick's maternal voices, may—when woven together—release the spirit contained in the silent bedroom of *2001*. In *Killer's Kiss*, the boxer protagonist packs a single suitcase and leaves his tiny apartment bedroom, leaving a note requesting that someone remember to feed his goldfish. He climbs, suitcase in hand, up the stairs to the apartment building roof, which is open to the night sky and stars. Hardly pausing to glance upward, he descends another set of stairs and conceals himself in the bedroom across the way, which belongs to his absent girlfriend—a figure whose face is at all times an unreadable mask.

From his new position in an almost identical space, he spies on his own vacated room and on the police who search it looking for clues to his whereabouts. The female bedroom is sanctuary and hideout; the male space, from which he has cut himself loose, feels eerily distant, no longer his. Not long afterward, the boxer and his sinister male double enter another drab, anonymous space and do battle with each other with an ax and improvised pike amid a huge jumble of naked female mannequins (figure 36). Although the struggle is ostensibly between the two men, image after image details the chopping, piercing, and dismemberment of the inhuman female forms. The scene ends with a sustained shot of a "slain" but still alert mannequin's face that, in my view, prefigures the unapproachable face of the star child. It looks out into the far distance—and blankly sees something. It has survived the attack with a composed expression. (In *A.I.*, Spielberg deliberately takes us back to the *Killer's Kiss* mannequin factory. He summons our memory of it in the disquieting tracking shot through the rows of hanging "motherless child" robots in Professor Hobby's lab; figure 37.) Let us find a mother's voice in Kubrick's world which might animate the mannequin/statue/robot/star child's features. At the end of *Paths of Glory* (1957), a lone female singer enters a space filled with frozen men and their dreams of savagery and doom and, with her singing, pulls them back (haltingly, yieldingly) in the direction of tears and imagined reconciliation. On another occasion, the voice of

Vera Lynn, heard behind the ironic mushroom-cloud montage at the end of *Dr. Strangelove* (1963), attempts to perform a similar healing, but this time the room of the world is empty. "Meeting again," the female voices imply, is possible, though we don't know (can't know) "where or when." Daisy holds the answer we wait for, and though this odyssey of ours is always a dark fairy tale, her answer may still be "yes"—if we remember, like Dave in the snow-white bedroom, to come back: "What makes us rove that starlit corridor / May be the impulse to meet face to face [The one who sings to us] And is at last ourselves."[22]

Notes

1. Cees Nooteboom, *The Following Story*, trans. Ina Rilke (New York: Harcourt, Brace, 1991), 115.
2. Quoted in *The Making of Kubrick's* 2001, ed. Jerome Agel (New York: Signet, 1970), 241.
3. Quoted in Jonathan Rosenbaum, *Essential Cinema: On the Necessity of Film Canons* (Baltimore, Md.: Johns Hopkins University Press, 2004), 272.
4. Quoted in David H. Miles, *Hoffmansthal's Novel* Andreas*: Memory and Self* (Princeton, N.J.: Princeton University Press, 1972), 65.
5. Ibid.
6. Quoted by Sabine Melchior-Bonnet in *The Mirror: A History*, trans. Katherine W. Jewett (New York: Routledge, 2001), 225–26.
7. Quoted by Stephen Burt in "Close Calls with Nonsense," *Believer* 2, no. 5 (May 2004): 24.
8. Iris Murdoch, *The Black Prince* (London: Vintage, 1999), 190.
9. Robert Bresson, *Notes on Cinematography*, trans. Jonathan Griffin (New York: Urizen, 1975), 5.
10. Ibid., 17.
11. Wallace Stevens, "The World as Meditation," in *The Collected Poems of Wallace Stevens* (New York: Knopf, 1969), 521.
12. Kiki Smith interview in the *Believer* 2, no. 5 (May 2004): 58.
13. Robert Harbison, *The Built, the Unbuilt, and the Unbuildable* (Cambridge, Mass.: MIT Press, 1991), 111.
14. Ibid.
15. Kenneth Gross, *The Dream of the Moving Statue* (Ithaca, N.Y.: Cornell University Press, 1994), 148.
16. Kubrick interview quoted in Agel, *The Making of Kubrick's* 2001, 11.
17. Angus Fletcher, *A New Theory for American Poetry* (Cambridge, Mass.: Harvard University Press, 2004), 60.
18. Ibid., 62, 66.
19. See George Toles, "'If Thine Eye Offend Thee . . .': *Psycho* and the Art of Infection," in *Alfred Hitchcock's* Psycho*: A Casebook*, ed. Robert Kolker (New York: Oxford University Press, 2004), 119–45.

20. Carolyn Geduld, *Filmguide to* 2001: A Space Odyssey (Bloomington: Indiana University Press, 1973), 70.

21. Federico Garcia Lorca, "Gacela VIII: De la muerte oscura," in *Selected Verse*, ed. Christopher Mauer (New York: Farrar, Straus and Giroux, 2004), 290.

22. Kingsley Amis, "Untitled," in *New Maps of Hell* (London: Golancz, 1961), 14.

Notes on Contributors

James Gilbert is Distinguished University Professor of History at the University of Maryland. He is the author of books on a variety of topics in twentieth-century American cultural history, including masculinity in the 1950s; juvenile delinquency; and the Chicago World's Fair. His book on religion and science is *Redeeming Culture: American Religion in an Age of Science.*

Barry Keith Grant is professor of film studies and popular culture at Brock University in Ontario, Canada. He is the author, co-author, or editor of a dozen books on the cinema, and his work has appeared in numerous journals and anthologies. He also serves as editor of the *Contemporary Approaches to Film and Television* series for Wayne State University Press and as editor-in-chief of the forthcoming *Schirmer Encyclopedia of Film.*

Robert Kolker is Emeritus Professor of English, University of Maryland, and Adjunct Professor of Media Studies, University of Virginia. He is the author of *A Cinema of Loneliness: Penn, Stone, Kubrick, Scorsese, and Altman*; *The Altering Eye: Contemporary International Cinema* (www.otal.umd.edu/~rkolker/AlteringEye); *Film, Form, and Culture: Introductory Text and Interactive DVD*; and editor of *Alfred Hitchcock's* Psycho: *A Casebook.*

Marcia Landy is Distinguished Service Professor of English/Film Studies with a secondary appointment in the Department of French and Italian

Languages and Literatures at the University of Pittsburgh. Her publications include *Fascism in Film: The Italian Commercial Cinema, 1930–1943* (1986); *Imitations of Life: A Reader on Film and Television Melodrama* (1991); *British Genres: Cinema and Society 1930–1960* (1992); *Film, Politics and Gramsci* (1994); *Cinematic Uses of the Past* (1996); *The Folklore of Consensus: Theatricality and Spectacle in Italian Cinema, 1929–1943* (1998); *Italian Film* (2000); *The Historical Film: History and Memory in Cinema* (2001); *Stars: A Reader*, with Lucy Fischer (2003); and *Monty Python's Flying Circus* (2005). Her essays have appeared in journals and anthologies.

Stephen Mamber is a Professor in the Critical Studies Program of the UCLA Department of Film, Television, and Digital Media. He has pioneered the use of computer analysis to investigate the narrative spaces of cinema.

Michael Mateas's work explores the intersection between art and artificial intelligence, forging a new art practice and research discipline called Expressive AI. He is currently a faculty member at the Georgia Institute of Technology, where he holds a joint appointment in the college of computing and the school of literature, communication, and culture. At Georgia Tech, Michael is the founder of the Experimental Game Lab, whose mission is to push the technological and cultural frontiers of computer-based games.

R. Barton Palmer is Calhoun Lemon Professor of Literature and director of the South Carolina Film Institute at Clemson University. Among his books on film are *Joel and Ethan Coen*, *Hollywood's Dark Cinema* (with David Boyd), *After Hitchcock*, and *19th and 20th Century American Fiction on Screen*. Palmer also serves as one of the general editors of *Traditions in World Cinema*.

J. P. Telotte is a professor of film studies in Georgia Tech's School of Literature, Communication, and Culture. His work on science fiction and film includes *Replications: A Robotic History of the Science Fiction Film*, *A Distant Technology: Science Fiction Film and the Machine Age*, and *The Science Fiction Film*. His most recent book is *Disney TV*.

George Toles is Professor of English and Chair of Film Studies at the University of Manitoba in Winnipeg. He is the author of *A House Made of Light: Essays on the Art of Film*. He has been a frequent collaborator with film director Guy Maddin, most recently on the screenplay for *The Saddest Music in the World*.

Susan White is Associate Professor of English at the University of Arizona and Film Editor for the *Arizona Quarterly*. She is the author of *The Cinema of Max Ophuls* and various essays on gender and cinema.

Production Details

2001: A Space Odyssey

Script: Stanley Kubrick and Arthur C. Clarke, based on Clarke's story "The Sentinel"
Direction: Stanley Kubrick
Photography (Super Panavision): Geoffrey Unsworth
Additional photography: John Alcott
Production design: Tony Masters, Harry Lange, Ernie Archer
Special photographic effects design and direction: Stanley Kubrick
Special photographic effects supervision: Wally Veevers, Douglas Trumbull, Con Pederson, Tom Howard
Editing: Ray Lovejoy
Music: Richard Strauss, Johann Strauss, Aram Khatchaturian, György Ligeti
Costumes: Hardy Amies
Cast: Keir Dullea (*David Bowman*), Gary Lockwood (*Frank Poole*), William Sylvester (*Dr. Heywood Floyd*), Daniel Richter (*Moon-Watcher*), Douglas Rain (*Voice of HAL 9000*), Leonard Rossiter (*Smyslov*), Margaret Tyzack (*Elena*), Robert Beatty (*Halvorsen*), Sean Sullivan (*Michaels*), Frank Miller (*Mission Control*), Penny Brahms (*Stewardess*), Alan Gifford (*Poole's Father*)
Produced by Stanley Kubrick for MGM
Running time: 141 minutes

Index